PSYCHOLOGICAL SYMPTOMS

PSYCHOLOGICAL SYMPTOMS

Frank J. Bruno, Ph.D.

John Wiley & Sons, Inc.
New York • Chichester • Brisbane • Toronto • Singapore

Copyright © 1993 by Frank Bruno

Published by John Wiley & Sons, Inc.

All rights reserved. Published simultaneously in Canada.

Reproduction or translation of any part of this work beyond that permitted by section 107 or 108 of the 1976 United States Copyright Act without the permission of the copyright owner is unlawful. Requests for permission or further information should be addressed to the Permissions Department, John Wiley & Sons, Inc.

Library of Congress Cataloging-in-Publication Data

Bruno, Frank, Joe, 1930–
    Psychological symptoms / Frank J. Bruno
      p.   cm.
    Includes bibliographical references and index.
                       ISBN 0-471-01610-1
    1. Psychiatry—Popular works.   2. Mental illness. I. Title
  RC460.8694   1993
  616.89—dc20   92-28510
                                              CIP

Printed in the United States of America

10 9 8 7 6 5 4

*To those who refuse to be
the permanent victims of
psychological symptoms*

Preface

Seven Things This Book Can Do for You

You are holding in your hands *Psychological Symptoms* and wondering whether or not to buy it or check it out from a library. Is this a book you *need* to read? Is it anything you can *use*? Allow me to speed along your decision by listing seven things this book can do for you:

1. *Explain symptoms.* If you fear that you are heading for a nervous breakdown or other serious mental problem, this book can help you understand the meaning of your psychological symptoms. If symptoms make sense to you, then you are much less likely to be their victim.

2. *Offer strategies.* If you feel helpless in the face of such common symptoms as anxiety, anger, depression, emotional helplessness, lack of pleasure in life, and loss of meaning in existence, this book offers practical coping strategies—strategies designed to give you a greater sense of control over both your emotions and your actions.

3. *Explain the behavior of others.* If someone close to you, such as a child or a spouse, is exhibiting signs of emotional problems or a mental disorder, this book can help you make some sense out of his or her behavior.

4. *Identify causes and explanations.* If you think of emotional problems and mental disorders as mysterious illnesses without logical explanations, this book will reveal to you that most behavioral difficulties have either biological or psychological causes that can be understood. The origins of various disorders are examined and evaluated in a major section of each chapter.

5. *Define language and terms.* If you are put off or confused by the language of psychiatry and clinical psychology, this book will make professional terminology accessible to you with clear definitions and practical examples.

6. *Explain therapy and treatment.* If therapy is indicated for your psychological symptoms, this book will make clear to you your options. Such treatment approaches as drug therapy and psychotherapy are discussed and evaluated in each chapter for each cluster of symptoms.

7. *Restore self-direction.* If you feel that your own behavior is increasingly out of control, the information in this book can help you restore a greater sense of self-direction. If you are to be the "master of your fate, the captain of your soul," you need solid *information* that is accurate and up-to-date.

In sum, this is a *practical* book. It is a book that will be useful to you if you are troubled or if someone you care about is troubled. Think of it as a helping hand during time of crisis.

FRANK J. BRUNO, PH.D.

Acknowledgments

A number of people have helped me make *Psychological Symptoms* a reality. My thanks are expressed to:

Herb Reich, Senior Editor at John Wiley & Sons, for his recognition of the value of the book and for being a supportive and creative editor.

Bert Holtje, my agent, for providing the idea seed from which this book germinated.

Peter Brown, Editorial Assistant to Herb Reich, for his practical assistance during the preparation phase of the manuscript.

My wife, Jeanne, for our many meaningful discussions about adjustment and personal growth.

My son, Franklin, for our conversations about words, language, and meaning.

George K. Zaharopoulos, a true teaching colleague, for his steadfast encouragement of my writing projects.

F.J.B.

Contents

Contents _____

Chapter 1

Suffering and Psychological Symptoms

You are suffering.

You recognize that you have an ongoing problem with one or more psychological symptoms such as anxiety, depression, helplessness, anger, indecisiveness, or obsessional thoughts. You are aware that your behavior is often self-defeating and self-destructive. Yes, you are suffering.

Is it really possible to be free of suffering? The answer is a carefully considered *yes*. However, this yes needs to be qualified. It is not, of course, possible to be free of *all* suffering. If you break a leg, you almost certainly will suffer. Physical pain is a fact of life—until healing or drugs ease the pain.

This book will speak about *mental and emotional suffering*—psychological, not physical, pain. It will focus on unnecessary suffering, the kind people bring on themselves through their own thoughts, perceptions, attitudes, evaluations, and memories.

Sigmund Freud, the father of psychoanalysis, was once asked, "What is the purpose of psychoanalysis?" He half-jokingly replied, "To replace neurotic suffering with ordinary human misery." In other words, Freud was saying that some suffering is self-induced and some suffering is just part of the life process. The principal goal of this book is to help you get rid of self-induced suffering, the worst kind.

However, if you get rid of neurotic—or unnecessary—suffering, are you left with misery? You may have negative emotions, but are these misery? If someone frustrates you, it is normal to feel a certain amount of anger for a time. If you lose someone you love, it is normal to experience grief and go through a period of mourning. But these are natural, realistic emotions. They are the kind of suffering that a relatively well-adjusted person can tolerate. Freud was overstating the case when he said that the human balance sheet—after you subtract neurotic suffering—contains misery. Quite the contrary. It now appears that the natural emotional state of a human being without significant psychological symptoms is a general feeling of mental and emotional well-being, comparable to the way your body feels on good days when you do not have aches and pains.

The kind of psychological suffering that is intolerable is the kind that goes on and on, that seems to have no end. The name *chronic* is usually given to this kind of suffering, and its roots do not grow in the soil of reality but in the soil of fantasy.

It is something you induce. And it is something you can bring to an end. In this book, you will learn effective ways to cope with the kind of psychological symptoms that bring you months and years of useless suffering.

Why You Have Symptoms

Why do you have symptoms? What do they mean?

The usual interpretation of symptoms in both psychiatry and clinical psychology is that they are the consciously experienced manifestations of an underlying mental or emotional illness.

This is known as the *medical viewpoint* because it borrows the basic structure of the illness concept directly from medicine. Suppose you feel feverish, nauseated, and weak. It soon turns out that you have a case of the flu. The flu is the illness, and the set of distress signals you experience are its symptoms.

Similarly, in the medical approach to psychopathology it can be argued that vague anxiety, unrealistic elation, obsessional thoughts, memory problems, compulsive eating, loss of normal pleasure in activities, and so forth, are symptoms of mental and emotional disorders. A symptom can be viewed as something like a fire alarm. If the sound of the alarm ringing irritates you (as it should), disconnecting the alarm does not stop the fire. You want to either escape from or put out the fire.

Suppose that you suffer from chronic anxiety and that you attempt to cope with it by taking tranquilizers on a regular basis. This is like disconnecting the fire alarm. The fire is allowed to rage and consume the building. Similarly, if you ignore the question of *why* you are suffering from chronic anxiety, an underlying neurotic process (i.e., the "fire") may be doing damage to your personality. If you decide to take tranquilizers to ease the immediate pain, you should still seek ways to deal with the underlying problem. This is only common sense.

The medical viewpoint has two versions. The first and oldest version is the *biological* version. The biological version holds that a mental or emotional symptom is caused by an underlying organic condition; for example, it is possible for depression to be caused by an imbalance of certain chemical messengers in the brain. This viewpoint can be traced back to 400 B.C. and Hippocrates, a Greek physician who is known as the father of Western medicine. Hippocrates held that an overabundance of the humor (i.e., fluid) black bile would cause melancholy (i.e., depression or sadness). When a person was in a good or a bad humor, the original reference was to the balance of body fluids. (Note that *melan* means "black" in Greek.) So to be *melancholy* means literally "to be afflicted with a black humor (or fluid)." Although it appears that Hippocrates had the details wrong, the modern view in psychiatry that some depression is caused by an imbalance in chemical messengers is essentially a modern version of Hippocrates' outlook.

The second version of the medical viewpoint is the *psychological* one. This version holds that a sickness can have its roots in emotional conflicts and pathological personality development. Such mental disorders are called *functional* in order to distinguish them from organic, or physical, ones. Suppose that John has the persistent idea that he can contract AIDS from touching doorknobs. He tries to ignore the thought, one that he himself regards as irrational. He develops the magical idea that he must count to seven immediately after touching a doorknob and that this will take away the danger. He finds that soon he *must* count to seven after touching any doorknob. Only this ritual will reduce his anxiety. John is suffering from an obsessive compulsive disorder. And its roots are primarily psychological and emotional, not organic.

However, the medical viewpoint is not the only one that can be applied to help us understand psychological symptoms. The *behavioral viewpoint* was inspired by the work of such great psychologists as Ivan Pavlov, John B. Watson, and B. F. Skinner. This viewpoint says that under certain conditions, no valid distinction can be made between a symptom and an underlying illness. Sometimes the symptom *is* the illness; for example, certain kinds of mental and emotional distress can be looked upon as "bad" habits. They perpetuate themselves and serve no practical function. Joseph Wolpe, father of a type of behavior therapy, spoke of "useless" fears. Many phobias (i.e., irrational fears) fall in this category. The more someone responds to a phobia by avoiding the feared thing or situation, the stronger the phobia seems to get. Going back to the fire-alarm analogy, it is as if a person keeps running out of a building that he or she imagines is burning. However, something is wrong with the alert system, and it keeps sounding false alarms! Thus, in the behavioral approach to psychopathology, the task becomes to find ways to short-circuit false alarms (i.e., meaningless psychological symptoms).

You will note that the medical and the behavioral viewpoints are not presented as logical opposites, as is often done, as if one were right and one were wrong. The truth is that both viewpoints represent valid approaches. One of the tasks in the face of an actual symptom is to determine if it represents a deeper problem or if it is something of a psychological false alarm.

Three more viewpoints merit consideration. These are the interpersonal, humanistic, and sociocultural ones. The *interpersonal* viewpoint says that a psychological symptom can arise from problems in a relationship. The most obvious example is depression because a love affair is going wrong or a marriage is on the rocks. It is assumed in the interpersonal viewpoint that the personality needs love and affection in somewhat the same way that the body needs water. Lack of emotional closeness—or intimacy—in primary relationships produces distress.

The *humanistic* viewpoint holds that a psychological symptom comes into being when a person has difficulty attaining certain crucial human values. Abraham Maslow, a principal founder of humanistic psychology, asserted that each person has an inborn need to be self-actualizing, to make the most of talents and potentialities. If one is unable to be self-actualizing, the result may be mental and emotional states such as anxiety, anger, or depression. Suppose Henry has a substantial amount of musical talent, but he has not invested the time and effort required to bring this talent to fruition. He makes a fair living as a life insurance salesman but feels that he is on the wrong road in life. His seemingly irrational outbursts against his wife and children are in part understandable in terms of his frustration with himself.

The *sociocultural* viewpoint asserts that many psychological and emotional problems are reflections of, as its name indicates, a troubled society and culture. An obvious example is that during a great economic depression there may be a rise in alcoholism and suicide. To provide a second illustration, the author Alvin Toffler coined the term *future shock* to describe the kind of mental and emotional confusion that can arise in some people when the pace of change in their social world exceeds their ability to cope. For one more example, *alienation* is a psychological symptom associated with the belief that one cannot fit into one's family or society in a meaningful way. The alienated person is convinced, "I am alone and a stranger in a world I never made."

So there are several ways of looking at psychological symptoms. None of these viewpoints is completely wrong or right. They are, in varying degrees, useful in explaining why people suffer. Each chapter of the book will include a heading called "Causes and Explanations." In those sections, the major viewpoints will underlie our efforts to make sense out of psychological symptoms.

Hope and Help

If you are suffering from a persistent psychological symptom is there any hope for you?

The answer is, of course, *yes*. For one thing, psychological symptoms are sometimes self-curing. They just go away of their own accord! Spontaneous recoveries, recoveries undoubtedly due to a natural self-healing process in the human body or personality, are relatively common. You have heard that there is no cure for the common cold, and that is correct. Nonetheless, a cold is not a permanent illness. The body's own immune system attacks the invading viruses, kills them, and the cold is gone in a few days. If you doubt that something similar takes place in the human personality, consider the fact that the most virulent of mental disorders, schizophrenia, is self-curing in about one-third of cases. (Schizophrenia is characterized by such symptoms as delusions and hallucinations and is popularly referred to as "madness.") Schizophrenia is said to follow the "rule of thirds." About one percent of the adult population is afflicted with the disorder. About one-third of this one percent will in time make a complete recovery, with or without treatment. About one-third will have periodic bouts with schizophrenic symptoms, but will often be relatively free of symptoms for long periods. And a final third will suffer from chronic schizophrenia, constantly plagued by symptoms. And there is hope even for this final third because there are treatments today that can reduce the worst symptoms of schizophrenia, often making life tolerable for patients and their families.

If there is real hope for even the most severe of mental disorders, imagine how much hope there is for conditions in which one's contact with reality is intact. If you are able to think relatively clearly, the dice are loaded in your favor. You can take advantages of the ideas in this book and apply them to yourself. If you decide to seek counseling or psychotherapy, you can benefit from what you learn.

You will find in each of the book's chapters two sections relating to hope and help for the symptom, or symptoms, under consideration. The first of the two sections is headed "Coping," and sets forth practical ways you can help yourself. The immediately following section is headed "Professional Help," and describes the kinds of treatment offered by psychiatrists and clinical psychologists. Discussions of both drug therapy and psychotherapy are included.

Terms and the Glossary

Whenever psychological terms are first introduced in the text proper, they are both italicized and defined. Usually the definition is followed by an example. In some instances, where it was deemed to be of particular importance for either emphasis or clarity of communication, a term is italicized and defined again.

Toward the back of the book, you will find the Glossary. It contains brief definitions of all important terms used in the book.

Key Points to Remember

- It really is possible to be free of mental and emotional suffering.
- Much mental and emotional suffering is unnecessary.
- It now appears that the natural state of the human being, without significant psychological symptoms, is a general feeling of mental and emotional well-being.
- Several viewpoints are used to explain psychological symptoms. They are not mutually exclusive. Each is useful in its own way.
- There is hope for you if you are suffering from one or several persistent psychological symptoms.
- Psychological symptoms are sometimes self-curing.
- The "Coping" section of each chapter will set forth practical ways to cope with psychological symptoms.
- The "Professional Help" section of each chapter will describe the kinds of treatment offered by psychiatry and clinical psychology for the symptoms under consideration.
- On page 246, you will find the Glossary.

Chapter 2

Alcohol Abuse: Mistreatment of the Self

In the classic film *The Lost Weekend*, the protagonist wakes up on a Monday morning and realizes in great distress that he has no memory of the past 48 hours. This is the "lost weekend" of the title. One of the symptoms associated with alcohol abuse is *blackouts*, or periods of amnesia that can span several hours or even several days.

Alcohol abuse has a peculiar association with the literary arts. Tom Dardis, author of *The Thirsty Muse*, says, "Of the seven native-born Americans awarded the Nobel Prize in literature, five were alcoholic." The five identified by Dardis are Sinclair Lewis, Eugene O'Neill, William Faulkner, Ernest Hemingway, and John Steinbeck. Other famous writers who abused alcohol include Jack London, F. Scott Fitzgerald, Thomas Wolfe, and Dashiel Hammet. The list could be greatly extended. (The term *alcoholic* may be a little too strong. It is better to speak of alcohol abuse or alcohol dependence.)

Jack London, author of *The Call of the Wild* and *The Sea Wolf*, insisted that he was not an alcoholic. He said that he drank heavily by choice, not by compulsion. He went so far as to write a book entitled *John Barleycorn* in which he described the evils of alcohol abuse, but he believed that he was somehow above its ravages. In spite of a robust constitution, he died at the age of 39 of kidney failure almost certainly caused by, or greatly aggravated by, alcohol abuse.

Alcohol abuse is a chronic self-destructive pattern of heavy drinking that produces significant damage to one's health, career, and family relations. *Alcohol dependence* is the inability to free oneself at will from a pattern of heavy drinking and can be thought of as an addiction to a drug. Indeed, alcohol *is* a drug. It is a central-nervous-system depressant, and some of the dependent individual's craving is based on an acquired physiological need.

One reason to avoid the term *alcoholic* is that it tends to label the individual. If it is said a person *is* an alcoholic, then it is assumed that he or she overuses alcohol because of a certain elusive quality of personality or inner being. On the other hand, if it is simply said descriptively that the individual abuses or is dependent on alcohol, the focus is on *behavior* and ways that the behavior can be modified. For these reasons, the principal term that will be used in this chapter is *alcohol abuse.*

The American Psychiatric Association describes three principal patterns of alcohol abuse. First, some individuals drink excessive quantities of alcohol every day. Second, some individuals save all of their heavy drinking for weekends when they do not have career responsibilities. Third, some individuals stay sober for long periods and then go on extended "benders" or "toots."

Alcohol abuse is a tremendous social problem in the United States. It is estimated that somewhat over 10 percent of adults have at least one prolonged bout with alcohol abuse. The cost in auto accidents, damaged careers, and unhappy homes is beyond measure.

Other signs and symptoms frequently associated with the principal symptom of alcohol abuse are:

1. Loss of interest in eating
2. Unsteadiness in the early hours of the day
3. Pains in the stomach
4. Pathological differences in the personality
5. Mental bewilderment and disorientation
6. Damage to the internal organs
7. Deficiency of vitamin B_1
8. Giving birth to an infant with fetal alcohol syndrome
9. The development of Korsakoff's psychosis
10. Delirium tremens

Some of the above items require comment. *Fetal alcohol syndrome* is characterized by one or more birth defects such as a cleft palate or an improperly formed heart. *Korsakoff's psychosis* is also known as *alcohol amnestic disorder* and is characterized by severe memory difficulties. *Delirium tremens* is caused by withdrawal from alcohol and is characterized by an elevated temperature, agitation, delusions, and hallucinations.

Causes and Explanations

The subtitle of this chapter is "Mistreatment of the Self," and that is one way to think of alcohol abuse. In classical psychoanalytic theory, it is held that the basic drive of aggression can sometimes be turned inward. Thus, a way to look at alcohol abuse is as a form of self-aggression. It can be seen as a slow form of suicide, sometimes called an *indirect self-destructive pattern*. (For more about this pattern, see Chapter 24.) An example of the interpretation of the kind of suicide under discussion is provided toward the end of the actor Errol Flynn's autobiography, *My Wicked, Wicked Ways*. He was totally disappointed in himself as a human being and sought to destroy himself with alcohol. He succeeded.

The genetic interpretation of alcohol addiction has been given a great deal of credibility in the last decade or so. Research suggests that there may be an inborn predisposition to become dependent on alcohol. This is based on studies in which adopted children upon reaching adulthood have drinking patterns more like one of their biological parents than either of their adoptive parents. Although it seems clear that there may be a genetic factor involved in alcohol abuse, it is very doubtful in an individual case that this factor is the sole explanation for the pathological behavior. Genes may set the person up for a pattern of abuse or addiction, but psychological factors are required to trigger the pattern.

It is possible to think of alcohol abuse as a pathological habit. This approach sees alcohol abuse as learned behavior. The learned behavior is shaped by one or more *reinforcers*, psychological payoffs for the behavior. What are these payoffs? An obvious one is anxiety reduction. Alcohol is a central-nervous-system depressant and acts upon it like a tranquilizer. Another reinforcer is sexual success. Alcohol often paves the way for sexual relations, reducing inhibitions and moral restraints. Another reinforcer is forgetfulness. It is possible to temporarily blot out one's troubles with alcohol. Still another reinforcer is fellowship. People who would otherwise be boring seem more likeable to someone who is inebriated. Another reinforcer is shyness reduction. Shyness is a common personality trait, and alcohol helps the individual to feel more self-confident in social relations.

In the case of the creative writer, alcohol may act as a reinforcer by providing, or seeming to provide, greater access to a wealth of images and otherwise unconscious ideas. The drug seems to remove blocks to the flow of inspiration. The late poet John Ciardi in an article in *The Writer's Digest* admitted that he used alcohol in this way. Raymond Chandler, author of *The Big Sleep* and other Philip Marlowe mysteries, kept a fifth of good whiskey in a drawer in his desk and spoke of it as a "friend" when he was writing. Many psychologists believe that alcohol is only a short-term aid to creativity. In the long run, its effects are corrosive and eventually destroy the ability to create.

What role does physiological addiction play in alcohol abuse? It is true that alcohol is an addictive drug; that is, the body builds up a requirement for the drug when a person is a habitual user. Thus, withdrawal from the drug produces uncomfortable physical symptoms such as stomach cramps, severe headaches, shakiness, and, in extreme cases, delirium tremens. The person is said to be "hooked" on the drug. However, this addictive property of the drug is not so important as is commonly assumed. A person can be detoxified in a hospital setting in a few weeks. The person is no longer physiologically addicted to the drug; the biological dependence is completely gone. However, the vast majority of such detoxified persons go back to the abuse of alcohol after leaving the hospital. Why? The individual remains *psychologically addicted* long after the physiological addiction is gone. The reinforcers associated with alcohol abuse are still there, and the individual seeks these in times of emotional need.

The game-playing aspects of alcohol abuse should not be overlooked. A *game* is a self-defeating pattern of social behavior involving two or more persons. Suppose Ralph abuses alcohol. Helen, his long-suffering wife, is the stable, responsible one in the family. She pays the bills, works when Ralph is unemployed, keeps a clean home, and sees to it that the children go to school. Ralph is playing the social role of Alcoholic, with a capital *A*. Helen is playing the social role of Victim, also with a capital letter. They both get something out of this game. Ralph uses the game to punish and humiliate Helen. It is one of his pathways for the expression of aggression. Helen uses the game to feel morally superior. By being stable and responsible, she enables Ralph to continue to abuse alcohol. Thus, she becomes what is termed a *codependent* in the disease process.

Coping

If you abuse or are addicted to alcohol, you may find value in the following list of practical coping strategies:

• Ask yourself if you are using alcohol to destroy yourself. If you become aware that you are using a bottle in much the way that a suicide victim uses a gun, then you have made an important step in the direction of recovery. If you feel helpless in the face of this kind of knowledge, you should seek outside assistance. When you cannot rescue yourself, it is only common sense to seek help.

• Examine the reinforcers that support or continue a pattern of alcohol abuse in your particular case. Look for better ways to obtain the same reinforcers. If, for example, you use alcohol to relieve anxiety, ask yourself how you can relieve anxiety in more constructive ways. For more on relieving anxiety, see Chapter Five. If you use alcohol to relieve shyness, consider taking a course in assertiveness training. Such courses are offered by many colleges extension programs and counseling centers.

• Avoid critical cues. Habits are usually triggered by certain well-defined stimulus situations. The most obvious example for alcohol abuse is a friendly bar where you often do a lot of heavy drinking. The best and most solid advice in the world is to avoid this bar. This is much easier said than done. Nonetheless, avoiding the environmental or social cues that set off a habit is one basic way to undermine it.

• Do not use alcohol to facilitate a creative process. Most people need good, fresh ideas in their work. Engineers, teachers, people in the advertising business, writers, and research scientists are all examples of persons who are paid to be creative. Just remember that the search for ideas in a bottle of booze is a devil's bargain. The long-run cost is much greater than the short-term benefit. There are many effective ways to increase one's creative flow without resorting to alcohol.

• Do not give up hope by saying to yourself, "It's all genetic. My father was an alcoholic, and so was his father. I'm doomed to follow the pattern." Think of the genetic factor as a tendency, no more. Attitudes, emotional conflicts, habits, and other psychological factors play paramount roles in the direction your behavior actually takes, and these are factors over which you can exercise a degree of control.

• Remain vigilant. Suppose you have been detoxified. You are no longer physiologically addicted to alcohol. Your body does not crave it. You are still at risk. Do not relax and let go of the kinds of coping strategies presented here. You have won a battle, but you have not won the war. You have to keep fighting for your sobriety.

• Ask yourself if you are playing the role of Alcoholic in a self-defeating life game. Are you using intoxication as a way to punish someone else? Reflect on any patterns in your relationships with significant-other people in your life, and look for more constructive ways to relate to them.

• If you are a codependent in the game of Alcoholic, ask yourself how you might be inadvertently playing into the hands of the problem drinker. Are you being used? Are you making it possible for the other person to continue a pattern of irresponsible behavior?

• If you discover that your drinking is out of control, that you cannot stop when you want to, and that alcohol abuse and addiction are having a destructive effect on your life, seriously consider becoming a member of Alcoholics Anonymous (AA). The organization's Twelve Step recovery program has helped many people. If you are a codependent or family member, Al-Anon and Alateen groups can be beneficial.

Professional Help

If you find that you cannot cope adequately with alcohol abuse and/or addiction, there are a number of ways in which the professions of psychiatry and clinical psychology can help you.

A therapist with a psychodynamic approach can assist you in exploring the reasons *why* you drink. Often these reasons are obscure and half-hidden in the mists of the mind. The therapist, through the use of interpretations, can act like a mirror, revealing the hidden self to consciousness. Many drinkers think that they know why they drink. This can be an illusion. Often the insight, or self-understanding, that is revealed in psychotherapy is effective in freeing the individual from compulsive drinking patterns.

Some psychotherapists focus on the behavior of drinking itself, seeking ways to modify it directly by a well-established set of habit-breaking procedures. One method that has met with mixed success is to teach patients to sip mixed drinks instead of rapidly consuming, for example, straight whiskey. In behavior therapy, individuals are reinforced with a second mixed drink if they can demonstrate slow consumption. This method has met with numerous objections because there are many students of alcohol abuse who are convinced that total abstinence is the only answer.

Another kind of behavior modification involves *aversive conditioning*, a learning procedure in which an unpleasant stimulus, such as mild electric shock to the fingertips, is administered on a random basis during the undesirable behavior, which would be when alcohol is being consumed. Mild electric shock tends to produce nausea and a generally unpleasant feeling in the body. Eventually the sight of alcohol tends to produce a similar reaction. Aversive conditioning can be helpful as a secondary therapy in some cases, but it needs to be combined with an insight-oriented approach and additional habit-breaking procedures.

A variant of aversive conditioning involves prescription of the drug *disulfiram*, marketed under the trade name of Antabuse.

If disulfiram is taken alone, it is generally not toxic. However, if an individual is taking regular doses and consumes alcohol, there will be a severe *disulfiram reaction* involving such unpleasant responses as nausea and vomiting. As long as the patient is taking the drug, there will be a tendency to avoid alcohol consumption. After the patient stops taking the drug, there is often a residual avoidance tendency due to negative associations with the disulfiram reaction.

An antianxiety agent is often prescribed during the withdrawal phase from alcohol addiction. The logic of this is that a patient often uses alcohol to reduce anxiety. The prescription drug provides a temporary bridge to a more sober style of life.

Psychiatrists are medical doctors, and their services are of particular value if you are physiologically addicted to alcohol. A program of detoxification requires medical supervision. If delirium tremens occurs, medical management is of particular importance for your physical health.

Key Points to Remember

- Alcohol abuse is a chronic self-destructive pattern of heavy drinking that produces significant damage to one's health, career, and family relations.

- Alcohol dependence is the inability to free oneself at will from a pattern of heavy drinking and can be thought of as an addiction to a drug.

- It is estimated that somewhat over 10 percent of adults have at least one prolonged bout with alcohol abuse.

- Other signs and symptoms associated with the principal symptom of alcohol abuse suggest a general pattern of deterioration in both the body and the personality.

- Delirium tremens is caused by withdrawal from alcohol and is characterized by an elevated temperature, agitation, delusions, and hallucinations.

- One way to look at alcohol abuse is to think of it as a form of self-aggression.

- Genes may set the person up for a pattern of abuse or addiction, but psychological factors are required to trigger the pattern.

- An important distinction is the one between psychological and physiological addiction.

- A codependent individual may inadvertently reinforce a pattern of alcohol abuse.

- A key coping strategy is to examine the reinforcers that maintain a pattern of alcohol abuse.

- If your drinking is out of control, you should seriously consider becoming a member of Alcoholics Anonymous (AA).

- Insight, or self-understanding, can be helpful in freeing the individual from compulsive drinking patterns.

- Aversive conditioning, involving the use of either mild electric shocks or the drug disulfiram, is sometimes a useful form of adjunct therapy.

- Psychiatrists are medical doctors, and their services are of particular value if you are physiologically addicted to alcohol.

Chapter 3

Alienation: "I Call No Place Home."

Below is an excerpt from the personal journal of Virginia J., a 27-year-old woman with two school-age children. She married her husband, Sawyer, when she was 17 and is a full-time homemaker.

> I've just had breakfast with Sawyer and the kids. They're off to work and school now. While they were eating breakfast, I stared at them like they were strangers—like they didn't belong to me and I didn't belong to them. They are my family, but they don't *feel* like *my* family. They are outside of me and I am outside of them. Sawyer said something while he was eating that was supposed to be funny, and the children laughed. I didn't laugh. I didn't even smile. Now I stare at the walls of the kitchen and think, "I don't belong in this room. I belong somewhere else. But where?"

The lines from Virginia's journal reveal that she is suffering from an unpleasant and confusing sense of alienation from her family. *Alienation* is the feeling that one does not belong to a given reference group. It is important to note that alienation is always alienation *from*. A person can be alienated from the family, from friends, or from the general society. It is possible to be alienated from a first group and feel that one belongs to a second group. Thus, an adolescent might feel alienated from the family but not alienated from a school team, a club, or a gang. The familiar term *generation gap* is associated with this kind of teenage alienation.

Alienation is highly distressing when the individual feels emotionally disconnected from *all* reference groups. Such an individual is lonely and lost—a complete outsider. He or she can say with complete conviction, "I call no place home."

The image of the alienated person has been popularized and glamorized in the twentieth century. In the film *Rebel Without a Cause*, James Dean portrayed a confused, rebellious adolescent who was alienated from his parents. The 1934 novel by James M. Cain, *The Postman Always Rings*

Twice, has been made into two films. The more recent version starred Jack Nicholson as Frank Chambers, a man alienated from traditional society and all it stands for. The existentialist author Albert Camus said that the style and theme of *The Postman Always Rings Twice* was an important influence when he wrote *The Stranger,* published in 1942. *The Stranger* portrays a man who seems to have no heart, no soul, no capacity to love or feel in the normal way. It is an ultimate portrayal of an alienated person.

There is nothing admirable or glamorous about alienation. It is a kind of pathology. It is an important psychological symptom suggesting that something has gone badly wrong in a person's life. An alienated existence is a joyless existence. Until an individual who suffers from alienation can "come in from the cold," he or she will pay a heavy emotional price.

Usually, the word *alienation* refers to the individual's emotional distance from a group or groups. However, it is possible to speak of *self-alienation.* A first characteristic of self-alienation is a loss of a robust sense of identity. The person feels confused about his or her self-image and what social role or roles should be played in life. A second characteristic of self-alienation is a sense of depersonalization, the general impression that one is more of a thing, object, or robot, than a human being.

Other signs and symptoms related to the major symptom of alienation are:

1. Loss of a sense of humor
2. The conviction that life is without purpose or meaning
3. Emotional numbness
4. A desire to run away from, or abandon, friends and family
5. The illusion, recognized as irrational, that one does not belong with *this* family or other group
6. A secret sense of superiority—others seem stupid or shallow
7. Social introversion
8. Lack of caring for others

Some of these related signs and symptoms merit comment. *Loss of a sense of humor* is common in cases of alienation because the individual has lost the capacity for joy. The person is in no mood for jokes and a look at the funny side of life. *The conviction that life is without purpose or meaning* is associated with a loss of attachment to values. Nothing seems worth doing; nothing seems important. Even fundamental values such as raising one's children or earning a living seem trivial. (For more about loss of meaning in life, see Chapter 16.)

Emotional numbness refers to a restricted range of feeling. The individual finds it difficult to become excited about anything. Most experiences bring neither pleasure nor displeasure. *Social introversion* refers to a tendency to pull into oneself. There is withdrawal from others. The kind of social introversion associated with alienation should not be confused with a similar trait associated with shyness. In the case of alienation, there is a quality of coldness and lack of concern for others. In the case of shyness, although there is withdrawal, there is often an intense wish to be accepted and liked. (For more about shyness, see Chapter 26.)

It is important to note that alienation often overlaps with other major psychological symptoms such as boredom, depression, and helplessness.

In psychiatry and clinical psychology, alienation is not regarded as a mental disorder in and of itself. However, it is recognized as playing a role in *antisocial personality disorder*, which is characterized by a lack of interest in the rights and feelings of others.

Causes and Explanations

To some extent, alienation is a malaise of modern times. There are no exact statistics, of course, because the concept of alienation is a very general, abstract one. Also, it is not a defined mental disorder as such. Nonetheless, it can be said with some confidence that alienation in the modern sense is uncommon in tribal societies, small villages, and in highly traditional cultures. Factors contributing to alienation include a complex, changing society that presents an overwhelming number of hard choices to the individual; moving frequently from job to job and place to place; the high divorce rate; the loss of the extended family as an important support system; the tendency in some organizations to treat people as replaceable units rather than as human beings with feelings and needs; a high population density, which can make the individual feel small and unimportant; and so forth. It is difficult *not* to feel alienated if one's sense of individual worth is violated. Often the individual feels small and powerless in the midst of torrents of social forces that are far beyond one person's control.

Experiences in childhood may contribute to a sense of alienation. If a child has parents that are (1) authoritarian and overcontrolling and (2) emotionally distant, the child will find it difficult to identify with the family and develop a sense of real belongingness. In psychoanalytic terms, such a child will not develop a traditional *superego*, a moral self that reflects the standards and values of the family. In adolescence and adulthood, it can be expected that such an individual will be estranged from the family. It can also be expected that such an individual will find it difficult to form close ties with others and develop the kind of emotional intimacy required in a successful marriage.

From the behavioral viewpoint, it is possible to argue that the kinds of withdrawal behaviors associated with alienation may be reinforcing to the individual, having their own psychological payoffs. If one feels uncomfortable and ill at ease in the presence of certain people, one may experience a sense of relief when there is an opportunity to escape from, or avoid, their presence. The sense of relief is reinforcing and increases the likelihood of withdrawal behavior. Thus, a vicious circle forms that strengthens the sense of alienation.

Alienation may arise in the context of a troubled interpersonal relationship. Marriage provides a common example. Virginia J., referred to in the opening paragraph of this chapter, married Sawyer in good faith without any sense of alienation toward him at the time of the wedding. Recall that she was 17 when she married. Although she was not openly estranged from her family, she often had daydreams in which she left home. The marriage to Sawyer provided a respectable way to do so. It should be noted that she already had latent tendencies toward alienation at the time she married. She entertained the fantasy that her marriage would meet all of her emotional needs. When Sawyer turned out to be somewhat authoritarian and egotistical with demanding emotional needs of his own, she hit a wall of frustration. The passage of time and inability to cope effectively with the demands of the relationship eventually led her to become increasingly alienated.

Finally, it can be said that alienation is one of the psychological costs associated with the inability to attain meaningful goals in life. If an individual has talents, aptitudes, and abilities that go unrecognized and unrewarded, there can be an increasing sense of a breach or a void between the individual and those people or organizations that are expected to provide gratification. This is why the stereotype of artists, such as poets, painters, and novelists, portrays them as bitter and rebellious. If their works are ignored and unpublished, with the passage of time, they tend to become alienated.

Coping

If you feel alienated from significant-other people in your life or from traditional society, you may find value in the following list of practical coping strategies.

• Be prepared to expect that one side of your personality will resist any efforts to overcome alienation. This is because you feel *justified* in your alienation. In a state of alienation, you tend to think of others as being in the wrong. Therefore, you can probably take some comfort in your alienation and nurse it. However, keep in mind that you lose much more than you gain. The price you pay is emotional isolation and the other psychological symptoms already described. *Decide* that it is well worth it to make some effort to overcome alienation.

• Do not allow yourself to become convinced that alienation is a sign of your unusual brightness or intelligence. It is true that unusually bright or reflective people often tend to become alienated. In a sense, their intense self-awareness digs for them a psychological hole. However, the really clever thing is not to dig your hole, but to construct a psychological ladder out of it. Jean-Paul Sartre, one of the founders of existentialism, discovered that he could overcome alienation—a problem he experienced as a young adult—by acting *as if* there were things worth doing and ideas worth believing in. He said people create value by their actions. He used his intelligence to cope with the alienation his very intelligence had created.

• Recognize that alienation is a defense system. It is a way of shielding yourself from rejection and psychological injury. The psychological game is that you reject others before they can reject you. However, you can be so overprotected in your defense system that you fear to venture forth from your emotional citadel. As a consequence, you lose out on opportunities to make emotional contact with others. Experiment with risking contact. As one saying goes, "Give the suckers an even break." Maybe they will not be so bad after all.

• If you are alienated from your family, you are probably magnifying all of their bad points and minimizing all of their good points. Try to look at them more objectively. Attempt to make a more balanced appraisal than the one you have been making. Find out more about them as persons, as individuals. If possible, learn something about your roots and the family history from grandparents, aunts and uncles, or other relatives. They may have some interesting stories to tell that will reveal the family to you in a richer, three-dimensional perspective.

• Refuse to be a victim of modern times. Just because society is vast and complex and many impersonal forces exist there, do not develop the point of view that you are just a piece of flotsam to be buffeted about. Instead, take the point of view that you have a will, that *you* are in control. If you now work for a big company, you do not have to stay there and accept its impersonal treatment of you. You can work for a smaller organization or eventually start a small business. The small fish in the big pond often feels alienated, but the big fish in the small pond does not. If you need to, you can play the game of life on a smaller scale.

• If you are married or involved in a close personal relationship, you will find that alienation increases when you refuse to speak up for yourself in an assertive manner. If you manifest a cold exterior and respond to real or imagined slights with sullen, brooding, moody, petulant, or sulking behavior, the emotional gap between you and your partner will increase. Firm assertiveness without hostility is, of course, better than a verbal fight. However, a quarrel—if it must come to that—is probably better than playing the role of victim. There is some truth to familiar comments such as, "First we fight, then we make up."

· If you have talents, aptitudes, and abilities that are going unrecognized and unrewarded, you may be asking for too much too soon. First, set subgoals for yourself. Make your level of aspiration realistic. Reach for what you can actually grasp. (One man, for example, is a very talented performer. He is an attorney by avocation and performs in local musical plays as an avocation. He meets his needs for self-actualization in a practical way.) Also, realize that success usually takes time. It is a process. Often larger recognition may come, but it comes slowly. Reject the impatience that aggravates a sense of alienation.

Professional Help

If you find that you cannot cope adequately with alienation, there are a number of ways in which the professions of psychiatry and clinical psychology can help you.

The general approach usually taken in psychotherapy with an alienated person can be broadly characterized with such words as *existential* or *humanistic*. This is to say that the focus is on the person's day-to-day struggle with life and his or her unique characteristics as a human being. A specific kind of existential therapy that is often helpful in cases of alienation is logotherapy, pioneered by the psychiatrist Viktor Frankl. *Logotherapy* employs a series of thoughtful discussions designed to help the troubled individual rediscover meaning in life. Although logotherapy was designed to deal primarily with the major problem of meaninglessness in life, this particular problem often overlaps with alienation. Therefore, logotherapy is well-suited to deal with both problems.

An existential or humanistic approach in therapy recognizes that the alienated person is a conscious, thinking, reflecting human being. The focus of the therapy is not so much on early childhood experiences as the here and now. The therapist and the client assume that the power of the will is real and that it can help the individual overcome alienation.

Cognitive therapy is often employed in conjunction with a general humanistic approach. In cognitive therapy, the client is asked to reevaluate long-held conscious ideas, ideas that may have become automatic. Usually the alienated person holds such ideas as, "I don't care about other people; they don't mean anything to me," or "I don't belong here with these people—they don't love me and I don't love them," or "I wish I lived in another time and another place." These, and similar ideas, are subjected to the spotlight of logic. They are often revealed to be overgeneralizations and oversimplifications.

The therapist will often encourage the alienated person to stop using alienation as a defense mechanism, as a way of avoiding reality. Instead, the individual is encouraged to turn around, face reality, and realize that one way to overcome alienation is to take responsibility for both life and relationships.

The therapist may introduce elements of assertiveness training. These are specific skills designed to help the individual become more effective in interpersonal relationships. Often alienated persons exhibit excessively passive and compliant behavior in the presence of others or excessively aggressive, hostile behavior. Both of these extremes intensify feelings of alienation. Assertiveness is an effective coping tool that holds forth the reward of greater emotional closeness with others. Assertiveness skills are of particular importance when applied to the problems of couples.

Behavior modification is sometimes employed in a specific and limited way in the treatment of alienation. The client is asked to ascertain ways in which behaviors associated with alienation, such as avoidance and withdrawal, tend to bring about the short-term gains of relief and psychological safety. These short-term gains are defined as reinforcers that maintain and sustain the individual's pathology. The therapist and the client together look for ways to break out of the vicious circle created by the chain of reinforcement.

You are likely to resist and even try to defeat the therapist's best efforts. The effective therapist will interpret this behavior to you and explain how you use resistance as a way of hanging on to alienation and its short-term benefits. Interpretation of resistance is often an effective tool in therapy, and it is of particular value when much of the difficulty revolves around a problem that affects the individual's character. Alienation is this kind of problem.

The therapist will help you to see that you are an individual with a will and the powers of self-direction and choice. You are not just a pawn of fate. These insights form an essential part of overcoming alienation.

The therapist will assist you in becoming a self-actualizing person. You should receive encouragement to make the most of your talents, aptitudes, and potentialities in *realistic* ways that match your opportunities and life situation.

The prescription of drugs is not a treatment for alienation. It is true that alienation is often associated with depression, and in some cases of depression drug therapy is appropriate. Nonetheless, alienation in and of itself as a problem is not due to organic or biological factors. It is the result of an attitude toward life, a negative one, arising from an incorrect appraisal of one's situation. Therefore, the alienated person can be effectively helped in therapy primarily by appealing to his or her thinking processes.

Key Points to Remember

• Alienation is the feeling that one does not belong to a given reference group. A person can be alienated from the family, from some other group, or from the traditional society.

• An alienated existence is a joyless existence.

• Alienation is a malaise of modern times.

• A parental style that is simultaneously authoritarian and emotionally distant can be a causal factor in eventual alienation.

• Withdrawal and avoidance behaviors may have their own short-term psychological payoffs and, in consequence, maintain and reinforce a state of alienation.

• Alienation may arise in the context of a troubled interpersonal relationship.

• If talents, aptitudes, and abilities go unrecognized and unrewarded, this can contribute to alienation.

• Realize that you may resist your own efforts to overcome alienation.

• Recognize that alienation represents a defense system.

• Learning something about your roots and the family history may be helpful in overcoming alienation.

• Refuse to be a victim of modern times. Do not accept the idea that you are a pawn of fate and powerless in the presence of impersonal forces.

• Sullen, brooding, moody, or sulking behavior aggravates alienation.

• Meet your needs for self-actualization in a practical way. Set subgoals for yourself.

• A specific kind of existential therapy often helpful in cases of alienation is logotherapy.

• Usually the alienated person holds ideas about life that cannot stand the harsh spotlight of logic.

• Alienation in and of itself as a problem is not due to organic or biological factors. Thus, the prescription of drugs is not a treatment for alienation.

Chapter 4

Anger: Seeing Red When the Light Is Green

Karl R. is an angry man. He growls at his wife for little or nothing. He is short-tempered with his children and is quickly critical of the slightest infraction of his rules. He is convinced the he is underpaid and overworked. Although he believes that his employer is a hard-hearted Scrooge, Karl himself barks orders unfeelingly to workers beneath him. His wife complains to her sister, "Even when you're pleasant to Karl, you're likely to get an angry response. He seems to see red even when the light is green." In short, Karl lives in a state of perpetual resentment, exasperation, indignation, and borderline rage. There appears to be little or no objective provocation for his constant emotional agitation.

Anger is an unpleasant emotional state characterized by high physiological arousal. The pulse quickens, the respirations increase, the pupils of the eyes constrict, blood rushes to the striated muscles of the body (the muscles that move the body's bones), and the adrenal glands pump out hormones. At the conscious level, there are commonly to be found ideas such as, "She shouldn't have said that to me," or "Who does he think he is?" or "I can't take any more of this," or "That bastard is always taking advantage of me." From the primitive biological point of view, the angry person is demonstrating a well-known response pattern called the *fight-or-flight reaction*. In a civilized setting, the angry person can seldom engage in a physical fight or run away. Therefore, an individual such as Karl is often forced to stew in his own emotional juice.

A distinction can be made between manifest anger and latent anger. *Manifest anger* is evident, and the individual is aware of it. *Latent anger* is repressed to an unconscious level, and the individual is not aware of it. Latent anger plays a role in chronic depression. (For more about latent anger, see Chapter 8, the chapter on depression.) The kind of anger being discussed here is manifest anger.

Manifest anger can be transient or chronic. Everyone is familiar with transient anger. It is a normal, appropriate emotion. It is usually a natural reaction to a frustration and tends to spontaneously evaporate in a short time. On the other hand, chronic anger represents a real problem in personal adjustment. It has three key attributes. First, it is *pathological.* It tends to poison the person's life and may even contribute to physical illness. Second, it is *excessive.* The anger expressed is out-of-bounds as a response to the frustration experienced. Third, it is *irrational.* Usually, an idea that is neither logical or reasonable is linked with it.

Other signs and symptoms frequently associated with the principal symptom of chronic anger are:

1. Impatience
2. Constant hurrying
3. Speaking in a harsh, abrupt manner
4. Egotistical and self-centered behavior
5. Inability to relax readily
6. High blood pressure
7. Inability to play or enjoy vacations
8. Verbal aggressiveness
9. Free-floating hostility

Some of these signs and symptoms merit comment. *Impatience* and *constant hurrying* are both aspects of a general attitude that is called *time urgency.* It is as if the chronically angry person is in a time pressure cooker. *High blood pressure* is common in angry people because the body is always on alert, always ready for action.

Free-floating hostility is characterized by being mad at everybody and everything. The chronically angry person is ready to hurl negative psychological thunderbolts at the slightest provocation. Thus, others are constantly discounted, abused, or even insulted. Privately, people are given such labels as *stupid, incompetent,* and *lazy.*

There is obviously a strong similarity between these signs and symptoms and a pattern of behavior that was first designated *Type A behavior* by the cardiologists Meyer Friedman and Ray H. Rosenman in the 1970s. Recent research suggests that one of the most serious components of Type A behavior is chronic anger.

Causes and Explanations

Chronic anger may have roots in early childhood experiences. In classical psychoanalysis, the id, the primitive, inborn self, is the source of aggressiveness. The superego, the moral self, comes into being as a result of socializing experiences. The moral self may not develop adequately because of ineffective parenting. In such a case, the id has too much influence on the adult personality and expresses itself too readily. Thus, the individual who manifests chronic anger is sometimes seen in psychoanalysis as a case of arrested emotional development. This is evidenced in familiar common-sense statements such as, "He's just a big baby," or "I wish she'd grow up," or "She's just a brat."

The psychoanalyst Karen Horney theorized that victims of chronic anger may not have had their emotional needs met in infancy and toddlerhood. This led them to suffer from an underlying condition called *basic anxiety*, the unverbalized impression that the world is unsafe and threatening. One way an adult can defend against basic anxiety is by repressing it and converting it to anger. Threats are anticipated and dealt with while they are still far away on the psychological horizon. Thus, Horney looks on much chronic anger as a defense against emotional insecurity.

Longitudinal studies by developmental psychologists on traits of temperament suggest that these traits are to some extent inborn and relatively stable. Some children are more aggressive than others, and this is just their basic disposition. Although this is not an explanation of chronic anger, such a trait of temperament, if present, may interact with other causes and amplify chronic anger.

If a child grows up in a family that allows itself frequent irrational outbursts of anger, then observational learning can play a role in a tendency toward chronic anger. The adult may be imitating the behavior of parents or older siblings. The individual was given tacit permission as a child to express aggressive impulses without sufficient restraint.

It is possible that the angry adult was a verbal or physical bully as a child or adolescent. Such behavior often intimidates others and may bring short-term psychological payoffs. If so, the behavior is reinforced and tends to become a trait of personality.

The aggressive adult may have been a hyperactive child. (Aggressiveness and hyperactivity are often linked in children.)

One factor that appears to play an important role in childhood hyperactivity is minimal brain dysfunction (MBD). *Minimal brain dysfunction* is *not* gross damage, nor does it impair basic intelligence. However, it appears to be related to a problem in the brain center that controls arousal. Although it is commonplace to say that hyperactivity is something that will be outgrown in adulthood, it is possible that hyperactive tendencies carry over to some extent in some persons and, in turn, magnify normal anger into chronic anger.

Chronic anger may be aggravated by interpersonal problems. Here is an example: Mabel J. is married to a man who is a whining, clinging, sorry-for-himself individual. His constant self-indulgent laments leave her feeling frustrated. Mabel has an aggressive temperament. Consequently, it is not much of a wonder that she makes her husband the target of hostile remarks. She is angry, in a constant state of emotional irritation, and she expresses herself accordingly.

A basic way to understand anger is to refer to the *frustration-aggression hypothesis*, which states that aggression is a natural response to frustration. Frustration is a state that occurs when the motivated individual is unable to (1) attain a desirable goal or (2) to escape from, or avoid, an unpleasant situation. If you intensely desire a promotion and it goes to someone else, you will be frustrated and in turn angry. If you feel trapped in an unhappy relationship, again you will be frustrated and, in turn, angry. Chronic anger may result when an individual believes, correctly or incorrectly, that life presents a constant stream of frustrating events.

The psychiatrist William Glasser, father of reality therapy, makes the point that anger is, to a large extent, self-induced. It is not only a reaction to a situation, it as a *voluntary action*. A person creates anger by his or her evaluations and choices and, thus, needs to take responsibility for the anger. This leads naturally to the topic of coping with anger.

Coping

If you suffer from chronic anger, you may find value in the following list of practical coping strategies.

• Be open to the possibility that you might be overvaluing the importance of your own emotional states and not placing enough importance on your responsibility to act like a mature, reasonable adult. Place an image in your mind of how you *should* act in emotional situations, and try to use it as a guide.

• Ask yourself if you are using anger as a way of coping with basic anxiety. If latent, or repressed, anxiety plays a role in your chronic anger, consider applying some of the coping suggestions in Chapter 5, the chapter on anxiety.

• Impose a *delay* between a situation that aggravates you and your actions in response to it. It has been standard to advise people prone to excessive, quick anger to "Count to ten." Although the advice is trite, it has value.

• Think of a self-imposed delay as a "time-out." During the time-out, *challenge* the anger-inducing ideas going through your mind; for example, if you are thinking, "Susan always keeps me waiting like this," ask yourself, "Am I right? Does she *always* do it?" You may realize that you are overgeneralizing and being unfair to Susan.

• Even if a tendency to be more aggressive than others is an inborn trait of your personality, you do not want to cling to the attitude that you are the trait's helpless victim. Instead, develop the attitude that you can *work around* the trait, that you can effectively diminish its influence with your intelligence and your will.

• Perhaps you are imitating the angry behavior that, as a child, you witnessed in your parents or older siblings. If so, ask yourself these questions, "Am I just a copycat? Do I have to do something just because I saw less thoughtful people do it as a child? Am I a programmed robot or a human being?" Reflective answers to these questions may help to set you free from the bondage of observational learning.

• Perhaps being a psychological bully helps you get your way. An alternative is to look for ways to *negotiate*, to exchange agreements, with important people in your life. This will be better for your relationships in the long run than the raw use of hostile power.

• If you think that you are perhaps somewhat hyperactive, you need some way to lower physiological arousal. This is why some chronically angry people abuse alcohol and sedatives. (Alcohol depresses central nervous system activity.) Dependence on drugs is an ineffective coping strategy. There are other methods to lower arousal. Depending on individual differences, those methods might be listening to music that you find soothing, taking a warm bath, having a snack, and so forth. Some individuals have found that taking a course of instruction in meditation techniques is useful in lowering arousal.

• If you feel that you *must* let anger out or else explode, try hitting a pillow or a punching bag. The physical movement will help you release some of the anger and may reduce its intensity.

• Remember that acting in an angry manner is a choice you make. Refuse to think, "I can't help myself." Instead think, "I'm in the driver's seat. And negative emotional displays are not in my own best interests."

Professional Help

If you find that you cannot cope adequately with chronic anger, there are a number of ways in which the professions of psychiatry and clinical psychology can help you.

A therapist can help you explore the unconscious motives behind your anger. It is possible that you are retaining psychological grudges held against your parents. It is possible that during your childhood they were abusive, unloving, insensitive to your feelings, or overcontrolling. The anger you continue to feel toward them is "unfinished business," and it is generalized to almost anyone who attempts to exert the slightest authority over you, including a partner, a teacher, or an employer. Although it is generally held that insight into unconscious motives is of value, it is also generally held that such insight is insufficient therapy in and of itself. You must act on an insight in a constructive way.

An insight-oriented therapist may help you to recognize how you employ an ego defense mechanism called *projection* to deny the unconscious roots of your anger. You are likely to perceive others as wanting to take advantage of you or to abuse you. This may in fact be your projection—a protective device in which you place on them your own hostility. Instead of recognizing that your anger arises from within, you see others as its source.

Taking a behavioral approach, a therapist may help you explore practical ways to avoid anger-eliciting situations and certain persons who irritate you. Also, the therapist will help you identify the psychological payoffs associated with chronic anger. You will learn that these have only short-term benefit, and together you will look for more effective ways to obtain such gratifications as emotional release or the cooperation of others.

Taking an interpersonal approach, a therapist will help you find ways to improve your relationships with others. This is usually done by focusing on your communication skills and by helping you become more assertive. In helping chronically angry people, the distinction between assertive behavior and aggressive behavior becomes particularly important. The assertive response to another person allows you to stand up for your rights without damage to the relationship. The aggressive response is almost always too emotional and self-indulgent. As a consequence, the response damages the relationship, drives others farther away, and increases your emotional isolation. This, in turn, makes you angrier. The therapist may make use of a behavioral approach known as *assertiveness training*.

Taking a cognitive approach, the therapist assumes that you are a thinking, conscious human being and that your ideas about life and other people have a lot to do with your anger. If you suffer from chronic anger, these ideas are almost always distortions. The therapist will help you recognize and identify these distortions. A common cognitive distortion is called *personal labeling*. The chronically angry person often mentally refers to other people with negative names such as *jerk, loser,* or *fool.* This dehumanizes the other individual, oversimplifies his or her personality, and allows for an easy rationalization of the anger.

Although there is no such thing as an antianger drug, it is true that sometimes anger is associated with chronic high arousal of the central nervous system. If this is the case, a psychiatrist may prescribe a minor tranquilizer in order to help you reduce overall tension and agitation. However, keep in mind that a psychiatric drug is not a cure for chronic anger, just a treatment. The drug can be a stepping stone to better adjustment if it is combined with effective psychotherapy. The drug should be used on a temporary basis for a particularly intense problem. In the end, the goal is to give up the drug and take responsibility for your own behavior.

Key Points to Remember

• Anger is an unpleasant emotional state characterized by high physiological arousal.

• A distinction can be made between *manifest anger* and *latent anger*.

• Chronic anger has three key attributes—it is *pathological*, *excessive*, and *irrational*.

• Examples of other signs and symptoms frequently associated with the principal symptom of chronic anger are impatience, constant hurrying, egotistical and self-centered behavior, high blood pressure, and free-floating hostility.

• The individual who manifests chronic anger is sometimes seen in psychoanalysis as a case of arrested emotional development.

• The psychoanalyst Karen Horney suggested that *basic anxiety* sometimes underlies chronic anger.

• If a child grows up in a family that allows itself frequent irrational outbursts of anger, then observational learning can play a role in a tendency toward chronic anger.

• Hyperactive tendencies in childhood may carry over to some extent in some persons and in turn magnify normal anger into chronic anger.

• The *frustration-aggression hypothesis* states that aggression is a natural response to frustration.

• Ask yourself if you are using anger as a way of coping with basic anxiety.

• Impose a *delay* between a situation that aggravates you and your actions in response to it.

• Learn to *negotiate*, to exchange agreements, with important people in your life. Do not bully them.

· If you feel that you *must* let anger out or else explode, try hitting a pillow or a punching bag.

· Therapy sometimes reveals that anger felt toward authority figures is an expression of "unfinished business" associated with parents.

· Taking a behavioral approach, a therapist may help you explore practical ways to avoid anger-eliciting situations and certain persons who irritate you.

· Taking an interpersonal approach, a therapist will help you find ways to help you become more assertive and less aggressive.

· A common cognitive distortion is called *personal labeling* in which you mentally refer to other people with negative names such as *jerk*, *loser*, or *fool*.

· A minor tranquilizer is sometimes helpful on a short-term basis to help you cope with overall tension and agitation; but a psychiatric drug is a treatment, not a cure, for chronic anger.

· Take responsibility for behavior. Acting angry is a choice that you make.

Chapter 5

Anxiety: Worrying About Worry

A. J. Cronin, author and physician, in his autobiography *Adventures in Two Worlds* relates the case of Willie, a baker who is told by Cronin that he may have cancer of the tongue. Two days is required for a pathology report. During the two days, Willie, normally a stolid man, dies a thousand deaths. His imagination conjures up horrible visions of an operation in which his tongue is cut out by the roots. He seriously considers suicide when he stands looking at the local river. He relates none of this to his wife or friends. He is told at the end of the two days that he has a harmless papilloma of the tongue.

Was it fear or was it anxiety that Willie experienced during his two-day emotional ordeal? The answer is that he experienced both. To the extent that he had real cause for alarm, he experienced fear. To the extent that irrational ideas or an overactive imagination distorted his thinking, he experienced pathological anxiety.

Fear is a rational emotional response to a real threat. *Pathological anxiety* is an irrational emotional response to an imagined threat. If you walk down a dark alley in an unfamiliar city and a stranger stops you with a drawn gun, you experience fear. If you walk down a familiar street in broad daylight, and begin to imagine that some disaster is about to descend upon you without warning, you experience pathological anxiety. The two are tangled together, of course. And it is not always possible to clearly distinguish them.

It is very appropriate to speak of "worrying about worry." Persons with neurotic tendencies tend to chew on their anxieties the way dogs chew on bones. There is a circular quality to their thinking, and the circle takes them downward until they are a quivering mass of apprehension. This is one of the characteristic aspects of pathological anxiety.

A type of anxiety often experienced by troubled persons is called *free-floating anxiety*. It is "free-floating" because it is attached to nothing. It can be described as a cloud that follows the person everywhere, as if it were on a string. And the anxiety casts a long shadow over existence, making the individual constantly on the alert.

The overanxious person is hypervigilant. Anything and anyone may pose a hazard. There is a persistent state of arousal. The pulse is elevated, respirations are rapid, and blood pressure is high. This is essentially a fight-or-flight reaction. But where is the enemy? What is the source of threat?

Anxiety is a most distressing symptom. It is no wonder that antianxiety drugs have become perhaps the most popular prescription medicines ever produced. It is intolerable to be in a steady state of anxiety. Escape is essential.

Other signs and symptoms related to the major symptom of anxiety are as follows:

1. Tight muscles
2. Uneasiness
3. Feeling tired
4. Difficulty breathing
5. Being cross and out of sorts
6. Problems in maintaining attention
7. Sleep disturbances

Some of these signs and symptoms merit comment. The anxious person has *tight muscles* because the fight-or-flight reaction has been activated, and the body is ready for action—action that seldom materializes. It is understandable that victims of anxiety *feel tired*. Their muscles and bodies are working overtime for no objective reason.

A *breathing difficulty* can refer to labored breathing or hyperventilation. The diaphragm, involved in the action of the lungs, is also a muscle. And it can be overly tight. When there is perpetual, low-grade anxiety the person often works too hard when breathing. On the other hand, if there is hyperanxiety or a panic attack, there is great excitement. And the individual may hyperventilate.

Chronic anxiety interferes with happiness. Therefore, it is understandable that its victims are often *cross and out of sorts*. A worried person may have a *problem in attending* to tasks, a lecture, or to something being read. The fantasies and random thoughts associated with the anxiety draw attention away from the objective, external world toward the subjective, internal world. Such individuals often seem to be "somewhere else."

Anxiety is a complicating factor in *sleep disturbances*. (For more about sleep disturbances, see Chapter 27.)

Assume that anxiety and its related symptoms are chronic. Also assume that the individual experiences substantial distress. In a case such as this, the psychiatric term used to describe the syndrome is *generalized anxiety disorder*. An older term, no longer in vogue, is *anxiety neurosis*.

Causes and Explanations

The classical psychoanalytic explanation of pathological, or neurotic, anxiety is based on Freud's personality theory. Freud said that there are three sides to the personality: the id, the ego, and the superego. The *id* is the primitive, inborn personality and is the source of all desires and wishes. The *ego* is the conscious personality and is in contact with the real world. The *superego* is the moral personality and evaluates one's behavior in terms of right and wrong.

The id is the source of many forbidden sexual and aggressive urges. In the socialized person, these urges are repressed, or blocked from consciousness. However, they want to break through and be acted upon. The individual senses this in a poorly defined way. Anxiety is the warning signal, the alarm bell that rings telling the individual "Watch out." But watch out for what? The answer is for the threat associated with one's own forbidden desires.

Anxiety, however, is experienced as a threat from the outside world, not the inner one. How is this possible if the source of danger is one's own impulses? The answer lies in a defense mechanism known as *projection*, a tendency to perceive the external world in terms of the conflicts experienced at an unconscious level.

Here is an example: Timothy O. is a married minister with a traditional, conservative outlook on life. He has been married 11 years and has three children. His wife is a sincere person and very supportive of his work. More than once, he has experienced fleeting sexual fantasies relating to women in his congregation, particularly those who have sought pastoral counseling. He thinks of his fantasies as nothing more than will-o'-the-wisps and is offended by what he imagines is the seductive behavior of some of the women. Of course, most of this is projection. He manifests most of the symptoms of a generalized anxiety disorder. The source of danger is his own forbidden sexual impulses.

A similar state of affairs can exist if the individual has forbidden aggressive desires. The wish to insult, injure, or even kill another may exist at an unconscious level of one's personality. The possibility that one may actually do the forbidden thing is experienced as undefined anxiety.

It is not presently believed that all pathological anxiety arises from the kind of dark, murky, unconscious motives identified by psychoanalysis. Another way to explain anxiety is offered by the behavioral viewpoint, a viewpoint based on learning theory. According to the behavioral viewpoint, anxiety represents a generalization of learning from past experiences, a tendency to confuse two similar objects or situations. Assume that Sally was very badly mauled and bitten by a dog when she was five years old. It is understandable that as an adult she is apprehensive in the presence of dogs. This dog phobia is not, of course, generalized anxiety, but a specific fear. However, further assume Sally has had many bad experiences in the past, particularly during the early developmental years. She was a victim of child abuse, came close to drowning, almost died of a kidney infection, and so forth. It is easy to understand why Sally frequently experiences pathological anxiety. She has had enough bad experiences in the past that she generalizes her fear to almost anything.

Life can also be complicated by *existential anxiety*, apprehension revolving around one's very being. Everyone knows that life hangs by a thread, that it can be lost at any time by an accident or an illness, and that even a long and productive life ends in death. The future may be filled with promise and joy. But even if this is your perception, in the far future only the grave beckons. These kinds of sour musings were proposed by Søren Kierkegaard, the father of existential philosophy, as the basis for a built-in anxiety that can never be completely eliminated.

People try to brush existential anxiety away, to deny its existence. And in some ways this only makes matters worse. Kierkegaard's point is that existential anxiety cannot be explained away nor denied. It must be faced with courage and accepted. Then the individual can go on living in spite of the burden of existential anxiety.

Biological processes can contribute to anxiety. There is evidence that some individuals have an inborn temperament that makes them prone to anxiety. They are more emotionally reactive as infants and children than their peers, and this tendency carries over into adulthood. Individuals who suffer from *hypoglycemia*, or chronic low blood sugar, may be more prone to anxiety than the average individual. When blood sugar is below normal, it is difficult to think, behave, and feel in a normal manner.

Coping

If you suffer from chronic anxiety, you may find value in the following list of practical coping strategies.

• Ask yourself if you are denying to yourself the existence of strong forbidden sexual and aggressive urges. Try to become more well acquainted with the unconscious level of your personality. Of course, if the unconscious level really *is* unconscious, how can you know what is there?

The unconscious level reveals itself in many ways—through dreams, conscious fantasies, idle thoughts, traits of character, and slips of the tongue. A personal journal of thoughts and reflections helps you to become more aware of your hidden self. The purpose of making contact with the darker side of your nature is *not* to act on it in an irresponsible way. On the contrary, the idea is to *integrate* your forbidden urges into consciousness in order to bring them under rational control. An understood impulse is less threatening than an incomprehensible one.

• Suppose that, in the near future, you will need to deal with a threatening situation such as a job interview, a party where you will know almost no one, or an important examination. Use a method called *stress-inoculation training*. Imagine yourself in the situation and run a mental movie. Try to make the images as vivid as possible. You will feel your anxiety rising. But each time you run the mental movie, your anxiety will diminish. You will find that the reduction of anxiety associated with the imagined situation will transfer to some extent to the real situation.

• It has been found that relaxation of the muscles is incompatible with anxiety. A warm bath will relax your muscles. You can also use a method known *progressive relaxation*. Sit in a comfortable chair or a recliner. You cannot relax a set of muscles at will, but you can tighten them up at will. So consciously tighten the muscles in one of your legs for 10 to 15 seconds. Then you will find that it is easy to let go, and they will automatically relax. Then progress to the muscles in the other leg. Working upward, relax your abdomen, each arm, each shoulder, and your neck. In this manner, you will be able to systematically relax your whole body.

• Examine your ideas about anticipated events. What are you thinking? Are your thoughts rational or irrational? Suppose you have been asked to give a talk or presentation before a group. Are you thinking, "My mind will go blank," "I'll probably make a fool of myself," "They'll all laugh at me," or something similar? If you are, challenge these thoughts with more realistic ones such as, "I'll get through it, even if I'm not perfect," "I'll probably do as well as most of the others would do," "This whole thing really isn't that serious," or something similar.

• Do you have an overactive imagination? Anxiety-prone people often make good creative writers and love to read fiction. Their ability to conjure up images makes them see the worst in the mind's eye, and they hypersensitize themselves to anticipated events. You can "fight fire with fire" by willing yourself to imagine pleasant, successful outcomes. In this manner you desensitize yourself to anticipated events. (For more about phobias, see Chapter 14.)

• Learn the art of meditation. This does not have to be an esoteric Eastern technique in which you try to become a yogi. You can simply sit in a comfortable chair, close your eyes, and think the word *relax* in rhythm with your respirations. Think "re-" as you breath in, and think "-lax" as you breath out. Three or four minutes of this will induce a *relaxation response*. The relaxation response was studied by Herbert Benson of the Harvard Medical School, and it is antagonistic to the fight-or-flight reaction associated with anxiety.

• If you think that hypoglycemia, or low blood sugar, might be contributing to chronic anxiety, avoid highly processed foods and foods that contain large amounts of sugars (e.g., soft drinks, candy, and most desserts). Concentrate instead on foods high in protein and complex carbohydrates. Although common sense might say that foods high in sugar help blood sugar to rise, this is not correct. The effect of high-sugar foods is to make blood sugar rise too rapidly at first. Then there is a kind of boomerang reaction called the *hypoglycemic rebound*, and blood sugar may drop below normal.

• Keep in mind that a certain amount of background anxiety is normal. This existential anxiety described by the philosopher Kierkegaard is simply one of the burdens of life and must be accepted with a certain amount of courage and serenity. Everyone feels this kind of anxiety.

Professional Help

If you find you cannot cope adequately with chronic anxiety, there are a number of ways in which the professions of psychiatry and clinical psychology can help you.

A therapist can help you develop greater insight into the unconscious level of your personality. The interpretation of dreams, painful memories, slips of the tongue, and traits of character can all lead to greater self-understanding. This general approach, often called a *psychodynamic* approach in therapy, was inspired by the early work of Freud. It is assumed that greater self-understanding tends to reduce the overall level of pathological anxiety because the troubled person is no longer completely at the mercy of unknown forces.

A common approach used in contemporary psychotherapy is to focus on irrational thoughts and explore the ways in which these inflame anxiety. The therapist points out specific ways to modify irrational thoughts, thus sprinkling some cool psychological water on the fires of fear. This general avenue goes by several names including *rational-emotive therapy*, *cognitive-behavior modification*, and *cognitive therapy*. The therapist will train you to modify your own thoughts when they are unrealistic or irrational.

The therapist may use guided fantasies with positive, safe outcomes as a way of defusing the anxiety associated with anticipated disasters, emotional or physical. This technique is called *systematic desensitization*, and it has been found to be one of the most effective ways to diminish chronic anxiety.

A psychiatrist may prescribe an *antianxiety agent*, also known as a minor tranquilizer. These drugs are of great value in the treatment of chronic, pathological anxiety. However, keep in mind that there is a reason they are prescription, not over-the-counter, drugs. In some cases, they may have adverse side effects, and benefits always have to be weighed against biological and psychological costs. Some individuals may abuse these drugs, and this will undermine the value of the drugs as therapeutic agents. Used properly, the drugs have a place in the treatment of anxiety.

Key Points to Remember

- Pathological anxiety is an irrational emotional response to an imagined threat.
- Free-floating anxiety is like a cloud that follows the person everywhere as if on a string, casting a long shadow over existence.
- Other signs and symptoms related to the major symptom of anxiety include tight muscles, feeling tired, and problems in maintaining attention.
- The classical psychoanalytic explanation of pathological anxiety is that it is a warning signal telling the individual to watch out for forbidden impulses.
- According to the behavioral viewpoint, anxiety represents a generalization of learning from past experiences.
- A certain amount of existential anxiety, apprehension revolving around our very being, is inevitable.
- A principal way to cope with pathological anxiety is to integrate unconscious impulses into consciousness.
- Anxiety is incompatible with muscle relaxation.
- A therapist can help you develop greater insight into the unconscious level of your personality.
- Systematic desensitization is a technique using guided fantasies with positive, safe outcomes as a way of diminishing anxiety.
- Used properly, antianxiety agents, or minor tranquilizers, have a place in the treatment of anxiety.

Chapter 6

Boredom: When Life Grows Dull

The literary classic *Madame Bovary*, by Gustave Flaubert, tells the story of a woman who is bored with her husband, bored with her fellow townspeople, and, in general, bored with her life. Her days are too tedious and predictable, and she is filled with romantic, idealistic fantasies. In order to escape from boredom, she enters into two love affairs, both of them disastrous. In the end, she commits suicide by taking arsenic. First published in 1857, *Madame Bovary* illustrates that boredom is no newcomer to the human race as a psychological problem.

Boredom is an unpleasant mental and emotional state characterized by discontent and lack of interest. Physiological arousal is low—any sense of excitement is completely absent.

A distinction can be made between situational boredom and chronic boredom. *Situational boredom* is specific, and everyone has experienced it. Examples are being bored with a classroom lecture, a movie, a book, another person, a long ride without interesting sights, a repetitive task, and so forth. *Chronic boredom* is general and pervasive. It is the kind that Madame Bovary suffered from. It is pathological and destructive. People who suffer from chronic boredom tend to be bored with significant others in their lives such as partners, parents, and their children. They also tend to be bored with their day-to-day routines and their vocations. This second kind of boredom is a sort of psychological cancer that eats away at the heart of one's existence. The principal concern of this chapter is with chronic boredom.

Note that boredom is always boredom *with*. As already indicated, there can be boredom *with* a lecture, a person, or a situation. Thus, boredom is often perceived as having a source. And the individual is often convinced that if he or she could escape from or avoid the source of boredom, then boredom would go away. Consequently, there is often a lot of blaming associated with boredom. The bored individual thinks, "He bores me," or

"She bores me," or "It bores me." The psychological contribution that one makes to one's own boredom is often missed.

Other signs and symptoms frequently associated with the general symptom of boredom are:

1. Frequent drowsiness
2. The slow passage of time
3. Vanity and self-absorption
4. Listlessness or fatigue
5. Moderate to severe depression
6. Lack of commitment to goals and plans
7. Wishful thinking
8. Preoccupation with romantic or heroic fantasies
9. Vague discontent

Commenting on some of the signs and symptoms identified, *drowsiness or sleep* is one way to escape from a boring situation. Situationally bored people might struggle to stay awake during a long lecture on a subject of little personal interest. Chronically bored people often sleep 10 to 12 hours a day if they have the opportunity, or they may take frequent naps.

Listlessness or fatigue may be so pronounced that the individual suspects that he or she has an illness. (If there is real reason to believe that an organic problem is present, this should, of course, be evaluated by a physician.)

Depression overlaps with boredom, and depression is itself a major psychological symptom. Although they can coexist and do affect each other, they are not identical. It is useful to look upon boredom as a major symptom in itself and to identify it as an important causal factor in depression. (For more on depression, see Chapter 8.)

Causes and Explanations

A major cause of boredom is lack of variety. Human beings appear to have a need for changes of stimulation. Imagine yourself confined to a small room with no windows, no telephone, no television set, no books to read, no interesting pictures on the wall, and no visitors. You probably would soon find yourself unbearably bored. As Robert S. Woodworth, a leading motivational theorist in the 1920s and 1930s, put it, "The eyes want to see and the ears want to hear." Various experiments in sensory isolation have demonstrated that if volunteer subjects are deprived of changes of stimulation, they will begin to have mild hallucinations. They may see spinning, glowing patterns or hear odd sounds.

Although a bored person may not be physically confined to a small room or systematically deprived of changes of stimulation, there are parallels. A young homemaker with three children and no car of her own commented, "I feel like I'm going stir crazy. Some days I'm so tired of it all I could scream." A woman who worked on an assembly line said, "When I go to work, I feel like I'm going to prison." If you perceive your life as greatly deficient in change of stimulation, if there is too much *sameness*, you are bound to be bored.

In some cases, unlike those cited above, boredom is associated with affluence. Galvin C. has no meaningful vocation, and he hires most personal services. He and his wife live well from the income of a large trust fund. He has time on his hands. He tries to cope with boredom by turning to popular entertainments such as luxury cruises and vacations at gambling resorts. But basically he is simply bored with life and knows it.

It is important to note that an interesting, varied environment is a matter of perception. Melanie thinks of a trip to an antique store as exciting and interesting. Paula, Melanie's sister, thinks of the same activity as boring. In contrast, Paula finds it stimulating and exciting to shop for clothes and look at the latest colors and styles. Melanie might as well be looking at gray uniforms. She takes no interest and is bored when she accompanies Paula.

A great deal of experimental evidence suggests that human beings have an inborn curiosity drive. This is true not only of human beings, but also of animals. Rats will actively explore areas of a maze that contain walls with vertical stripes and avoid areas that display gray walls without patterns. Apparently, as the rats run by the vertical stripes, they experience changes of visual stimulation. Infants will spend more time gazing at a black-and-white checkerboard with nine squares than at a more simple one with only four squares. As the infant's eye scans the checkerboard, each shift from black to white or from white to black is a specific change of stimulation. The curiosity drive seeks as its goal changes of stimulation in the same way that the hunger drive seeks food. If the curiosity drive is not met adequately, boredom is the result.

Of course, in adult human beings, the curiosity drive is selective. This is because they have interests. Travel to faraway places will not satisfy the curiosity drive of an individual who finds it boring to leaf through the pages of an issue of *National Geographic*. An astrophysicist might be curious about the latest data supporting the theory that there are black holes in space. The same information might bore someone else. However, both persons have a curiosity drive. And both persons need the kinds of changes of stimulation that will satisfy them.

A personal factor that may cause boredom is high intelligence. The psychoanalyst Eric Fromm said that the human being is the only creature that can be bored. This is not strictly speaking correct. One of the principal problems with the care of some animals in zoos is that they become bored. This is particularly true of relatively intelligent animals such as apes and bears. However, snakes and crocodiles do not appear to have a problem with boredom. Very bright individuals often take most of the information out of a stimulus before others do, and they are ready to move on when others are still interested. Informally, they get "saturated" with objects or other persons quickly and become bored with them.

A final factor in boredom is the "too much too soon" phenomenon. An individual is treated in youth like a prince or a princess. He or she has "had it all" or "seen it all." The good things of life are not earned but obtained with little or no effort. Boredom may set in at an early age. Diana Barrymore, daughter of the famous actor John Barrymore, wrote an autobiography with the very title *Too Much, Too Soon* in which she describes a self-destructive life style arising in part from boredom. The motion picture actor Errol Flynn in his autobiography *My Wicked, Wicked Ways* portrays his life in a similar manner.

Coping

If you suffer from boredom, you may find value in the following list of practical coping strategies. The list has applications to both situational boredom and chronic boredom.

• Make a systematic attempt to introduce more frequent and regular changes into your life. These should be changes that you can implement readily without too much effort. Here is an example: over a period of several weeks, Anatole R. called an old college friend he had not talked to for years, took a short vacation to a place he had never been to before, and visited for the first time a large, well-known used-book bookstore about 100 miles away from his home. The general idea is that if you are in something of a rut, try to break out of it.

• Find something *important* to do. Much boredom is associated with the idea that one's work or other activities are meaningless. Your life should not be seen as an endless round of routine with no long-range purpose. Rediscover meaning in your work, or consider making a career change. You might consider offering your services as a volunteer to a hospital or a school.

• Learn something new. Take an evening course at a community college in almost anything that presents a challenge and a mild psychological threat. By a psychological threat is meant something at which you just might fail. You will be forced to rise to the occasion, to use your intellect. The introduction of different ideas into your life helps to counter boredom.

• Take a child to a movie. Kay G. took her seven-year-old granddaughter to see the Walt Disney version of *Snow White and the Seven Dwarfs*. Kay saw the film in the 1930s and remembered it with fondness. She would have not enjoyed seeing it alone. However, taking her granddaughter to see it allowed her to share a memory and reexperience the story vicariously through a child's eyes.

• In general, learn to use fantasy in a constructive, creative way. Madame Bovary acted on her romantic fantasies in a destructive way. Instead, think of your fantasies as a kind of second psychological life, as a source of rich gratification. You do not have to insist that they materialize in the real world; the individual with a healthy personality makes a clear distinction between fantasy and reality.

• Recognize that feelings come and go. Some boredom is natural. Learn to tolerate it. Go on with your daily activities in spite of the boredom, and it will often lift and vanish.

• Think of boredom as coming from your child self. Imagine that you are the parent of an actual child who says, "I'm bored. There's nothing to do." How would you answer? Apply the answer to yourself.

• When you are bored, do not just sit and stare. Get up and engage in some motor activity. It can be almost anything from taking a short walk to sweeping a kitchen floor. Motor activity is antagonistic to boredom. It is much more difficult to be bored when you are moving. You cannot will away your boredom, but you can will your actions. The activity will feed back on the boredom, reducing its intensity.

• Use your intelligence. As earlier indicated, it has often been observed that intelligence is associated with boredom. It is possible that you have used your mind destructively to throw yourself into a psychological pit. The intelligent thing to do is certainly *not* to passively accept the pit as a trap. If your intelligence got you in, it can get you out. The really bright person realizes that the trap of boredom is a self-made one, and it can be dismantled with intelligence just as it was constructed by intelligence. Brainstorm the problem. Make your own list of coping strategies that are likely to work for you.

Professional Help

If you find that you cannot cope adequately with boredom, there are a number of ways in which the professions of psychiatry and clinical psychology can help you.

In the first place, it should be realized that very few people come to a psychiatrist or a psychologist offering boredom as their principal psychological symptom. It is much more likely that the chronically bored person will complain of depression. The therapist needs to ascertain to what extent boredom does or does not play a role in a particular client's complaint of depression. If boredom plays a major role, then it needs to be addressed.

There is no categorical advice that will cure boredom. The kinds of coping strategies outlined in the prior section may or may not be received with interest. Some individuals will resist them completely, discount all of them, and go right on being bored. When this happens, the therapist has to take a more general, less directive approach.

In stubborn cases of chronic boredom, many therapists make use of the humanistic viewpoint. The client is seen as a whole person functioning poorly in a complex life situation. Therapeutic discussions deal with the problem of boredom indirectly. The client is helped to reevaluate his or her philosophy of life. The meaning that life holds is explored. Attempts are made to help the troubled person rediscover lost meanings. A life of work and activity without meaning is, without question, boring.

The approach described in the above paragraph, when it is the principal treatment modality, is called *logotherapy*. Logotherapy is based on the premise that human beings have an inborn will to meaning. As a kind of therapy, it was pioneered by the psychiatrist Viktor Frankl. (For more on logotherapy, see Chapter 16, the chapter on meaninglessness.)

An important theme in the humanistic viewpoint is self-actualization. *Self-actualization* refers to an inborn need to maximize one's talents and potentialities. According to Abraham Maslow, a principal founder of humanistic psychology, people have "whisperings within" that suggest what direction they need to take in life in order to make the most of their abilities. Self-actualizing individuals, individuals who are deeply involved in a process of personal growth, tend at some times to have spontaneous peak experiences. *Peak experiences* are moments of genuine joy or ecstasy. A life with few or no peak experiences is gray and dull. In order to help a client overcome boredom, the therapist will explore ways for the client to become more self-actualizing.

Taking an approach advocated by Alfred Adler, a principal founder of early psychoanalysis, the therapist may focus on the importance of social interest and the creative self. *Social interest* is asserted by Adler to be an inborn tendency in human beings. It is a need to care not only for themselves, but also for their fellow human beings. Expressions of social interest can be seen in raising children, in providing a service of value for others, and in having a concern for the welfare and future of humankind. As earlier indicated, bored people often lack social interest and instead are vain and self-absorbed. How can lost social interest be rediscovered? Adler argues that each individual has a *creative self*, an inborn ability to take charge of life and become autonomous. Through the use of the creative self, it is possible to reaffirm and rediscover social interest. The therapist can work with the client in an attempt to bring the creative self into play.

Boredom in and of itself does not call for the prescription of a drug. There is no such thing as antiboredom medication. However, it is true that there are antidepressant drugs; and if boredom is a secondary complaint associated with a major complaint of depression, then one of these drugs may be prescribed and in turn may be helpful. (For more about drug therapy for depression, see Chapter 8.)

Key Points to Remember

• Boredom is an unpleasant mental and emotional state characterized by discontent and lack of interest. Physiological arousal is low—any sense of excitement is completely absent.

• *Situational boredom* is specific. *Chronic boredom* is general and pervasive.

• Some of the other signs and symptoms associated with boredom are frequent drowsiness, vanity and self-absorption, wishful thinking, and preoccupation with romantic or heroic fantasies.

• A major cause of boredom is lack of variety. Human beings appear to have a need for changes of stimulation.

• A personal factor that may cause boredom is high intelligence. Learn to use your intelligence not only to create boredom, but to avoid and escape from it.

• A factor in some cases of boredom is the "too much too soon" phenomenon.

• Make a systematic attempt to introduce more frequent and regular changes of stimulation into your life.

• Learn something new.

• When you are bored, get up and engage in some sort of motor activity.

• Taking a humanistic viewpoint in therapy, the client is seen as a whole person. Exploring the client's philosophy of life can often be helpful.

• Self-actualizing persons, persons deeply involved in personal growth, find life exciting and interesting.

• The creative self can be used to rediscover social interest.

Chapter 7

Delusions: When Fantasies Become Real

Waldemar T. is convinced that he can walk through walls.

Phillipa M. believes that she has six fingers, one of them invisible to others but visible to her.

Orson L. thinks that in the year 2001 Earth will be destroyed in a collision with an enormous comet, that a great ark of space will be built, that he will be one of its passengers, and that he will help set up a colony for humankind on Mars.

What do Waldemar, Phillipa, and Orson all have in common? They suffer from delusions. A *delusion* is believing in something that most members of an individual's family or culture regard as irrational or false. One of the words used by ancient Greek writers to identify delusions was *phantasia*, and this is the root of our word "fantasy." A delusion may be regarded as a fantasy that is taken to be a reality.

In some cases, delusions seem to come and go without apparent rhyme or reason. As indicated above, Phillipa believes today that she has an invisible finger. Yesterday, she said that her head was made out of a pumpkin. Tomorrow, she may insist that she is only 2 inches tall. She is a hospitalized mental patient and suffers from schizophrenia. Her thinking is very disorganized and confused.

On the other hand, it is possible for an individual to have a highly organized, consistent delusional system. When this happens, a diagnosis of *delusional disorder*, also known as *paranoid disorder*, is made. An example of this kind of disorder is provided by a case history entitled "The Jet-propelled Couch," reported by the psychoanalyst Robert Lindner in his book *The Fifty-Minute Hour*. Kirk Allen, a physicist, believed that he led a dual existence. One existence was his mundane Earth life. In a second, more important existence, he was the lord of a planet in a distant universe. In this second existence, arrived at through telepathic means, he ruled an interplanetary empire and wore important robes of office. Kirk had accumulated 12,000 pages of "records" documenting his role as a star king. Maps, charts, and biographical data were amazingly consistent.

A highly organized system such as Kirk's is relatively rare. Much more common are the more or less inconsistent delusions associated with such mental disorders as schizophrenia and organic mental syndromes.

Three common kinds of delusions are bizarre delusions, nihilistic delusions, and delusions of being controlled. *Bizarre delusions* are those that are ridiculous to most people—Madge says that her eyes are made out of grapes, that her hair is cotton candy, and her ears are fashioned from leftover stew meat. *Nihilistic delusions* stress the themes of death and decay—Sawyer says that he is a walking, talking corpse brought back to a sort of half-life by Dr. Frankenstein. *Delusions of being controlled* are characterized by the idea that external forces in the form of energies or persons are running one's thoughts and behavior—Tyrone has told his psychiatrist more than once that invisible wires held by the Puppet Master make him do things against his will.

Other signs and symptoms frequently associated with the general symptom of a tendency to have delusions are:

1. Irrational thinking
2. Inability to use facts to modify the delusion
3. Hallucinations
4. Confabulation
5. Distortions of body image
6. Disorientation
7. Magical thinking
8. Distress

Those signs and symptoms merit comment. *Irrational thinking* does not follow the laws of logic as most people understand them. Thus, an individual who is thinking in an irrational way may insist that $2 + 2 = 5$ or that taking an aspirin will give the person the power to fly like a bird.

The *inability to use facts to modify the delusion* means that the disturbed person may superficially accept facts but fail to employ them correctly. When Phillipa insisted that she had an invisible sixth finger, her therapist, Dr. W., asked, "Can I feel your invisible finger? Is it solid?"

"Of course, it is."

"Let me feel it."

"All right." Phillipa presented her invisible finger to the therapist.

Dr. W. felt in the general region of Phillipa's hand and said, "I feel nothing. What do you make of that?"

Phillipa answered, "I see your point, Dr. W. Invisible fingers are *not* solid."

Hallucinations are false perceptions. The individual may see something or hear something that cannot be detected by others. Invisible companions, bugs crawling under the skin, the presence of dead friends or relatives, or the smell of nonexistent onions frying are all examples of hallucinations.

In *confabulation*, the troubled person answers a question with false information. This is common in organic deterioration of the brain associated with such conditions as Alzheimer's disease or alcohol amnestic disorder. Jocelyn, age 84, is asked the date of her birth. She answers after some thought, "June 12, 1940." She is doing her best to appear competent and in charge of her faculties.

People with delusions sometimes have *distortions of body image*. These can themselves be kinds of delusions. Persons with more or less normal bodies may think they are withered, shrunken, gigantic, misshapen, wrinkled, or obese.

Disorientation suggests that the person is poorly oriented in time and space. Individuals displaying this condition may not know what day, month, or year it is. They may not know where they live or how to find their way home.

Magical thinking is characterized by a tendency to ignore the importance of natural causes and their effects. Thus, a person thinks that an airplane flies because he or she wishes it into the air, or that it will stop raining because he or she turns counterclockwise three times.

Finally, it is important to realize that *distress* is commonly associated with delusions. There is a myth that mental patients are happy with their delusions, that they provide an escape into a pleasant fantasy world. This can, of course, be true in some cases. However, it is more common for a patient to feel tormented and controlled by delusions, which the patient perceives as real and as beyond the control of his or her will. Consequently, the patient often feels like a victim of the delusions.

Causes and Explanations

One of the principal mental disorders associated with delusions is schizophrenia. *Schizophrenia* is a severe mental disorder characterized by illogical thinking; often there are other signs and symptoms such as hallucinations. However, it is important to understand that a mental disorder such as schizophrenia is not in and of itself a "cause." The important question is: What causes schizophrenia? There is no single or simple answer to the question. Instead, a number of causal factors appear to play a role.

First, studies of identical twins and other siblings suggest that genetic factors play a role in the disease. Second, these genetic factors may contribute to an inherited brain defect making it difficult to profess information in a conventional way. Third, there is evidence that the neurotransmitter *dopamine*, a chemical messenger, is overactive in the brains of schizophrenic patients. Fourth, emotional wounds inflicted in early infancy may aggravate the likelihood that the disease will appear later in life. Fifth, parents who confuse a child and who are emotionally distant may also aggravate tendencies to develop schizophrenia. Sixth, environmental triggers such as going bankrupt, getting divorced, or losing a loved one may be necessary to "light the fuse" of the disease.

All of these causal factors, interplaying with each other in a complex way, may play a role in the disease and, in turn, its delusions.

One important way to explain delusions is to appreciate that they frequently have a meaning. Often, a delusion, or delusional system, represents a psychological need for power in the form of wishful thinking. Waldeman T., the man who said he could walk through walls, was a mild-mannered, financially unsuccessful salesman for a plumbing company. Kirk Allen had been emotionally crushed in many ways in his early childhood. And he had been sexually abused by a governess. He felt weak and powerless in his actual life, but in his life as a great star king, he ruled a galaxy.

Frequently, delusions can be understood as metaphors. Sawyer, who said he was a walking, talking corpse, was in essence saying that he felt *as if* he were dead. A deep state of depression and demoralization was expressing itself. Delusions, if their meanings are sought, provide a kind of window into the troubled person's state of mind.

Delusions can be caused by an actual pathology of the brain and nervous system. Alzheimer's disease, brain tumors, strokes, general paresis (caused by syphilis), and alcohol amnestic disorder provide examples of such pathology. An older name for *alcohol amnestic disorder* is "Korsakoff's psychosis" in honor of the Russian neurologist who first studied it. In alcohol amnestic disorder, there is damage to the brain caused by years of alcohol abuse. (For more on alcohol abuse, see Chapter 2.)

The toxic effects of drugs can induce delusions. Irrational ideas are often present in the altered states of consciousness induced by such drugs as morphine and heroin. Some drugs are actually called *psychedelics* or *hallucinogens* because of their ability to greatly alter normal brain processes. Examples of these drugs are cannabis (i.e., marijuana), hashish, mescaline, psilocybin, lysergic acid diethylamide-25 (LSD), and phencyclidine (i.e., "angel dust"). Finally, it should not be forgotten that alcohol is a drug. Not only can a person have delusions when intoxicated, delusions are a common symptom of delirium tremens, which is caused by withdrawal from a dependence on alcohol.

Coping

It would at first appear contradictory to give advice on how to cope with delusions. The argument is that persons with delusions by definition believe their irrational ideas to be both real and true; therefore, they cannot be argued or reasoned out of them. This is correct. Nonetheless, persons with delusions often recognize their borderline and impossible character. Although they will usually resist *outside* reasoning, they often struggle within themselves against delusions. The psychoanalyst Robert Lindner points that it is incorrect to believe that in every instance persons with delusions are so "far gone" that they do not know they are mad. Lindner notes that, for the most part, deranged persons are aware of their disturbance, aware either because it directly induces personal suffering or because they are made to suffer for it by others.

Also, it should be noted that the severity of delusions waxes and wanes. Persons with schizophrenia often experience a spontaneous remission of symptoms, sometimes for prolonged periods of time. Antipsychotic drugs also bring about a reduction in the severity of symptoms. During periods of increased mental clarity, disturbed individuals are accessible to rational thinking, including their own.

If you suffer from delusions, you may find value in the following list of practical coping strategies.

• In some cases, delusions have a quality similar to the experiences in a lucid dream. A *lucid dream* is a dream in which you become aware that you are dreaming. It is then possible to break out of the dream or control it. This often happens with delusions. A part of your consciousness whispers, "This can't be real. These ideas are impossible." Under these conditions, it is possible for you to take some control over the delusions.

• When you are in good reality contact, when your delusions have retreated to the corners of your mind, take advantage of a behavior therapy technique called stress-inoculation training. *Stress-inoculation training* involves preparing yourself ahead of time for a stressful situation. Play a mental movie of future situations in which a delusion interferes with your ability to function effectively. Visualize how you will cope in a practical manner, and work around the delusion. Stress-inoculation training can forearm you against your own unbidden delusional tendencies.

• Make sure that your nutrition is adequate, that you obtain enough protein, carbohydrates, vitamins, and minerals. There is a substantial amount of evidence suggesting that clear thinking is associated with a healthy brain and nervous system. One way to look at the mind is to think of it as the brain and nervous system in action. A healthy mind requires an equally healthy body. To be more specific, certain chemical messengers in the brain (e.g., norepinephrine) are required for rational thought. These are synthesized out of substances provided by food. The B-complex vitamins have been found to be of particular importance.

· Do not act on the basis of an idea that you think is true and that most other people think is false. Consider that it just *might* be a delusion. Do not jump from a roof just because *you* think you can fly. Do not try to live without food just because *you* think you are immortal and do not need it. Listen to the small voice within you that says, "I might hurt myself. Maybe other people are right."

· Avoid the use of psychoactive drugs. These include amphetamines, cocaine, morphine, heroin, cannabis (i.e., marijuana), and lysergic acid diethylamide-25 (LSD). These drugs interact with a tendency to have delusions and sometimes greatly increase the level of irrational thought.

· Be aware of the concept of *consensual reality*, that is, the way a well-defined group (e.g., a family, a tribe) sees the world. Although from a strict philosophical point of view one cannot say that the group's outlook *is* reality, from a practical point of view one can act *as if* it is reality. Therefore, even if you do not believe in the group's perception of reality as a fact, be practical. Work *with* their reality, not against it, if you want to reduce your level of conflict and suffering.

If a partner, child, or other person close to you suffers from delusions, below are coping strategies that may be of some value.

· Do not challenge a delusion directly. Do not tell the troubled person such things as, "That's silly" or "That's nonsense." Do not discount the delusion and attempt to minimize its importance. Such blunt frontal attacks tend to galvanize resistance and push the individual farther into the delusion.

· Try to encourage the other person to be as practical as possible in spite of the delusion. Describe the logical consequences of actions. Orient the individual toward reality by pointing out that a given behavior may lead to imprisonment, bodily injury, or property damage. Working *with* the assumptions of the delusion, help the person steer clear of its buried dangers.

Professional Help

If you find that you cannot cope adequately with delusions, there are a number of ways in which the professions of psychiatry and clinical psychology can help you.

If delusions are both chronic and severe, a period of hospitalization may be recommended. It is for good reason that an older term for a mental hospital is an *asylum*. Among the meanings of *asylum* are "a temporary refuge," "a sanctuary," "a secure retreat." The mental hospital provides a time-out from the stresses and demands of everyday life. In the vast majority of cases, hospitalization is temporary. The goal is to return the individual to the larger social world. Often, treatment is continued on an outpatient basis. Outlined in the following paragraphs are ways of helping the individual that can take place on either an inpatient or outpatient basis.

One of the standard treatments for delusions has been electroconvulsive therapy (ECT). This involves the passage of a weak electric current through the frontal part of the brain. Introduced in 1937 by the Italian psychiatrists Ugo Cerletti and Lucia Bini, ECT was a common treatment for schizophrenia for about two decades. Although it is still sometimes recommended for schizophrenia, the present thinking is that the disease can be more readily managed through the use of drug therapy. The principal value of ECT appears to be not in the treatment for delusions, but in the treatment of major depression. (For more on depression, see Chapter 8.)

A principal treatment approach for delusions is drug therapy. As a general category, the kinds of drugs used are called *major tranquilizers*, or *antipsychotic agents* (*psychotic* describes an extreme mental or emotional derangement of either biological or emotional origin). A substantial amount of relatively recent research has established that these drugs are effective because they regulate in the brain the action of the chemical messenger dopamine. There are approximately ten of these drugs that are commonly prescribed. Examples of two are haloperidol (i.e., Haldol) and chlorpromazine (i.e., Thorazine). These drugs can have potent adverse side effects; therefore, they are available only when prescribed by a psychiatrist or other physician.

An approach to the treatment of delusions recommended by some therapists is *orthomolecular psychiatry*. This approach is also called *megavitamin therapy*. Orthomolecular psychiatry was pioneered by the biochemist Linus Pauling and the psychiatrist David Hawkins. As indicated earlier, the B-complex vitamins in particular seem to play an important part in the synthesis of the brain's neurotransmitters. Pauling and Hawkins prescribed large doses of vitamins, emphasizing the B-complex group, and reported beneficial results. Orthomolecular psychiatry has not become a primary kind of treatment for delusions, nor is it recommended by a majority of therapists. Nonetheless, a number of professionals think that it may help some individuals in some cases. The individual in megavitamin therapy should be under a physician's care because of the possible risk of toxic effects of megadoses of vitamins.

Psychotherapy should be combined with drug therapy in the treatment of delusions. When patients are lucid and thinking more clearly, this is an opportunity for the therapist to intervene and help individuals develop ideas and attitudes that will help them cope more effectively with future delusional tendencies. In connection with the psychotherapy, the therapist will often recommend that the troubled person join a support group made up of people with similar symptoms. Patients often find it of great value to exchange ideas for practical ways to cope with delusions. It also helps persons who suffers from delusions to realize that they are neither totally odd nor completely alone.

Key Points to Remember

- A *delusion* is believing in something that most members of an individual's family or culture regard as irrational or false.
- Some of the other signs and symptoms frequently associated with the general symptom of a tendency to have delusions are: irrational thinking, hallucinations, disorientation, and magical thinking.
- One of the principal mental disorders associated with delusions is schizophrenia.
- Excessive activity of the neurotransmitter dopamine, a chemical messenger in the brain, is a causal factor in delusions.
- Delusions often have a meaning. Frequently, they can be understood as metaphors.
- Use stress-inoculation training to forearm yourself against unbidden delusional tendencies.
- Do not take action on the basis of an idea that you think is true and that most other people think is false.
- Avoid the use of psychoactive drugs.
- Do not directly challenge the delusions of other people. However, try to encourage them to be practical in their actions.
- If delusions are both chronic and severe, a period of hospitalization may be recommended.
- A principal treatment approach for delusions is drug therapy.
- Psychotherapy should be combined with drug therapy in the treatment of delusions.

Chapter 8

Depression:
The Anatomy
of Melancholy

Members of an introductory psychology class were recently asked to use the word *depression*, or some variation of the word, in a written sentence. Here are some of their answers:

I get depressed when it rains, when I have fish for dinner, and when my wife is in a bad mood.

When I get depressed, it seems that all of the joy goes out of life.

I think I'm sort of half-depressed most of the time.

Depression is like a dark storm cloud on the horizon that just keeps coming and coming and won't go away because you're wishing for it to.

I'm seldom depressed because I have found ways to avoid the feeling before it gets too much of a grip on me.

I get depressed when I have to do a lot of things I don't like to do.

I get depressed too often, and it frightens me.

I remember that I was about 13 years old the first time I was consciously depressed.

It is evident from the above responses that depression is a common experience, one that is familiar to most people. As one of the students wrote, "Everybody knows what it is to get depressed." However, not everyone knows what it is to be unable to shake depression for prolonged periods of time, for depression to enter into one's life like an uninvited guest who stays for weeks and months. This kind of depression, what psychiatrists refer to as *major depressive episode* or *severe depression*, is a principal concern of this chapter. However, mild and moderate episodes of depression are included in the discussion. These can be early signs of a more severe problem and should not be neglected.

Many famous persons have suffered from depression. Well-known examples are Abraham Lincoln, the political leader Winston Churchill, the philosopher Ludwig Wittgenstein, and the novelist Virginia Woolf. One viewpoint is that extremely intelligent, creative people engage in too much self-analysis and self-criticism. Their consciousness is like a harsh spotlight turned inward. A second viewpoint is that people in general suffer from depression, but when a famous person suffers from depression, it is more likely to receive publicity. There is probably an element of truth in both viewpoints.

Depression has been called "the common cold of mental illness." Surveys indicate that during any given time period, about 4 percent of the adult population is suffering from some degree of depression.

One of the more famous literary works in the English language is *The Anatomy of Melancholy*, written more than 300 years ago by the scholar and librarian Robert Burton. It was a success in Burton's time and has been reprinted many times. It provides an early, thoughtful analysis of the nature of depression. The word *melancholy* is derived from the Greek *melan* meaning "black" and is more or less synonymous with depression. It is derived from the belief of Hippocrates (ca. 460–377 B.C.), often referred to as "the father of medicine," that depression is caused by too much black bile in the body. (See also Chapter 1, page 3.)

Other signs and symptoms frequently associated with the general symptom of depression are:

1. Crying
2. Loss of the ability to laugh
3. A negative, brooding outlook
4. Thoughts of suicide
5. Changes in eating habits
6. Lack of sexual desire
7. Fatigue

Some of these items can benefit from a few comments. *Loss of the ability to laugh* refers to the fact that depressed persons are very likely to lose their sense of humor. They do not think anything is funny and they frequently seem to miss the point of jokes. In fact, watching a situation comedy or an amusing movie may make them *more* depressed.

A negative, brooding outlook is associated with what are sometimes called *cognitive distortions*. These are irrational thoughts, oversimplifications such as, "We are all going to die anyway—so what's the sense of living" or "If I have a good income, it all goes to pay taxes and I can't get ahead."

Thoughts of suicide are to be taken seriously. Unfortunately, chronically depressed persons are at increased risk for suicide. If you have such thoughts yourself and cannot seem to shake them, you are well advised to seek help from a psychiatrist, a clinical psychologist, or other trained professional person. If a friend or family member is depressed and speaks of suicide, this may be what is sometimes called "a cry for help." You should guide the individual toward professional assistance if you are at all able to do so.

Changes in eating habits suggest either overeating or the avoidance of food. People who are mildly depressed often tend to overeat in order to give themselves solace. However, when people are profoundly depressed, they tend to lose their appetites.

Depression is associated with lack of joy and pleasure in life. Therefore, it is not at all uncommon for depressed persons to *lose interest in sexual activity*. It is difficult to become sexually excited when life looks bleak and the future seems dark.

Fatigue can, of course, have an organic basis. However, when people are depressed they often think that there is something physically wrong because they "lack energy" and have "no get up and go." It is well known that this kind of lassitude and tiredness may have a psychological root in some cases.

Causes and Explanations

There are a number of causal factors associated with depression. One or several of these may be involved in a particular case.

A large body of contemporary research suggests that in some cases depression can have a biological basis. There is evidence suggesting that some depressed persons tend to have low levels of the neurotransmitter (i.e., a chemical messenger) *norepinephrine* in their brains. The cause of the low levels is open to some debate and discussion. It is possible that there is a genetic tendency toward low levels. However, it is also possible that a psychological variable termed *learned helplessness* is linked to the low levels.

The classical psychoanalytic theory of depression sees its source as repressed anger. The logic runs something as follows. Depressed persons tend to be conventional, socialized, and traditional in their personal lives and marriages. They are trained to be polite, courteous, and "nice." In

Freudian terms, they have superegos that are overly strict and self-punitive. (The *superego* is the moral agent of the personality.) Consequently, they have a hard time expressing normal aggressive feelings in the face of life's many frustrations. They bottle up their hostile feelings, and this gets converted into depression.

Psychoanalysts also speak of the "secondary gains" of an illness. Although the secondary gains are not principal causes of an illness, they can aggravate it. In the case of depression, an example of a secondary gain is escape from responsibility. A person who suffers from depression may soon learn that a sympathetic spouse will take care of the cooking, the washing, the children's needs, and the paying of bills when he or she says, "Honey, I'm depressed. Can you do it today?" In terms of learning theory, it can be argued that the well-meaning, helpful spouse inadvertently reinforces the tendency to become depressed. Unfortunately, the psychological symptom carries with it a sort of payoff.

Research conducted by psychologist Martin E. P. Seligman has revealed the existence of a behavioral phenomenon called *learned helplessness*. Learned helplessness exists when individuals *believe* they are helpless in situations in which they are capable of functioning effectively. Behind learned helplessness is a history of failure in similar situations. The individual overgeneralizes and thinks that having been helpless in situation A, he or she is also helpless in situation B. Here is an example: Fern's first husband was abusive and overcontrolling. She was, in fact, a victim. Now, ten years later, she is married for a second time. When problems arise, she does not assert herself and plays the role of victim. She believes that she is helpless, and this is possibly not the case at all. As indicated earlier, there is evidence to suggest that learned helplessness may be a causal factor in actual changes in the levels of the neurotransmitter norepinephrine.

According to Abraham Maslow, one of the principal founders of humanistic psychology, lack of self-actualization can be a factor in depression. Maslow suggests that *self-actualization* is an inborn tendency to make the most of our talents and potentialities. When, because of obstacles or other reasons, people fail to live up to their natural gifts, they feel that they are wasting their lives and, in turn, are likely to become depressed.

There is evidence to suggest that a diet high in refined sugars can contribute to a chronic condition in some people called *hypoglycemia*. Hypoglycemia is low blood sugar. (In people prone to hypoglycemia, the eating of foods with a high sugar content, such as candy or pie, *does not*, as common sense might suggest, create a condition of chronic high blood sugar. There is a rebound effect. The blood sugar is temporarily high, and then it falls below a normal level.) Hypoglycemia is associated with both fatigue and depression.

Finally, existential depression cannot be dismissed. *Existential depres-*

sion comes from the everyday built-in frustrations of life, from the normal occasional feeling of being lonely and emotionally isolated, and from the awareness that eventually everyone is going to die. Existential depression is, to some degree, a part of life. It was first clearly identified by the Danish philosopher Søren Kierkegaard about 150 years ago. (You will recall that Kierkegaard also introduced the concept of *existential anxiety*. See Chapter 5.) Existential depression is, within limits, normal and must be accepted. However, if pathological depression—the kind that was defined and discussed earlier—is present, then the interplay of two kinds of depression can have a multiplicative effect, making the individual seemed doomed to a life without either hope or joy.

Coping

If it seems to you that you suffer excessively from depression, you may find value in the following list of practical coping strategies.

• Take a certain amount of responsibility for your depression. Do not think of it as something that just happens to you. You may have a tendency toward depression, but the tendency does not necessarily have to have you. Depression may be something you induce, or aggravate, because of your attitudes or beliefs. Ask yourself, "Am I making this worse? What can I do to make it better?"

• In connection with the previous paragraphs, examine your consciously held ideas. As indicated earlier, persons prone to depression tend to have a negative outlook and cognitive distortions. Cognitive distortions are warped, oversimplified ways of thinking. They can be thought of as bad mental habits. An example of a prime cognitive distortion is *all-or-none thinking*. You lose your job and think, "I'm a failure." You give yourself a capital F in life, ignoring the fact that you are successful in other ways. Or you are disappointed in a restaurant meal and think, "The evening is ruined." Learn to challenge your own thinking. Do not take it for granted that you are thinking the truth just because you yourself are thinking it.

• Adopt the attitude that optimism can be learned. In the same way that helplessness can be learned, a positive outlook can also be learned. Seligman, identified earlier, has recently conducted research suggesting that an optimistic viewpoint can be acquired, that it is antagonistic to a negative one, and that much of one's outlook is in fact within one's own power. Learned optimism is the result of a whole process of emotional maturation and cognitive development. It is a process that never stops and that goes on all of our lives. It can be nurtured by the seeking of the kinds of experiences, ideas, and information that reveal options and choices in life in contrast to experiences, ideas, and information that suggest dismal outcomes. There is no single suggestion that will foster learned optimism. All of the coping strategies in this chapter, and many of the ones in other chapters, will contribute to learned optimism. Effective psychotherapy can also contribute to learned optimism.

• Do not bottle up your anger when you do not have to. Do not allow yourself to stifle your feelings over and over again. This is *not* a recommendation to allow yourself temper tantrums and petty rages. The way to handle the kind of frustrations that generate anger is to be neither passive nor aggressive, but assertive and reasonable. A spouse or other important person in your life may be playing a role in your depression because you are too inhibited, too "nice" to speak your mind or stand up for your rights. Your own inhibitions, for no practical reason, block you from dealing with significant other persons in an effective way. Stop playing the role of emotional victim, allowing yourself to be used and abused.

• Do not indulge yourself with the secondary gains that can come from acting depressed. If people do your work for you or are too sympathetic when you are depressed, it is possible that you may learn to pull your "depressed act" when you want to avoid a responsibility or when you feel a little sorry for yourself. Be alert to the ways in which acting depressed can pay off psychologically, and try to discriminate this process from depression itself. Unfortunately, acting depressed can itself aggravate and induce depression.

• Adopt a program of moderate, regular exercise. A brisk 20-minute walk three or four times a week, or the equivalent, appears to be sufficient to give you a substantial number of benefits. One of these benefits is the formation within the central nervous system, including the brain, of a group of chemical messengers called *endorphins* (i.e., "endogenous morphines"). Endorphins are natural opiates, a part of the body's normal chemistry, and they induce a wholesome sense of well-being. They tend to improve your mood and act as a barrier to depression.

• Avoid the excessive consumption of foods containing high concentrations of refined sugar, such as candy, soft drinks, pie, cake, ice cream, jam, and so forth. As indicated earlier, these can induce or aggravate a tendency toward hypoglycemia. Hypoglycemia is associated with depression.

• Make a file or notebook of quotations or sayings that portray life in positive terms. Memorize one or several that appeal to you and recite them mentally when you detect the first hints of depression. This process helps to counter negative cognitive distortions. An example of a positive saying, by an anonymous author, is, "An optimist sees opportunity in every calamity. A pessimist sees calamity in every opportunity."

Professional Help

If you find that you cannot cope adequately with depression, there are a number of ways in which the professions of psychiatry and clinical psychology can help you.

Taking a psychodynamic approach, a therapist may help you explore the unconscious roots of depression. The psychoanalytic assumption is that you keep in too much anger and convert it into depression. If so, you will develop greater insight into experiences that have contributed to this tendency. By exploring your childhood years and your relations with your parents, you are likely to obtain a certain amount of emotional release and freedom from an overly demanding superego, the agent of your personality that represents social standards.

Taking a behavioral approach, a therapist will help you to become more assertive. Your therapist may recommend an approach known as *assertiveness training* in which you learn communication skills that make it possible for you to stand up for your own rights without becoming unduly aggressive yourself. Assertiveness training will help you to feel less used and abused by others, and this in turn tends to lift depression.

Taking a humanistic approach, a therapist will help you explore ways in which you can become more self-actualizing. If some of your depression arises from the belief that you are wasting your talents and potentialities, the humanistic approach can be very effective. There are times when you and the therapist working together can discover, or rediscover, the best general pathway in life for you.

A substantial amount of recent research on psychotherapy has demonstrated that cognitive therapy is particularly effective in the treatment of many cases of depression. *Cognitive therapy* pinpoints specific cognitive distortions and focuses on ways to correct them by introducing clear, rational thinking. Your therapist is very likely to apply aspects of cognitive therapy to your treatment.

In cases of major depression that resist all attempts at counseling or psychotherapy, there are two biological approaches that are often used. These are electroconvulsive therapy (ECT) and drug therapy. ECT involves the induction of an electrical current through the frontal lobes. In the past, this used to induce an obvious seizure. Contemporary ECT is usually given with a muscle relaxant in order to avoid the potential hazards (e.g., skeletal damage) associated with a seizure. ECT can have adverse side effects such as pinpoint bleeding in the cortex and short-term memory loss.

Nonetheless, there are psychiatrists who argue convincingly that it is one of the best tools available against major depressive episodes characterized by complete demoralization and a risk of suicide.

Drug therapy, not ECT, has become the principal biological approach in the treatment of pathological depression. There are two general classes of drugs prescribed by psychiatrists for depression. These are (1) the tricyclic agents and (2) the monoamine oxidase (MAO) inhibitors. Both work by increasing the overall levels of norepinephrine in the brain. Tricyclic agents stimulate the brain to produce more norepinephrine. MAO inhibitors interfere with the action of monoamine oxidase, a brain chemical that is destructive to norepinephrine. Drugs often have adverse side effects, and these must be carefully evaluated in discussions with a psychiatrist.

Key Points to Remember

• Depression is a common experience, one that is familiar to most people.

• *Major depressive episode* or *severe depression* is characterized by the inability to shake depression for prolonged periods of time, for depression to enter into one's life like an uninvited guest who stays for weeks and months.

• Surveys indicate that during any given time period, about 4 percent of the adult population is suffering from some degree of depression.

• Some of the other signs and symptoms frequently associated with the general symptom of depression are crying, a negative outlook, thoughts of suicide, and fatigue.

• There is evidence suggesting that some depressed persons tend to have low levels of the neurotransmitter (i.e., a chemical messenger) *norepinephrine* in their brains.

• The classical psychoanalytic theory of depression sees its source as repressed anger.

• In the case of depression, an example of a secondary gain, or psychological payoff, is escape from responsibility.

• Learned helplessness can be an important factor in some cases of depression.

• Take a certain amount of responsibility for your depression.

• Examine consciously held ideas for cognitive distortions.

• In order to counter learned helplessness, adopt the attitude that optimism can be learned.

- Do not bottle up your anger when you do not have to.

- Taking a psychodynamic approach, a therapist may help you explore the unconscious roots of depression.

- Taking a humanistic approach, a therapist will help you explore ways in which you can become more self-actualizing.

- Two biological approaches used to treat depression are electroconvulsive therapy (ECT) and drug therapy.

Chapter 9

Drug Abuse: Recreational Self-Destruction

In 1822, the English essayist and poet Thomas DeQuincey published *Confessions of an English Opium Eater*. It contained a description of his recreational and self-destructive use of opium. About 100 years ago, Sigmund Freud used cocaine, at that time a legal stimulant in Austria, to give him more energy when he was a medical student. When one of his friends died of complications associated with the abuse of cocaine, Freud became a lifelong opponent of its use. The examples of DeQuincey and Freud indicate that there is nothing new about either the use or abuse of drugs.

A distinction should be made between drug use and drug abuse. *Drug use* refers to the use of a drug for either therapeutic or recreational purposes. Such use may be limited or moderate, even in cases of drugs that have addictive potential. *Drug abuse* refers to the use of a drug in such a manner that it is interfering with everyday functioning and taking a toll on one's body and life. This chapter is about drug abuse and what you can do about it if it is one of your problems.

The term *addiction* is often used in connection with drug abuse, and it requires definition. *Addiction* exists if the individual (1) abuses a given drug and (2) is dependent on it. The dependence can be physiological or psychological. In the case of physiological dependence, withdrawal from the drug will produce distressing organic symptoms. In the case of psychological dependence, withdrawal from the drug will produce distressing emotional reactions, such as crying, anger, anxiety, or depression. In many cases, addiction is, of course, both physiological and psychological.

It should be noted that alcohol is a drug and that it is often abused. The term *drug abuse* in this chapter excludes the use of alcohol because it is the sole topic of Chapter 2.

It is impossible to accurately estimate the magnitude of the drug-abuse problem in the United States. However, various studies and surveys suggest that at least 30 to 40 percent of young adults have experimented with drugs, including illegal ones. Perhaps 5 to 10 percent of these individuals become chronic drug abusers. It is sometimes said that drug abuse has reached epidemic proportions, that it is a kind of psychological plague.

Other signs and symptoms frequently associated with the principal symptom of drug abuse are:

1. Changes in physiological measures such as blood pressure, pulse, and body temperature
2. Changes in pupil size
3. Changes in reflex responsiveness
4. Awkward movements
5. Hallucinations and delusions
6. Variations in central-nervous-system arousal ranging from great excitement to stupor
7. An artificial increase in self-confidence and the ability to socialize
8. Mental bewilderment and disorientation
9. Impulsive behavior
10. A decline in physical health

In connection with those signs and symptoms, it is important to identify the kinds of drugs that are frequently abused.

Stimulants are drugs that *increase* central-nervous-system arousal. Users often feel, for a time, that they can "lick the world." There is loss of fatigue, a sense of euphoria, and sometimes an increase in sexual drive. Three specific kinds of stimulants are *amphetamines*, *cocaine*, and *inhalants* (e.g., glues, solvents, and lighter fluid.) *Caffeine* and *nicotine* are also stimulants. However, they are considered to be relatively mild in contrast to amphetamines, cocaine, and inhalants. In the case of stimulants, psychological addiction to them is usually more significant than physiological addiction.

Sedatives are drugs that *decrease* central-nervous-system arousal. Users often feel temporarily more relaxed. Unpleasant aspects of reality can be obscured and briefly shut out of life. One of the medical uses of sedatives is to help people sleep. It was mentioned earlier that alcohol is a drug, and it is included in the class "sedatives." A *barbiturate* (e.g., pentobarbital) is also a kind of sedative. Sedatives have a high potential for both physiological and psychological addiction.

Narcotics, like sedatives, decrease central-nervous-system arousal.

Narcotics tend to induce drowsiness, stupor, and a reduction in the ability to feel pain. *Opium, morphine,* and *codeine* are narcotics. (It should be noted that morphine and codeine are derived from opium.) *Heroin* is a synthetic narcotic that mimics the effects of opium and drugs derived from it. One of the medical uses of narcotics is to help people cope with pain. Narcotics have a high potential for both physiological and psychological addiction.

Hallucinogens distort reality by inducing changes in thinking, mood, and perception. Sometimes, users temporarily think such thoughts as "I see the reality beyond reality" or "I hold the key to the truth of the universe." Frequently individuals feel that their minds have been greatly expanded. *Mescaline, psilocybin, lysergic acid diethylamide-25* (LSD), and *phencyclidine* (PCP or "angel dust") are hallucinogens. *Cannabis* (i.e., "marijuana") is classified as a somewhat weaker hallucinogen than the prior ones identified. Like stimulants, psychological addiction to hallucinogens is usually more significant than physiological addiction.

Causes and Explanations

One of the principal causes of drug abuse is the ready availability of such drugs and the profit motive for the pusher. As indicated earlier, drug abuse has reached epidemic proportions in society. Drugs are "pushed," and this is one of the principal reasons they are both used and abused.

Peer-group pressure is an important contributing factor to drug abuse. The novice is told that it is something that "everybody does" and is encouraged to experiment. He or she wants to belong and to be accepted by others. There is also the element of curiosity, the attraction of a new experience. The first step in the direction of eventual drug abuse is often taken in this way. If drug use is common among members of one's reference groups (e.g., a team, classmates, a club, a group of co-workers), the likelihood that one will become a user is greatly increased.

Sometimes, the first steps in the direction of drug abuse are taken for medical reasons. Amphetamines are commonly prescribed for weight control. Barbiturates are sometimes prescribed for insomnia and sleep disturbances. *Tolerance,* the inability of the drug to produce its expected effect, is associated with both amphetamines and barbiturates. Individuals who find that a drug is no longer producing the expected effect may find themselves taking increasingly large doses to get that effect, and this often contributes to both abuse and addiction.

It was thought at one time that there was a characteristic pattern associated with addictive personalities. Research has not been able to establish such a pattern. It cannot be said that drug abusers are higher or lower in intelligence, creativity, shyness, ambition, or other personality traits than people in general. Nonetheless, having said this, there are certain predisposing factors associated with drug abuse.

Chronic anxiety is one such factor. (For more about chronic anxiety, see Chapter 5.) People who worry constantly about anything and everything may find temporary relief from distress in such drugs as sedatives and narcotics.

A second predisposing factor is depression. (For more about depression, see Chapter 8.) One of the symptoms associated with depression is chronic fatigue and lack of energy. Consequently, persons who are depressed, in some cases, find stimulants such as amphetamines or cocaine to be appealing drugs. Such substances keep them going when they are low and have to get something done in spite of their own resistance.

A third predisposing factor is self-destructiveness. (For more about self-destructiveness, see Chapter 24.) Some individuals commit out-and-out suicide. Far more common is what the psychoanalyst Karl Menninger called *chronic suicide*, the killing of oneself by inches and degrees. This is also termed *indirect self-destructive behavior* by suicidologists. Slow suicide is far more common than quick suicide. Consciously or unconsciously, drug abuse may be a way of seeking death.

A fourth predisposing factor is low self-esteem. Persons with a negative self-concept, who are displeased with themselves and their accomplishments in life, are somewhat more likely than others to seek escape from themselves in drugs.

A fifth predisposing factor is the possibility that some individuals have a biological makeup that renders them somewhat more likely than others to abuse drugs and become addicted. This general approach is associated with the *genetic hypothesis*, the hypothesis that some persons inherit a high tendency to abuse certain drugs. Some evidence in favor of this hypothesis comes from the studies of families and twins. Other evidence is derived from studies of the nature of neurons and neurotransmitters in the central nervous system.

A general theme running through drug abuse is *escape*. Drugs provide a brief exit from reality, from the demands and responsibilities of everyday existence.

Coping

If you abuse drugs, you may find value in the following list of practical coping strategies.

- To the best of your ability, try to avoid social situations that are associated with drug abuse—it is much easier to say "No" to an invitation to a party or get-together than it is to resist social pressure when you are there. As one counselor who formerly abused drugs often says to his clients, "Remember that birds of a feather flock together. I used to say to myself that I want to stop flying with these particular birds."

- Refuse to play the role of patsy, or sucker. Holly Q., a woman who abused cocaine for several years, says, "One day it dawned on me that I was making a bunch of crooks rich. The big shots probably didn't abuse drugs. I got the picture of myself as a loser, a patsy. I resented them, and I got angry at myself. This really helped me to quit."

- Learn all you can about drugs, their chemical actions and their adverse side effects. An overdose of cocaine can lead to cardiac arrest and death. Large doses of amphetamines can induce delusions and a dangerous rise in blood pressure. Slurring of speech, brain damage, injury to the body's reflexes, and suppression of bone-marrow functioning are just a few of the other effects that have been associated with highly toxic drugs. And, of course, most people know that the sharing of needles for intravenous injections has been implicated in the transmission of acquired immune deficiency syndrome (AIDS).

- Do all that you can to bolster your self-esteem. Maybe drugs can make you feel temporarily better about yourself or help you avoid facing your personal failings and deficiencies. But in the long run, you have to actually *do* something in the real world. The best way to achieve this is with real accomplishments that are worth something to yourself and others. Keep in mind, however, that you do not have to take giant steps—take small ones that you can readily manage, like holding on to a job, finishing a course of study, paying your bills, and doing someone a favor.

- Avoid the fallacy of what I call *genetic fatalism*. Genetic fatalism is the viewpoint that your behavior cannot be helped because it is determined by your genes. It is too easy to say, "It's not my fault. I'm predisposed by my genes to abuse drugs." Although it is true that some research suggests the possibility of a genetic factor in drug abuse, this data establishes a weak association at best, not a one-to-one cause and effect. It is highly doubtful that your genes "doom" you to anything. To blame your genes for your behavior is a cop-out, a rationalization that you should reject.

- If you use drugs to cope with anxiety or depression, see Chapters 5 and 8, respectively, for more effective ways to cope with these emotional states.

- Face the fact that drug abuse is a pathway to self-destruction. If you are not ready to live with a damaged body, reconsider what you are doing to yourself.

• Memorize key sentences. David W. memorized the following key sentence: "Drug abuse is a road to hell and oblivion." He says, "At moments of temptation I would recite the sentence in my mind and really think about what it means and what I was doing to my life. It helped me to resist my impulses." Fay H. memorized: "I don't want to live in the gutter. I want to live on the sunny side of the street." William B. memorized, "It is a terrible thing to waste a person. I'm not going to waste myself." Memorize key sentences that you run across in your reading, or make up key sentences that are particularly meaningful to you.

• Remember that you cannot escape from reality. Drug abuse, at best, provides only a temporary vacation from reality. In the end, you have to return to the everyday world. And when you return, you return somewhat like a psychological pauper—poorer in both health and emotional adjustment, a victim of yourself. It has been argued that drugs provide doorways into other worlds, alternate realities. That is one viewpoint. Another one, harder to face, is that there is *only one* real world—the world of jobs, ups and downs, successes and failures, friends, lovers, spouses, and children— the everyday world of real people.

• Reject the idea that drugs make you a more creative person. Some people who have the desire to paint pictures, write stories and novels, compose music, and so forth, have become convinced that drugs help them to break out of mind sets and stimulate original thinking. Even if that is true, it is a Devil's bargain. But is it true? The essayist and poet Ralph Waldo Emerson wrote, "The spirit of the world, the great calm presence of the creator, comes not forth to the sorceries of opium or of wine."

Professional Help

If you find that you cannot cope adequately with a tendency to abuse drugs, the professions of psychiatry and clinical psychology offer real help and hope.

In the case of psychiatry, if you are physiologically addicted to a drug, you may require a period of hospitalization in order to detoxify your body. This requires medical supervision, and psychiatrists are medical doctors. Most addicted persons go through a period of resistance to hospitalization. They deny reality and say, "I can do it myself." They often learn that they are fooling themselves and that they require the period of respite and relief—a "time-out"—that a hospital setting provides. Hospitalization is often an important first step in the direction of freedom from drugs. It is hard to deny reality when you are in a hospital. You say to yourself, "I'm here. And it's pretty obvious that I need help."

In the case of clinical psychology, a psychotherapist can provide emotional support. When you are going through the storm and stress of withdrawal, the psychological strength and rational outlook of the therapist can help you keep going in the right direction. It helps to have someone with whom to talk over problems. However, the emotionally supportive therapist provides more than "tea and sympathy." The therapist provides *empathy*, a process of both intellectual and emotional understanding. Empathy has several functions: It helps you (1) to feel less alone and isolated, (2) to clarify your thinking and your feelings, and (3) to see yourself and your behavior in more objective terms by providing a psychological mirror into which you can look.

Key Points to Remember

• *Drug use* refers to the use of a drug for either therapeutic or recreational purposes. *Drug abuse* refers to the use of a drug in such a manner that it is interfering with everyday functioning and taking a toll on one's body and life.

• *Addiction* exists if the individual (1) abuses a given drug and (2) is dependent on it.

• Some of the signs and symptoms frequently associated with the principal symptom of drug abuse are changes in physiological measures, changes in reflex responsiveness, hallucinations and delusions, an artificial increase in self-confidence, and impulsive behavior.

• *Stimulants* are drugs that increase central-nervous-system arousal.

• *Sedatives* are drugs that decrease central-nervous-system arousal. *Narcotics*, like sedatives, decrease central-nervous-system arousal.

• *Hallucinogens* distort reality by inducing changes in thinking, mood, and perception.

• It was thought at one time that there was a characteristic pattern associated with addictive personalities. Research has not been able to establish such a pattern.

• Predisposing factors in drug abuse include anxiety, depression, self-destructiveness, low self-esteem, and one's biological make-up.

• A general theme running through drug abuse is escape from reality. Remember that in the long run you really cannot escape from reality.

• Refuse to play the role of patsy.

- Do all that you can to bolster your self-esteem.
- Avoid the fallacy of genetic fatalism.
- Memorize key sentences that provide insight or inspiration.
- If you are physiologically addicted to a drug, you may require a period of hospitalization in order to detoxify your body.
- A therapist can provide you with emotional support.

Chapter 10

Food Abuse:
Living to Eat

More than two thousand years ago, the philosopher Cicero said, "We should eat to live, not live to eat." People who abuse food often desperately wish they could live by Cicero's dictum, but they cannot. Some who abuse food feel helpless in the presence of food—as if bewitched by it. Their behavior is ruled by appetite and desire, not hunger—at least not biological hunger.

It should be noted that overeating is not the only way in which food is abused. Some people manifest overcontrolled behavior in the presence of food. Such individuals become phobic and will resist food to the point of emaciation.

Consequently, *food abuse* exists when an individual responds to food in pathological and self-defeating ways. Thus, the excessive eating of food may take the place of sexual satisfaction, help reduce anxiety, be a way to cope with boredom, be a substitute for love and attention, be a way to express anger, and so forth. Conversely, the compulsive avoidance of food may be a sign of the fear of obesity, an irrational belief that being thin keeps one from ever having to grow up, a way of expressing power in a family situation, and so forth. These maladaptive aspects of food abuse can result in morbid changes in the body including *obesity* at the one extreme and *emaciation* at the other.

It is important to stress that obesity is *not* synonymous with food abuse. A person can abuse food and still be very thin or have a normal weight. *Compulsive eating*, one kind of food abuse, is characterized by the pathological eating and digestion of calories significantly beyond one's metabolic needs. And, of course, compulsive eating is a contributing factor to obesity. However, it is only one factor. Other contributing factors to obesity include body type, metabolic rate, and body chemistry. These factors, biological in nature, to some extent reflect a genetic predisposition. People are not "doomed to be fat" by their genes, however. Eating in moderation, eating foods high in fiber and low in saturated fat and refined sugar, and a reasonable amount of exercise help modify the impact of "obesity genes" in a beneficial way. Although compulsive eating is but one factor, as already indicated, in obesity, it is probably in the vast majority of cases the principal factor. Therefore, it has to be indicted as one of the principal patterns of food abuse.

Other signs and symptoms associated with the principal psychological symptom of food abuse include the following:

1. Obsessively thinking about food
2. A failure of the will—an inability to exercise voluntary control over eating
3. Sneaking food, hiding food, and lying to others about how much one eats
4. Using food somewhat like a drug—as a way of coping with life's problems
5. Going on and off diets (riding a diet merry-go-round)
6. Gaining, losing, and regaining significant amounts of weight (the yo-yo syndrome)
7. Extreme dissatisfaction with one's body image
8. A magical belief that all of one's weight or eating problems can be solved with a new kind of pill, a series of shots, hypnosis, or plastic surgery.

Although the above signs and symptoms are clearly associated with overeating and obesity, it is worth noting they are also associated with the pathological avoidance of food. Persons who fear becoming fat or who are prone to starve themselves tend, like those who overeat, to think obsessively about food. Also, they compulsively avoid food or compulsively diet; consequently, they have lost voluntary control over their eating. And they often have a distorted body image imagining themselves to be fat when instead they are too thin.

It is a good idea to be familiar with some of the principal eating disorders that afflict adolescents and adults. The American Psychiatric Association's *Diagnostic and Statistical Manual of Mental Disorders* identifies two that are of principal interest. These are anorexia nervosa and bulimia nervosa. *Anorexia nervosa* is characterized by the refusal to eat enough food to maintain a normal body weight. The vast majority (about 95 percent) of the victims of anorexia nervosa are either adolescent or young adult females. The false belief that one is fat, cessation of menstrual flow, and lack of interest in sexual activity are some of the other common aspects of the disorder. Anorexia is one of the few life-threatening mental disorders because its victims sometimes die of complications associated with malnutrition. *Bulimia nervosa* is characterized by binge eating. This is frequently followed by purges such as self-induced vomiting, taking a laxative, or going on a fast. Depression and self-criticism after binging, eating easy-to-eat foods such as cookies and ice cream, an addiction to diets, and preoccupation with weight are some of the other common aspects of the disorder.

Some psychiatrists and clinical psychologists identify a condition called *bulimarexia*, although it is not at present a part of the standard nomenclature. Bulimarexia combines the two conditions of anorexia nervosa and bulimia nervosa. There are patients who, for example, will spend a few months in an anorexic state and then a few months in a bulimic state. They may alternate these states several times.

An important causal factor in the eating disorders is compulsive eating, although compulsive eating is not a recognized eating disorder. This is obvious in bulimia nervosa. It is not so obvious in anorexia nervosa. However, one interpretation of anorexia nervosa is that it is a defense against compulsive eating. The patient is aware of the intense cravings for food and overcompensates by excessive self-prohibition. The wish to eat is repressed to the unconscious level, and this emerges on the conscious side as a fear and avoidance of food. In psychoanalysis, this is called a *reaction formation*, the appearance of a wish at the conscious level in a form opposite of the way it is held at an unconscious level. In short, compulsive eating is an important factor in both bulimia nervosa and anorexia nervosa.

Causes and Explanations

One of the principal reasons that people abuse food is that they are connecting food with certain emotional satisfactions. It is quite possible, for example, for food to symbolize love. Therefore, someone who feels unloved often turns to food as a substitute for love. Associated with this is the fact that food can provide a degree of erotic gratification. In terms of psychosexual development, its first stage is often identified as *oral*. In infancy and toddlerhood, eating, biting, sucking, and chewing are very important. Individuals who lack adequate genital gratification as adults may find themselves returning to earlier levels of psychosexual development in a search for at least some erotic pleasure.

However, it should be noted that the wish to eat often arises in the face of almost any emotional lack. Depression, anxiety, anger, and boredom are common causal factors in food abuse. In the case of depression, the activity of eating provides a bright moment when one has the "blues" or the "blahs." In the case of anxiety, food often acts as a natural tranquilizer by activating the parasympathetic division of the autonomic nervous system and lowering arousal. In the case of anger, eating provides the biting and chewing that people often feel like doing when they are in a rage. In the case of boredom, eating is simply something to do.

Food abuse is sometimes related to family style. There are "fat families" in which the parents and the children all abuse food. In such cases the children have "permission" from the parents to overeat and also to be obese—it is "O.K." to be fat. In same cases, parents even "push" food on children as a way of proving that they love their children and also as a way of validating their own obesity or food abuse. Related to the prior points, there are families in which one child is unconsciously "picked" by the parents and other children to be "the fat one." Such a child provides a ready vent for the hostilities and superior feelings of other family members by being a scapegoat.

Maladaptive habits play a significant role in food abuse. A *habit* is an unthinking pattern of behavior, and "bad" habits are those that tend, in the long run, to work against a person's best interests even though they may provide momentary gratification. Thus, a person may have gotten such bad habits as eating a quart of ice cream every night after dinner, having two donuts every day at 10 A.M. after having had a complete breakfast at 7 A.M., drinking five soft drinks a day, and so forth. These kinds of bad habits are common, and they tend to have a momentum all their own. As already suggested, such habits bring pleasure, and they are hard to break because their constant repetition gives them what psychologists call "habit strength."

A tendency toward *hypoglycemia*, or low blood sugar, can be a contributing cause to food abuse. If one has a tendency toward hypoglycemia, he or she will frequently feel sluggish, fatigued, and lacking in alertness. This is because a given meal may not sustain the blood sugar at an optimal level for the four-to-six-hour intervals between meals. A "quick fix" for the problem is to eat a candy bar, drink a soft drink, have some ice cream, or to ingest something similar with a high sucrose content. Unfortunately, although this gives prompt relief, it will only tend to aggravate the problem. The blood sugar will rise too rapidly, peak, and plunge again. This is called the *hypoglycemic rebound*. It is evident that food with a high sugar content can have addictive properties. The short-term gratification provided by sucrose to a person with hypoglycemia is so great that it is easy to get "hooked" on the wrong foods.

In the case of anorexia nervosa, a common contributing cause to the problem is a power struggle within the family. An analysis can be applied to unmarried adolescent females who live at home. Parents are naturally concerned with their daughter's unwillingness to eat and her consequent emaciation. They recognize that the behavior is unhealthy. If they are somewhat overcontrolling and authoritarian, they will insist in a harsh and directive way that she eat. The adolescent, on the other hand, is fighting the battle of autonomy. She wants to be in control of her own life and does not want to be told what to do. A psychological tug-of-war takes place, and "winning" to the adolescent means not eating and following her own dictates.

A final contributing cause to food abuse in the United States is the way in which food is advertised and marketed. It is identified with fun and childish behavior. Television commercials often show adults regressing and gobbling food in delight. The kinds of foods that are the most advertised are those that are high in sugar or heavily processed. Foods in their natural states are not vigorously marketed. The advertised foods are the ones that are more likely to be abused by the individual.

Coping

If you tend to abuse food, you may find value in the following list of practical coping strategies.

• Work on separating food from emotional satisfactions. Say to yourself, "Food is not love," "Food is no substitute for sexual gratification," "Food does not help me cope in the long run with depression, anger, or boredom," "It is childish to express my anger by eating. I'm only hurting myself." Instead, look for realistic ways to gratify your emotional and sexual needs. As one client in psychotherapy put it, "When I look for love in the foods I eat, I'm looking for love in all the wrong places."

• If you are using food as a tranquilizer, look for other more effective and less self-defeating ways of reducing anxiety. (For more on anxiety, see Chapter 5.)

• If you believe that you have been "picked" by your parents or other family members to be "the fat one," consciously reject this role. Recognize it as a victim's role, as the result of accepting a status passively and without sufficient examination.

• Make a functional analysis of your maladaptive eating habits. This involves listing each habit on a piece of paper and identifying what triggers the habit, such as a given time of day, the behavior of other people, a mood, a special occasion, the sight or smell of food, and so forth. Now brainstorm each habit and try to come up with ideas for modifying or breaking it. Jot these down as they occur to you. Work on one habit at a time, starting with the easiest one first.

• If you believe that you suffer from hypoglycemia, look for long-run, not short-run, relief. You can accomplish this by avoiding snacks high in sucrose and refined carbohydrates. Instead select snacks high in fiber and/or protein. Examples of good snack foods are both nonfat and low-fat milk, whole wheat bread, an apple or an orange, a few unsalted or dry roasted peanuts, or a broiled chicken breast. Such foods will give you relief, sustain your blood sugar at an optimal length for a longer period of time, and help you stop abusing food.

• If you suffer from anorexia nervosa and are in a power struggle with a parent or parents, become conscious of the fact that you are acting as your own worst enemy. You are, as a familiar saying goes, "cutting off your nose to spite your face." If you lose your health while "proving" that your parents cannot boss you around and tell you what to do, what is the real benefit to you? The answer is, "None." Look for healthy ways to assert your autonomy. There are times when you might feel you must go against your parents' wishes, but do not make food the weapon and the dining table the battleground. It is a sham battle that makes no sense and has little basis in reality. Fight for your real rights, not symbolic ones.

• Be aware of the fact that advertising is designed to appeal to your childish self, to your impulsive nature. When you go to a grocery store, make a list not only of foods you intend to buy, but of foods you intend *not* to buy. Learn to resist suggestion.

Professional Help

If you find that you cannot cope adequately with a tendency to abuse food, there are a number of ways in which the professions of psychiatry and clinical psychology can help you.

Taking a psychodynamic approach, a therapist will help you become familiar with the specific ways in which you abuse food to satisfy emotional needs. An assumption of classical psychoanalysis is that you unconsciously confuse food with other psychological and emotional hungers. Suppose that you hunger for love, or sexual gratification, or success, or fame, or power. And suppose that one or more of these hungers is going unsatisfied. It is possible that you are blindly stuffing up the emptiness with food. Psychotherapy can provide insight into the specifics of this process in your particular case, and this self-understanding is often a first step in setting you free from the tyranny of food.

Still taking a psychodynamic approach, it is possible that your therapist will be able to help you trace your tendency to abuse food back to early experiences often rooted in infantile oral needs. If you suffered a severe emotional wound during infancy or toddlerhood, such as child abuse, neglect, or the loss of a parent, it is possible that you have developed oral fixations. Again, your therapist can help you evaluate if these fixations are a problem in your particular case.

Taking an interpersonal approach, your therapist will help you understand your role in the family. This may help you to evaluate dysfunctional communication processes and to find ways to improve them. If you have been "picked" to be fat, your therapist can help you find ways to reject this role and find a more life-enhancing role in the family. If you suffer from anorexia nervosa, the interpersonal approach can assist you in shifting the family gives and takes from a power struggle to a set of realistic negotiations. And this, in turn, can help you develop a more natural and accepting attitude toward food.

Taking a behavioral approach, a therapist will help you to break and modify maladaptive habits. The same kind of functional analysis of habits discussed earlier can be made with the help of a skilled behavior therapist. Such therapists are experts on how habits are made and unmade, and they can help you pinpoint your maladaptive habits as well as develop effective interventions. The basic laws of conditioning and learning can be applied in a beneficial way to the problem of food abuse.

If your food abuse problem is aggravated by hypoglycemia and you need professional help, you may want to look outside of the fields of psychiatry and clinical psychology in the direction of a family physician or an endocrinologist for additional therapy. Bariatric physicians also specialize in treating medical problems related to obesity and food abuse.

There is no drug that can be prescribed by a medical doctor or a psychiatrist to specifically treat food abuse. In some cases, an antianxiety agent may be prescribed when food is being used as a tranquilizer. In other cases, amphetamines may be prescribed to suppress appetite. However, many patients quickly build a tolerance to amphetamines, and they are often useless as a form of treatment in, for example, a few weeks. On the whole, drugs are of limited value in treating individuals who abuse food.

In general, it can be said that the best approach in therapy is one that fosters understanding of *why* you abuse food combined with practical methods indicating *how* you can break and modify your habits.

Key Points to Remember

· Obesity is *not* synonymous with food abuse.

· Compulsive eating, one kind of food abuse, is characterized by the pathological eating and digestion of calories significantly beyond one's metabolic needs.

· Food abuse exists when an individual responds to food in pathological and self-defeating ways.

• *Anorexia nervosa* and *bulimia nervosa* are two of the principal eating disorders. *Bulimarexia*, not a formally recognized disorder, is a combination of the characteristics of anorexia nervosa and bulimia nervosa.

• One of the principal reasons that people abuse food is that they are connecting it with certain emotional satisfactions. They should work on separating food from emotional satisfactions.

• Food abuse is sometimes related to family style.

• Maladaptive (i.e., "bad") habits play a significant role in food abuse.

• A tendency toward *hypoglycemia*, or low blood sugar, can be a contributing cause to food abuse. Hypoglycemia can be combatted by avoiding snacks high in sucrose and carbohydrates and instead selecting snacks high in fiber and/or protein.

• A power struggle within the family is a common contributing cause to anorexia nervosa. If you are in such a power struggle, seek more effective ways to declare your autonomy.

• A contributing cause to food abuse in the United States is the way in which food is advertised and marketed. Seek ways to resist suggestion.

• Make a functional analysis of your maladaptive eating habits and look for ways to break or modify them.

• A therapist can help you become familiar with specific ways in which you abuse food to satisfy emotional needs.

• A therapist can help you evaluate and modify dysfunctional communication processes in the family.

• A therapist can help you break and modify maladaptive habits.

Chapter 11

Helplessness: Is It Real or Learned?

Imagine that you are a passenger on an ocean liner in the North Atlantic. The ship strikes an iceberg and begins to sink. There are not enough lifeboats to accommodate everyone. And there is a shortage of life preservers. Shortly, you find yourself forced to jump off of the deck into the freezing water. You know that unless you are picked up, and this is unlikely, you will survive only a few minutes. Nothing you do in the water will make the slightest difference. You will almost certainly die. This is what it means to be really helpless.

Briefly, *helplessness* exists when an individual's actions have no positive effect on outcomes. However, it is important to make a distinction at the outset of this chapter between actual helplessness and a *sense* of helplessness. The first is real; the second is imagined to be real. The first is an objective process; the second is subjective in nature.

Seldom in life is anyone as helpless as an individual would be in the disaster situation described above. Nonetheless, many individuals act *as if* they are as helpless as the victim of the liner disaster. A sense of helplessness is not a specific mental disorder. Rather, it is a symptom of a general *process* underlying various other symptoms and difficulties such as depression, various failures, lack of assertiveness, and even physical illness.

A sense of helplessness can be specific or general. A person can feel helpless in various important roles in life, such as lover, spouse, parent, child, student, professional, and employee. Also, helplessness can be related to certain kinds of situations and demands, such as shopping for clothes, buying presents, chatting at a party, making repairs, and so forth. Although these kinds of specific helplessness are important, the focus on this chapter is on general helplessness. *General helplessness* is the conviction that one is helpless most of the time in most social roles and in most situations.

Some of the other signs and symptoms frequently associated with a general, pervasive sense of helplessness are:

1. The idea that one's life is out of control
2. The feeling that one is just a pawn of fate
3. A loss of a sense of personal power
4. An inability to initiate plans and set goals
5. Episodes of depression
6. Lack of self-confidence and self-reliance
7. A negative outlook on life
8. Passive behavior when confronted with a challenge
9. Learning blocks
10. Brooding about whether or not there's any sense in being alive
11. The impression that other people and situations, not decisions and actions, control the events in one's life

Causes and Explanations

In order to understand helplessness as a psychological process, it is essential to introduce a concept termed *learned helplessness*. The concept of learned helplessness was proposed, and introduced into the literature and language of behavioral science by the research psychologist Martin E. P. Seligman about 20 years ago. Since that time, both he and others have conducted a number of studies and experiments designed to clarify how the process operates in both animals and human beings.

Here is a description of a typical experiment with rats that is designed to demonstrate how learned helplessness works. A large group of rats—say, 60—are assigned to two smaller groups, Group A and Group B. The rats are assigned at random to the two groups—30 to each group—to eliminate biases that might arise from individual differences. The rats in Group A, one at a time, are subjected to *escapable shock*. The rats are trained in a device called a "shuttle box." The shuttle box has an electrified floor on both Side 1 and Side 2 of the box. A low hurdle separates the two sides. If a rat is in Side 1 of the box, a buzzer sounds as a warning. Then, 20 seconds later, a shock is administered. Soon, the rat learns to jump to Side 2. After a suitable time period, the buzzer sounds again. If the rat is resting in Side 2, it will soon jump to Side 1. Eventually, no matter what side of the box the rat is in, it will jump to the other side as soon as it hears the buzzer. The rat has learned, through a process called *operant conditioning*, to avoid shock when it hears the buzzer. Notice that the rats learn to do more than just escape from shock; they *avoid* it by jumping when they hear the buzzer and *not* waiting 20 seconds to be shocked. Therefore, they seldom are shocked.

The important point is that the rats in Group A are *not* helpless. Their actions have a positive effect on outcomes. Put another way, their behavior has meaningful consequences.

The rats assigned to Group B are not so fortunate. A transparent plexiglass barrier separates Side 1 from Side 2. When the buzzer goes off and the shock is administered, they at first try to escape, of course. However, they soon learn that all attempts are futile. After several pairings of the buzzer with the shock, they simply give up and huddle helplessly while they endure pain. The important point here is that rats in Group B are actually helpless. They are, so to speak, "victims of fate."

What has just been described concludes the *training phase* of the experiment. The next phase, the *test phase,* will elucidate the concept of learned helplessness. During this second phase, the rats are tested individually in a deep tank of water. Rats are good swimmers. Rats in Group A generalize their sense of control from the training phase, and they will swim vigorously until they are rescued. Rats in Group B generalize their *actual* helplessness in the shuttle box to the tank of water in which they are *not* helpless. They will quickly give up—enduring the water for only a few minutes—and they will drown and die if not rescued. This is learned helplessness.

In brief, *learned helplessness* exists when a behavior pattern acquired in a first situation where there was actual helplessness is generalized to a second situation where the individual is not helpless.

Perhaps you are thinking, "But this is rats. What is the human comparison? People are not subjected to inescapable electric shocks." True. But people are sometimes subjected to the psychological equivalent—situations that doom them to failure. Take this example: Amelia B. was unfortunate enough to have a cold, unfeeling teacher when she was in the fourth grade. The teacher made Amelia feel stupid when she had trouble learning some of the basic concepts in arithmetic. In the eighth grade, she had a similar experience. A teacher treated her as if she were stupid and openly referred to her as a "hopeless case" in front of other children. Amelia decided that she was "no good at math." This became what George Kelly, a clinical psychologist and personality theorist, called a *personal construct,* a well-defined conscious idea about oneself. The idea that she was no good at math was an important factor in what become an attitude of learned helplessness in this particular area of human abilities. Today Amelia is 20 years old, a college student majoring in history. Amelia avoids all math courses. She is even afraid that she will never graduate from college because she goes to a school that requires one basic math course in order to receive a four-year degree.

Is Amelia actually helpless? The odds are very high that the correct answer is, "No." She is not the same person that she was when she was in the fourth grade or the eighth grade. But she *believes* she is helpless. She has generalized early failure experiences to the present and is a victim of learned helplessness.

This is the way learned helplessness works. A series of early failure experiences is generalized to the present. In the present, the individual is not helpless. Nonetheless, the generalization interferes greatly with effective behavior.

A predisposing factor that may play a role in creating a general sense of helplessness in some individuals is a history of abuse. This may have been a pattern of abuse in childhood; or it can even be a history of abuse relatively recently, for example, in a marriage. Keep in mind that abuse need not be physical; it can be verbal. The individual—child or adult—who is made to feel over and over again that he or she is worthless, unimportant, incompetent, and unlovable will often respond by developing a self-image that is defined by these very traits.

Coping

If it seems to you that you suffer excessively from a feeling of general helplessness, you may find value in the following list of practical coping strategies.

• Say to yourself, "I want to think clearly about my feelings." The first step in coping with learned helplessness is to introduce an element of rational thought, of logic, into your responses to situations. You want to practice taking a psychological step back and reflecting on yourself and your behavior in objective terms. Feelings of learned helplessness come from a wounded child self. Your wounded child cannot solve your emotional problems—it can only feel hurt. You have to elevate your psychological processes to the adult level where you can become an effective agent of your own change, not a victim.

• Recognize that learned helplessness is basically a generalization phenomenon. This means that situation B is confused with situation A because of some perceived similarity. Generalization is a basic aspect of learning. Pavlov, the Russian physiologist who first studied classical conditioning, discovered that if a dog is trained to salivate at a tone of a given pitch, it will also salivate at tones of a slightly lower or higher pitch. On a less formal level, the humorist Mark Twain once noted that his pet cat had been burned by a hot stove and was now afraid not only of hot stoves but also of cold stoves. Say to yourself, "This situation today is *not* the same as yesterday's situation. This college math class is *not* the math class I had in the fourth grade." Candace E., a woman who had been abused in a marriage says, "I had to learn to say to myself when I began dating again that *this man* is *not* Constantine, my first husband. I was treating all men as if they were identical." You have to learn to discriminate "hot" stoves from "cold" ones.

· Recognize that personal constructs about the self do not necessarily reflect reality. They are *ideas* that guide behavior, and people often act *as if* they were absolutely true. However, it is both sensible and correct to adopt the viewpoint that personal constructs should be open to new information and gradual modification. Personal constructs such as, "I'm not popular," "I'm too shy to ever have a good time at a party," "I could never be a life insurance salesperson or a real estate broker because I don't meet people easily," "I am no good at English composition," "I have no musical ability," or "I can't draw" may all be proven incorrect in the long run. Betty Edwards describes in her book *Drawing on the Right Side of the Brain* how students in her art classes—students who thought they could not draw— learned to draw effectively through the use of special techniques.

· Be aware of the important difference between actual helplessness and learned helplessness. Unnecessary suffering is caused by learned helplessness, not by actual helplessness. Yes, there are times when a person is really helpless, and they may be a cause of unavoidable anguish and suffering. However, in many, many cases, you mistakenly act helpless when you are not. This is learned helplessness. Work on your ability to recognize learned helplessness in yourself. Ask yourself, "Am I *really* helpless? Or do I just think I am?"

· Value the power of human consciousness. The experiments described with learned helplessness in rats presented them as helpless victims—and they were. But rats do not possess human consciousness. They cannot understand the concept of learned helplessness. You can. Rats are doomed, trapped by their own limited psychological processes when they acquire learned helplessness. You, on the other hand, are set free by your understanding. You can break free from learned helplessness.

· Actively reject the idea that you are just a pawn of fate. Memorize the last two lines of William Henley's inspiring poem *Invictus* (*Invictus* means "unconquered"): "I am the master of my fate. I am the captain of my soul." Voluntarily "run the tape" of these lines through your conscious mind when you begin to feel helpless.

· Recognize that there is a psychological phenomenon that opposes learned helplessness. It is called *learned optimism*. Recently, Martin E. P. Seligman, the psychologist who first studied learned helplessness, has been studying learned optimism. In the same way that human beings can acquire a set of self-defeating generalizations and personal constructs, they can acquire a set of self-enhancing generalizations and personal constructs.

One of the key factors in learned optimism is how you explain your own behavior to yourself. Suppose Milton H. earns an A on a history test. He says to himself, "I studied hard and it paid off." George J. also earns an A on the same test. He says to himself, "I lucked out. The teacher is an easy grader." Milton's explanatory style reflects learned optimism. George's explanatory style reflects learned helplessness. If this seems dubious, consider the following. If in a future test both students receive a low grade, Milton is likely to think, "I need to burn the midnight oil—study a little harder." George is likely to think, "I've had it. The teacher has decided to lower the boom on me." In brief, you can cultivate optimism by your own efforts. The coping strategies presented in this section describe some of the ways to do it.

   • Focus on the word *learned* in the phenomenon of *learned helplessness*. What has been learned can be unlearned. Acquired behavior can be given up. Psychologists define *learning* as "a more or less permanent change in behavior, or a behavioral tendency, as a result of experience." Note that learning is "more or less" permanent. Yes, it resists change—has an inertia all its own. But it can, and does, change. Learned helplessness is acquired because of a history of maladaptive experiences. It can be modified with a new, self-directed history of adaptive experiences.

Professional Help

If you find that you cannot cope adequately with a general feeling of helplessness, there are a number of ways in which the professions of psychiatry and clinical psychology can help you.

   Taking a psychodynamic approach, a therapist may help you to identify the maladaptive experiences in your childhood or in recent years that gave rise in you to a sense of helplessness. You will discover that in these situations you probably were actually helpless. You were abused, unloved, misunderstood, discounted, criticized, bossed around, and presented with impossible situations. By identifying these situations, labeling and remembering them, you will find that they have less of a grip on you. To some extent, you can find freedom from them by understanding them and your emotional reactions at the time.

   Behavior therapy is a particularly important approach in the case of learned helplessness because behavior therapy is based on principles of learning and conditioning. Taking a behavioral approach, your therapist will look for ways to help you decondition and extinguish your maladaptive learning. This can be done in various ways. One way is through *systematic desensitization*. The therapist can desensitize you by painting word pictures and inducing guided fantasies in which you see yourself coping effectively with situations in which you would normally feel helpless (e.g., giving a talk, taking a test, asking for a date, chatting with strangers at a party). You can also be desensitized by the *in vivo* method. This involves "homework assignments" in which you cope with mildly threatening situations at first and work your way up to more demanding ones.

Taking a cognitive approach, your therapist will help you to examine your conscious ideas about yourself and helplessness. Ideas such as "I'll never make any of my dreams come true," "It's not what you know, it's who you know," "You cannot get anywhere unless you get some lucky breaks," or "I'm a victim of Murphy's law—whatever can go wrong, will" reveal a victim's outlook on life. Every one of them says beneath the surface, "I'm helpless." In therapy, your self-defeating ideas will be closely examined and discussed for their irrational content, and you *will* discover that they *are* irrational. Then they will stop controlling you.

Taking an interpersonal approach, your therapist may help you to detect ways in which you respond to overcontrolling, authoritarian personalities in your social world in a helpless, self-defeating, passive way. You will be helped to discover ways in which you can become more assertive and stand up for your rights. *Assertiveness training* is often used in which you are helped to acquire a set of social skills that enable you to function in more effective and adaptive ways.

Taking a humanistic approach, your therapist may help you to realize that one of our uniquely human attributes is the power of the will. William James, the dean of American psychology, held that the human will is one of the prime mental faculties. A belief in the capacity of the will to make real choices, to go forward in life, is an important feature of mental health. James himself said that he often felt depressed and victimized until he asserted both the reality and the importance of the human will. Humanistic psychologists tend to agree with James. Again, this is a part of learned optimism and should play an important part in your recovery from the ravages of learned helplessness.

Drug therapy plays little or no part in the professional treatment of learned helplessness. It is true that learned helplessness and depression are often connected. Therefore, in some instances an antidepressant might be prescribed. But this is for the *symptom* of depression, not the *process* of learned helplessness. Learned helplessness, in and of itself cannot, be overcome with a drug. It must be overcome by the coping strategies and the approaches to psychotherapy already described.

Key Points to Remember

- It is important to make a distinction between actual helplessness and a sense of helplessness.

- A sense of helplessness can be specific or general.

- Some of the other signs and symptoms frequently associated with a general, pervasive sense of helplessness are the idea that one's life is out of control, a loss of a sense of personal power, episodes of depression, and a negative outlook on life.

- Learned helplessness exists when a behavior pattern acquired in a first situation where the individual was actually helpless is generalized to a second situation where the individual is not helpless.

- According to George Kelly, a personal construct is a well-defined conscious idea about oneself.

- A predisposing factor that may play a role in creating a general sense of helplessness in some individuals is a history of abuse.

- The first step in coping with learned helplessness is to introduce an element of rational thought, of logic, into your responses to situations.

- Recognize that learned helplessness is basically a generalization phenomenon.

- Recognize that personal constructs about the self do not necessarily reflect reality.

- Actively reject the idea that you are just a pawn of fate.

- The psychological phenomenon called learned optimism opposes learned helplessness.

- A therapist may help you to identify the maladaptive experiences in your childhood or in recent years that gave rise in you to a sense of helplessness.

- Taking a behavioral approach, your therapist will look for ways to help you decondition and extinguish your maladaptive learning.

- Taking a cognitive approach, your therapist will help you to examine your conscious ideas about yourself and helplessness.

- Like William James, assert both the reality and the importance of the human will.

Chapter 12

Indecisiveness: Going In Mental Circles

Do you make decisions, even trivial ones, with great difficulty? If your answer is *yes*, you have plenty of company. Many people suffer from what has been called "decideaphobia"—the fear of making decisions. It should be noted that "decideaphobia" is an informal term and has no actual clinical status. It is not usually listed as one of the common phobias (For more on phobias, see Chapter 14.) This does not make it less real among its victims.

Indecisiveness can cause the individual to suffer great distress and emotional turmoil. Tolstoy and Kierkegaard were two such individuals. Leo Tolstoy, author of *War and Peace*, was a wealthy Russian nobleman. In his older years, he wanted to give his land and his book royalties away to needy persons and his poor serfs, but his wife and children were against the move. He spent many years in self-torture and self-doubt because he was unable to live up to his own idealistic principles. The philosopher Søren Kierkegaard was engaged to be married, broke off the engagement, proposed again, and broke off the relationship again. Finally, he and the woman in question gave up on each other. Then he lived with endless regrets. He even wrote a book titled *Either/Or* in which he argued brilliantly in favor of the importance of being decisive in life. Both Tolstoy and Kierkegaard paid a heavy emotional price for their indecisive behavior.

When indecisiveness is related to important decisions, such as what to do about property or marriage, it is at least somewhat understandable. Everyone, even fairly well-adjusted persons, has been "stuck" in the decision-making process at one time or another.

However, there are people who have a hard time deciding what movie to go see, what to order from a menu, what to do with a free evening, what clothes to buy, where to go on vacation, what to listen to on the radio, what book to read, what people to be friendly with, and so forth. Their days are filled with titanic emotional struggles. And these struggles make them perpetually miserable.

A distinction between normal indecisiveness and pathological indecisiveness should be made. *Normal indecisiveness* takes place when alternatives are very difficult to evaluate, and outcomes are of substantial consequence. *Pathological indecisiveness* takes place when alternatives are seen in distorted and irrational terms, and the importance of outcomes is exaggerated.

Here is a normal approach to the making of decisions: (1) gather information, (2) think, (3) make a decision, and (4) act on the decision. Here is a pathological approach to the making of decisions: (1) gather information, (2) think, (3) enter into an indecisive state, (4) gather more information, (5) think some more, and (6) become more indecisive.

Other signs and symptoms frequently associated with the general symptom of pathological indecisiveness are:

1. Going in mental circles
2. Taking "forever" to make a decision
3. Excessive fear of making the wrong decision
4. Gathering huge amounts of information
5. Lack of an intuitive sense of what is the right thing to do
6. An absence of willingness to let a random element—a bit of chance— enter into outcomes.
7. Short-circuiting actions after they are begun
8. Compulsively asking others for advice

As already indicated, a substantial amount of distress may accompany the signs and symptoms of indecisiveness.

Causes and Explanations

There are a number of causal factors associated with indecisiveness. One or several of these may be involved in a particular case.

In broad general terms, *indecisiveness* can be characterized as an *approach-avoidance* conflict, a conflict in which a goal, or object of desire, has both positive and negative value to the individual. Attaining the goal will bring gains, but it will also bring losses. If a "Tolstoy" gives away his land, his self-esteem will rise. But he will also take a tumble from "riches to rags" and reap the hostility of his wife and children. If a "Kierkegaard" marries his beloved, he will reap the joys of marriage. But he will also have to contend with another personality and accept new responsibilities. In an approach-avoidance conflict, the individual usually begins by moving in the direction of the goal. But when the goal is too close, the "heat" becomes more than the individual can stand, and he or she goes the other way.

When far enough away from the goal, the individual turns around and goes through the whole process again.

Victims of indecisiveness often have compulsive personalities. They want to order, organize, and plan everything. They do this in order to reduce general anxiety, to keep things "safe." This is essentially a neurotic process, a self-defeating pattern, with only limited effectiveness.

Indecisiveness is aggravated by too much information. The gathering of ideas and facts that should help one make a decision reaches such an overwhelming level that the individual is drowning in an ocean of data. The mind is dazzled, as if in a house of mirrors, and has a difficult time sorting out what is, and what is not, really important and relevant to the decision.

The person who displays pathological indecisiveness may have a fear of being laughed at by others. Persons with a strong social interest may attach too much importance to the opinions of others. It is not so much that the individual will be actually laughed at or openly called a "fool" or "idiot." It is more a case of playing to an imaginary audience. The individual can imagine what will be said behind his or her back.

A factor that affects decision making is the number of choices open to the individual. If a person has only one good choice, then a decision is easy to make. However, the modern world overwhelms people with choices— there are just too many. Telephones come in many styles and colors. One can search among 20 or 30 birthday cards for the one that is "just right." There are 15 different movies available in one night in the person's local area. A family restaurant menu has a large selection of different entrees. The cases go on and on. Life presented fewer choices in the early part of this century. Telephones were black and of only one style. The same could be said of Model-T Fords. Only a limited number of jobs and vocations existed. It was easy to make a decision. The availability of choices is supposed to be a positive factor of living in today's Western world. But the opportunity to make choices also brings with it the stress of indecisiveness.

In some cases, indecisiveness is associated with irresponsibility. The indecisive person may be unwilling to accept the responsibilities that are part and parcel of a marriage, a career, buying a house, becoming club president, a promotion, and so forth. In such cases, the child self is saying, "I don't want to do this. Don't ask me to carry this burden."

A cause of indecisiveness is the false belief that decisions are irrevocable—that all bridges have been burned once one takes action. This is seldom the case. Even in the most difficult of circumstances, there is usually some way out. Married people get divorced; cars are sold when their owners no longer like them; majors are changed in college; and so forth. One may find that the exit is narrow, but that is not the same thing as finding that there is no exit. Very seldom, no matter what the decision, is there no subsequent option except to live with it for life.

A predisposing factor in indecisiveness is being raised by parents who modeled compulsive, rigid, overly organized ways of behaving. The child and adolescent is raised with the irrational idea that "everything, including choices and decisions, must always be perfect and right." Parental values become a part of the parent self, and they are hard to shake—even when they are clearly inappropriate.

A certain amount of difficulty in making a decision can be traced to a conflict between what psychoanalysts call the id and the superego. The *id*, the primitive part of the personality, says "Do it!" Sexual and aggressive behaviors are examples of id impulses. The *superego*, the social and moral part of the personality says, "That's nasty," or "That's not right." The struggle between the two agents of the personality represents a kind of psychological civil war. Much of this war takes place "underground," at the unconscious level of the personality. The conscious manifestation of the struggle is indecisiveness.

A person who suffers from indecisiveness tends to be what Carl Jung, a founder of psychotherapy, called a thinking-sensation type. A *thinking-sensation* type refers to a person who relies mainly upon rational analysis and what can be seen and heard when making a decision. In contrast, there is the feeling-intuition type. A *feeling-intuition* type refers to a person who relies mainly on moods, emotions, hunches, and "gut reactions" when making a decision. According to Jung, to some extent, the two types are reflections of inborn temperaments. One can see manifestations of the types in the behavior of toddlers and preschoolers.

Common sense tells us that fear of failure is one cause of indecisiveness. And this is, of course, true. However, it should be noted that, paradoxically, *fear of success* can also be a cause of pathological indecisiveness. Success may bring a host of responsibilities, opportunities, and new risks. Orlando S. wrote a novel, boxed it, took it to the post office, but did not mail it to a publisher. He did this several times over a period of two years. He resisted sending it not because he feared rejection, but because he feared that sudden success would upset his marriage and vocation. He was threatened by the idea of having to be a guest on talk shows. The images he associated with success were, to a large extent, unrealistic personal fantasies; nonetheless, they acted as barriers to submitting the book.

Coping

If it seems to you that you suffer from pathological indecisiveness, you may find value in the following list of practical coping strategies.

- Realize that approach-avoidance conflicts are *psychological* conflicts, not objective conflicts. They tend to be perceived as being "out there," arising from the world itself. But they are "in here," arising from one's own perceptions and value judgments. Ludwig Wittgenstein, one of the leading philosophers of the twentieth century, was once asked, "What is the purpose of your philosophy?" He answered, "To show the fly the way out of the fly bottle." Applied to psychological conflicts, Wittgenstein's enigmatic answer may be interpreted as follows. The psychological traps in life are like the bottle that traps the fly. The exit is perfectly clear, and nothing blocks it. But the fly cannot escape because the containing walls look *just like the exit*. The fly is "bewitched" by the situation. Similarly, when you are "trapped" in a seemingly insolvable approach-avoidance conflict, you are "bewitched" by your own thought processes, ideas, and the self-talk you use in making a decision. If these are not clear and rational, you are "stuck." So an important first step is to realize that the conflict has no objective existence, that it is your own mental creation. In the same way that irrational thinking created it, it can be destroyed by clear, rational thought.

• Ask yourself if you have a compulsive personality. Do you try to overorganize your life? Be aware that indecisiveness may have roots in such behavior and that, in the long run, it is both ineffective and self-defeating.

• Stop the practice of gathering too much information. Get some important facts, but place a reasonable limit on their number. Before buying a new refrigerator, for example, do not look at 20 brands, collect 20 sales brochures, and then go look at each of the models two or three more times. Such a process is not only too time-consuming and exhausting, it is confusing. First decide on the qualities you want in a refrigerator (size, color, style, price range). Let some consumer research magazines advise you on the one or two best brands. Then visit two or three stores to comparison shop, and make your decision. The process should be simple, but informed.

• Stop worrying so much about what other people think. Their thoughts and values should be irrelevant to everyday decisions that have nothing to do with them. Ask yourself, "Who has to live with this decision—them or me? Will they be affected by it?" Stop imagining that they are laughing at you or talking behind your back. Even if they are, you may be completely incorrect about what they are saying or thinking. Realize that, in fact, it is you who are judging yourself, not they.

• Tell yourself that there are just too many alternatives and that it *is absurd*. Get a little angry about it. It is *unfair* that you should be asked to make selections among so many shapes and colors and styles. What looks on the surface like something that meets the needs of consumers is, in fact, just a result of competition in the business world and high-profile marketing. Too many alternatives do not meet human needs at all. Learn to pay less attention to all of the options. There are just too many, and frequently they are just arbitrary anyway.

• Accept responsibilities that must be accepted like the adult you are. In the end, you will probably accept the responsibility anyway, so why run away or go in circles? It takes courage to accept some of the burdens that life places on you. However, once the courage to act decisively is mustered, you will feel better about yourself.

• Keep in mind that very few, if any, decisions are completely irrevocable. You do not necessarily have to live all of your life with a bad decision. Yes, there may be a price to pay for taking a wrong turn. But what else can you do? You have to go forward and just do your best. As one psychologist said to his clients, "Do your best and just muddle through. We all do."

• Stop overidentifying with your parents. Remember that they are themselves and that you are you. If they were too rigid and compulsive about decisions, that was just their way. But it was not necessarily the right way for you. Do not let your parent self run your life. Make your own decisions from your adult self.

• In a conflict between your id and your superego, try to get your ego into the act. The *ego* in psychoanalytic theory is the realistic side of the personality, similar to what was referred to as the "adult self" in the previous paragraph. The ego acts like a mediator in a labor-management dispute. It suggests a realistic middle way. In other words, neither the id or the superego should "win." Ernest Jones, a psychoanalyst and Sigmund Freud's principal biographer, said, "The art of living is the art of compromise." Learn this art.

• If you are a thinking-sensation type, try to "tune in" and become sensitive to the feeling-intuitive side of your personality. It will help you make decisions with more comfort and confidence.

• Realize that the fears you associate with success are in most cases just unrealistic fantasies. In most cases, you have much more to gain than to lose from successes. Fear of success falls into a category that has sometimes been called "fear of fear" or, in other words, fear of nothing at all.

Professional Help

If you find that you cannot cope adequately with indecisiveness, there are a number of ways in which the professions of psychiatry and clinical psychology can help you.

Taking a behavioral approach, a therapist may use *systematic desensitization* to help you cope with the anxiety-arousing elements of a decision, particularly if you and the therapist agree that your anxiety is excessive. Using systematic desensitization, the therapist paints a word picture that places you in the future, actually experiencing the consequences of your decision. Repeated exposure to the imagined situation brings about a gradual reduction in the situation's ability to invoke anxiety. Desensitization can also be used to help you reduce anxiety associated with the fear of being laughed at for making an incorrect decision. Remember that both fear of failure and fear of success can be associated with resistance to making a decision, and desensitization therapy can be used to reduce the intensity of both fears.

When indecisiveness is associated with irresponsibility, an approach known as reality therapy can be helpful. *Reality therapy*, pioneered by the psychiatrist William Glasser, helps the individual to evaluate options in a rational manner, showing the individual that the responsible course of action is almost always also the best course of action. Sometimes persons avoid long-term responsible decisions with the rationalization, "Live today for tomorrow we may die." However, as O. Hobart Mowrer, a former president of the American Psychological Association, pointed out in the introduction to Glasser's *Reality Therapy*, "Usually we don't die tomorrow."

Taking a psychodynamic approach, a therapist may help you to explore the events in your childhood that contributed to the formation of a compulsive personality, a personality type often associated with indecisiveness. Possibly, you will develop insight into why you resist decisions and how this helps you to perceive the world as a safer, less dangerous place. Interpretation of traits of behavior associated with your personality is known as *character analysis* in psychotherapy, and such an analysis can often help to liberate you from useless behavior patterns.

Continuing to take a psychodynamic approach, a therapist may help you, using a modality known as *ego analysis*, to find practical ways to resolve an ongoing "feud" between your id and your superego, a feud that interferes with effective decision making. The aid of your rational, realistic ego is enlisted by the therapist in an effort to resolve the impulsive tendencies of the id and the punitive tendencies of the superego. The therapist analyses ways your ego can effect a compromise and walk a middle line.

If your therapist sees merit in Carl Jung's way of looking at psychotherapy, he may help to make better contact with the feeling-intuitive part of your personality. Jung believed that each person has such a part to his or her personality, but that it is inhibited and blocked in the person who, on the conscious side, has overdeveloped the thinking-sensation dimension of the personality. The idea of this kind of approach in psychotherapy is *not* to give up the functions of thinking and sensation, but to bring them into better balance with the functions of feeling and intuition.

There is no specific drug therapy for indecisiveness. Nonetheless, as has been indicated several times, indecisiveness is often associated with chronic anxiety. Consequently, a psychiatrist may, in some cases, prescribe an anti-anxiety agent for the symptom of anxiety itself, not indecisiveness. This may in turn, through anxiety reduction, help the individual to make a decision.

Key Points to Remember

• *Pathological indecisiveness* takes place when alternatives are seen in distorted and irrational terms, and the importance of outcomes is exaggerated.

• Other signs and symptoms frequently associated with the general symptom of pathological indecisiveness include going in mental circles, gathering huge amounts of information, and compulsively asking others for advice.

• In broad general terms, indecisiveness can be characterized as an *approach-avoidance* conflict. It is helpful to realize that approach-avoidance conflicts are *psychological* conflicts, not objective ones.

• Indecisiveness is aggravated by too much information.

• Fear of being laughed at by others may aggravate indecisiveness. Stop worrying so much about what other people think.

• Irresponsibility may be a factor in indecisiveness. Learn to accept responsibilities that must be accepted like the adult you are.

• A person who suffers from indecisiveness tends to be what Carl Jung called a *thinking-sensation* type. If you are such a type, try to "tune in" and become sensitive to the *feeling-intuitive* side of your personality.

• Stop the practice of gathering too much information.

• Tell yourself that, in some choice situations, there are just too many alternatives and that it is *absurd.*

• Realize that the fears you associate with success are in most cases just unrealistic fantasies.

• Taking a behavioral approach, a therapist may use *systematic de-sensitization* to help you cope with the anxiety-arousing elements of a decision, particularly if you and the therapist agree that your anxiety is excessive.

• When indecisiveness is associated with irresponsibility, an approach known as reality therapy can be helpful.

• Taking a psychodynamic approach, a therapist may help you to explore the events in your childhood that contributed to the formation of a compulsive personality, a personality type often associated with indecisiveness.

• If your therapist sees merit in Carl Jung's way of looking at psychotherapy, he may help you to make better contact with the feeling-intuitive part of your personality.

• A psychiatrist may, in some cases, prescribe an anti-anxiety agent for the symptom of anxiety itself, a symptom often associated with indecisiveness. And this may have an indirect beneficial effect on the capacity to make decisions.

Chapter 13

Interpersonal Difficulties: "*You* Are My Problem!"

May Y. complains that her husband Jack treats her like a child. She says that he is authoritarian, overcontrolling, and insensitive to her feelings. May and Jack have interpersonal difficulties.

Paul and Sylvia, an engaged couple, have developed a habit of bickering over anything and everything. They both criticize and complain about each other to each other at the slightest provocation. Paul and Sylvia have interpersonal difficulties.

Mary L. is 16 years old. Her mother, a single parent, says that Mary must be home from dates by 11:00 P.M. Mary is furious with her mother, and says, "I don't see why I can't stay out until two or three in the morning like all of my friends can." Her mother is in a state of despair and bewilderment and wonders, "Why can't Mary see that I'm just trying to protect her?" Mary and her mother have interpersonal difficulties.

For more than 50 years, a large audience has been entertained by the conflicts and misunderstandings of Scarlett O'hara and Rhett Butler in the novel *Gone with the Wind*, the movie of the same name, and *Scarlett*, the sequel to the original novel. That same audience is entertained by the communication gaps between spouses in soap operas and laughs at the put-downs and insults exchanged by characters in sitcoms. There is something fascinating about interpersonal difficulties.

All sorts of informal phrases and terms reflect reactions to interpersonal difficulties. Examples are "I have a broken heart," "Stop treating me like a dog," "I can't get away from the old ball and chain," "She's a witch," and "He's a rat."

Here is a more or less formal definition of an *interpersonal difficulty*: a difficulty characterized by self-defeating and/or self-destructive patterns of behavior between two or more persons. In brief, it is a troubled human relationship.

The word *games* is sometimes used to label interpersonal difficulties. This usage was suggested by Eric Berne, a psychiatrist and the father of transactional analysis. *Transactional analysis* is a personality theory and a method of therapy that explains personal problems in terms of flawed communication patterns.

Ask an emotionally disturbed or otherwise troubled person, "*Who* is making you feel this way?" or "*Who* is your problem?" You are likely to receive answers such as, "It's my husband. He makes me depressed." Or, "It's my wife. She makes me live like a perpetually angry man." Or, "It's my mother. She makes me fat by forcing food on me." Or, "It's my daughter. She drives *me* crazy because she's boy crazy." All of these answers suggest the important presence of interpersonal difficulties.

Other signs and symptoms frequently associated with the general symptom of an interpersonal difficulty are:

1. Feeling used and abused
2. A sense of emotional isolation
3. Lack of effective communication and frequent misunderstandings
4. Episodes of emotional agitation, such as anxiety or depression
5. Bouts with depression
6. Avoiding the individual who is the source of personal frustration
7. Wondering if the other person is thinking and acting in good faith
8. An I-it relationship

Some of the items on the above list can benefit from a few comments. *Feeling used and abused* is one of the prime signs of an interpersonal difficulty. One person often feels that he or she is the victim of the other person's meanness, smallness, cruelty, selfishness, or pettiness. The "victim" feels "kicked around" and worthless. In contrast, the "persecutor" also has a price to pay. He or she will suffer from a *sense of emotional isolation*, the feeling that one is all alone in the world. The persecutor is like a lonely dictator or king—a boss, a ruler—with no friends.

The term *good faith* suggests that a person is honest and authentic in his or her dealings with others. *Bad faith* suggests that a person is manipulative and without conscience in his or her dealings with others. The distinction was suggested by Jean-Paul Sartre, a French existential philosopher. An *I-it* relationship is one in which a first person feels like an "I"—a living self—but does not, in fact, recognize or realize that this is true of a second person. In an *I-thou* relationship, a first person respects the other person as a living being, a living self. The distinction between the two kinds of relationships was made by the theologian Martin Buber. Obviously, Sartre's ideas and Buber's have great similarities.

Causes and Explanations

There are a number of causal factors associated with interpersonal difficulties. One or several of these may be involved in a particular case.

It is possible to "fall in love with love." This factor plays an important role in troubled relationships involving couples. The title "Falling in Love with Love" was penned by the lyricist Lorenz Hart in the 1930s, and it is the basic theme and message of a song he wrote with Richard Rogers. The essential idea is that a person who is "in love" is often *not* actually in love with another person but with romance, with the *idea* of being in love. This is a sort of bewitched, enchanted state. When the individual awakens, there is bound to be trouble. The awakened, or disenchanted, individual takes a new look at the partner. "What did I ever see in him (or her)?"

Related to the "falling in love with love" phenomenon is a pattern that has been called the *idealization-frustration-demoralization (I-F-D) syndrome*. The existence of the syndrome was proposed by Wendell Johnson, author of *People in Quandaries* and a noted semanticist. In the beginning of a relationship, there is a high probability that the other person and the relationship itself will be idealized. "Everything" is wonderful, and the future looks bright with promise. The lover lives in a sort of cotton-candy world made up of sweetness and fluff. The woman is beautiful and understanding beyond belief. She is a Cinderella. The man is handsome and intelligent beyond all possibility. He is a Prince Charming. In brief, this first phase is characterized by unrealistic expectations.

Then there are frustrations. There are disappointments, misunderstandings, violations of little agreements, revelations of inadequacies, and so forth. One's hopes and dreams are blocked. The fancies and fantasies of the idealization phase fail to materialize.

The last stage is demoralization. The individual is angry, sad, and depressed. He or she thinks a horrible mistake has been made. Maybe the relationship should end. If married, maybe there should be a divorce. The future looks bleak and joyless.

A factor in interpersonal difficulties is the natural human need for recognition. Most people want to be loved, liked, and paid attention to; they hate to be completely ignored. If one is in a relationship that is characterized by neglect, by lack of warmth and interest, then one will "misbehave" in order to obtain recognition. Even though the response to whining, nagging, complaining, and criticizing may be anger or a return of criticism, it is *better than being ignored*. No one, except perhaps a hermit, wants to live in a social vacuum. If a person cannot get positive recognition, he or she will often do something to generate negative recognition.

Human relationships are made worse when one person is willing to take all of another person's "garbage" and nonsense with a sort of "poor me" act. This is allowing oneself to play the role of defeated little child. It is seldom necessary or demanded by the actual facts of a situation. It is a kind of passive choice made out of a general feeling of low self-esteem. It is people who play this victim's role that tend to feel the most used and abused in troubled relationships.

Also, human relationships are made worse when one person is always "dishing it out" to the other person. This is allowing oneself to play the role of "boss" or "ruler." Again, it is seldom necessary or demanded by the actual facts of a situation. It is a kind of active choice made out of a general feeling of arrogance. It is people who play this "bossy" role that tend to feel the most isolated and alone in troubled relationships.

A causal factor in interpersonal difficulties is the very understandable reaction of "an eye for an eye." This represents a desire for equity. "You steal from me, and I'll pay you back by stealing from you." "You kill my cattle, and I'll kill your dogs." "You insult me, and I'll insult you." This is the psychology that underlies bickering. The first person says, "You're a cheapskate." And the second person responds, "You're a spendthrift." The first person says, "You can't cook," and the second person responds, "You must not have any taste buds." The first person says, "You don't understand me," and the second person says, "I understand you all too well." There is no communication—just an exchange of negative comments meant to provide first aid to one's own psychological wound. In transactional analysis, these kinds of exchanges are called *crossed transactions*, transactions in which each person tries to shove the other person down to a lower psychological level.

A factor that has a highly adverse effect on a relationship is a *hidden message*, a message that is communicated at a psychological level by an expression, a tone of voice, or a position of the body (e.g., standing with crossed arms or a clenched fist). The hidden message often contradicts spoken words. At a verbal level, a person says, "Sure, I'd love to go see that movie with you." At the psychological level, the message is, "I hate action-adventure movies." At a verbal level, a person says, "Of course, I love you." At a psychological level, the message is, "I'm not so sure—I have my doubts." In transactional analysis, messages with two levels, a verbal one and a psychological one, are called *duplex transactions*. Such transactions play a particularly important role in the pathological patterns that Berne identified with the word *games*.

A need for power on the part of one person can greatly complicate and confuse a relationship. Some people have a need to dominate others. They are just not happy unless they are telling others what to do and running the show. Unfortunately, there are other people who have a need for self-abasement. They unconsciously seek to be taken advantage of, to be used. This is the result of an underlying sense of low self-esteem or a sense of guilt for real or imagined wrongdoings. If a person with a need for power connects with a person with a need for self-abasement, then a stable, but pathological, relationship often forms. The nature of the relationship is described as *sadomasochistic*. (This may be, but is not necessarily, sexual in nature.)

Suggestibility and projection are related factors in interpersonal difficulties. Unfortunately, it is possible to be "bewitched" or "spellbound" by a person. *Suggestibility* takes place when the statements, promises, and opinions of the other person are taken as very important, absolutely true, and very wise. *Projection* takes place when a first person perceives a second person as having powers and attributes not actually possessed by the second person, merely wished for by the second one. The interaction of suggestibility and projection is a powerful one that leaves its victim feeling weak, helpless, and psychologically limp.

Coping

If it seems to you that you suffer excessively from interpersonal difficulties, you may find value in the following list of practical coping strategies.

• Recognize that you may be enchanted by romance, that you are possibly "in love with love." Take a hard look at your own attitudes. You may be placing impossible, perfectionistic demands on a partner. If your expectations are too high, you will be bound to be disappointed and hurt.

• Do not obtain recognition by "misbehaving"—by whining, griping, complaining, nagging, pouting, or giving the other person the cold shoulder. These manipulative strategies often backfire. Obtain your recognition by your positive actions—do something the other individual can approve of, compliment, or praise. In some cases, it is all right to simply *ask* for recognition saying something such as, "I would like some attention," or "Listen to me for a few minutes," or, "I need a hug."

• Refuse to play the role of victim. Do not crumple into a psychological lump and let yourself be kicked around and abused. It may be the short-run way to solve a problem and to avoid a conflict. However, in the long run, you are likely to pay a heavy price—such as depression or demoralization.

• Refuse also to play the alternate role of "boss" or "ruler." No one loves a dictator. You may get your way in the short run. However, in the long run, you are likely to pay a heavy price—such as loneliness or emotional isolation.

• Give up the "eye for an eye" attitude. A human relationship is not a war. If you exchange insults, the hostility between you and the other person will escalate and get out of control.

• Stop sending hidden messages. Do not hide your frustration, anger, or hostility behind false, sweet words. Say what you mean in an honest, self-disclosing, rational way.

• Ask yourself if you have an excessive need for power. If the answer is *yes*, face the fact that your need for power is aggravating your interpersonal difficulties.

• Conversely, ask yourself if you have an excessive need for self-abasement. If the answer is *yes*, face the fact that your need for self-abasement is aggravating your interpersonal difficulties.

• Examine the possibility that you may be projecting powers on other persons that they do not actually have. If you can stop projecting, you will not be as suggestible and feel so much at the mercy of another's efforts to control you.

Professional Help

If you find that you cannot cope adequately with interpersonal difficulties, there are a number of ways in which the professions of psychiatry and clinical psychology can help you.

Taking a psychodynamic approach, a therapist may help you ascertain the sources of your attitudes towards others. A common observation is that repressed hostility toward one or both parents may result in a transference of this same hostility to another person who plays a role that is similar to that of parent—a person who has hostility toward a parent may have a problem relating to a supervisor, a teacher, or even a spouse. (A spouse is sometimes unconsciously perceived as a parent of sorts.) The therapist will help you get in touch with your hostility. Understanding its roots will give you better control over it.

Still taking a psychodynamic approach, a therapist may help you to comprehend how excessively low self-esteem may be contributing to an excessive deference to others. This is a common pattern. Conversely, in some cases, excessive arrogance and/or egotism may be contributing to an excessive control of others. Again, this is a common pattern. In either case, a therapist will help you comprehend the pattern and find ways to break out of it.

Taking a behavioral approach, a therapist will help you become more assertive. (This point was made in the "Professional Help" section of Chapter 8 on depression.) *Assertiveness training* is a method of teaching communication skills that make it possible for you to be neither too passive nor too aggressive. The assertive response is usually the optimal response, and it will, in most cases, have a beneficial effect on a relationship.

Taking a cognitive approach, a therapist will assist you in becoming more aware of how you may be, in an irrational way, romanticizing a relationship beyond realistic bounds. It is possible that you are placing impossible, unrealistic demands on another person or upon yourself. Either-or thinking, a cognitive error, makes one think that a relationship should be perfect. Few, if any, relationships fit anyone's idealized version of what they should be. Therapy will make it easier for you to give up unrealistic expectations.

Taking a humanistic approach, a therapist can help you to reject the trap of an I-it relationship. The therapist will help you appreciate that the other person is a *real* person just like you—a "thou." This enhanced appreciation of the full humanness of significant-other people in your life is of extreme importance.

Earlier in this chapter, an approach known as *transactional analysis* was identified. As was noted, the psychiatrist Eric Berne was the father of this approach. Transactional analysis teaches people to understand the nature of communication patterns and, in turn, to talk to each other more clearly, effectively, and constructively. When there are personal problems between two or more people, it is helpful if the individuals can learn how to communicate between their adult selves. (Berne spoke of ego states and referred to what here is called the "adult self" as the "Adult ego state." The capitalized form is used in transactional analysis to distinguish an actual person from an ego state.)

A therapist may employ transactional analysis, or a modification of it, to enhance your communication skills. Transactional analysis is best learned in interactions with other people. Consequently, transactional analysis is frequently employed either with a couple or in a group setting.

Family therapy is often used to help a family that is functioning in a pathological, self-defeating manner. Family therapy, like transactional analysis, is instructional in nature. Individuals in the family learn how they are destructive toward each other and how they can become fully functioning members of the family.

Key Points to Remember

- An *interpersonal difficulty* is a difficulty characterized by self-defeating and/or self-destructive patterns of behavior between two or more people.
- The word *games* is sometimes used to label interpersonal difficulties.
- Other signs and symptoms frequently associated with the general symptom of an interpersonal difficulty are feeling used and abused, a lack of effective communication along with frequent misunderstandings, and an I-it relationship.
- It is possible to "fall in love with love." Take a hard look at your own attitude.
- The *idealization-frustration-demoralization (I-F-D) syndrome* often has an adverse effect on a relationship. Try to give up unrealistic expectations.
- Hunger for recognition can cause a person to "misbehave" if that person believes he or she can obtain recognition in no other way. Look for more effective, mature ways to obtain recognition.
- Human relationships are made worse when one person is willing to take all of another person's "garbage" and nonsense with a sort of "poor me" act. Refuse to play the role of victim.
- Human relationships are made worse when one person is always "dishing it out" to the other person. Refuse to play the role of "boss" or "ruler."
- A causal factor in interpersonal difficulties is the very understandable reaction of "an eye for an eye." Reject this attitude.
- A factor that has a highly adverse effect on a relationship is a *hidden message*. Stop sending such messages.
- Either a need for power or a need for self-abasement can complicate and confuse a relationship. Do your best not to act on these needs in an abusive way.
- Taking a psychodynamic approach, a therapist may help you to ascertain the sources of your attitudes towards others.
- Taking a behavioral approach, a therapist will help you to become more assertive.
- Taking a cognitive approach, a therapist will assist you in becoming more aware of how you may be in an irrational way romanticizing a relationship beyond realistic bounds.
- A therapist may employ transactional analysis to enhance your communication skills.

Chapter 14

Irrational Fears: A Plague of Phobias

Neil P. is attending the first day of a college philosophy course. The professor announces that every student will have to give a 15-minute oral report based on the life of a great philosopher. Neil groans inwardly and thinks, "Oh, no! I can't do that." He pictures himself giving the report: he is stumbling over his words and is being laughed at. His heart begins to race, his throat feels dry, and his palms become sweaty. The anxiety is very distressing. "If they laugh at me, I'll die." This thought makes him more anxious. He seriously considers dropping the class. Neil is not alone. An irrational fear of public speaking is very common, and it falls into a general class known as the *social phobias*.

A *phobia* in psychiatry and clinical psychology is defined as "an irrational fear or an obsessive dread." (The clinical term is derived from the ordinary Greek word *phobia*, which means, in that language, simply "fearing.") The three basic kinds of phobias are (1) agoraphobia, (2) social, and (3) simple. *Agoraphobia* is characterized by a set of related fears including the fear of being alone, a fear of public places, and a fear of traveling any significant distance from home. The victim of this phobia imagines that in a certain situation he or she will be trapped and unable to escape. Therefore, the individual may avoid public vehicles (e.g., buses and airplanes), crowds, theatres, heavily traveled roads, and so forth. In extreme cases, the individual either becomes a self-made "house prisoner" or stays very close to home.

A *social phobia* is characterized by a fear of placing oneself in situations where others have an opportunity to observe or judge one's behavior. As already indicated, the fear of public speaking is a social phobia. Other examples include a fear of meeting strangers, a reluctance to accept an invitation to a party, excessive self-consciousness when using a public rest room, embarrassment when placing a food order with a waiter or waitress, inability to fill in an application for a job when being watched, and so forth. Often there is the thought, "I'm making a fool of myself."

Simple phobias are those in which the source of the fear can be readily defined and identified. They are "simple" only in the sense that the source of the fear is not complex. Another term for simple phobias, perhaps a better one, is *specific phobias*. Each simple phobia has been given a name derived from a Greek root. Here are some frequently identified simple phobias: (1) *acrophobia*, a fear of heights; (2) *algophobia*, a fear of pain; (3) *astraphobia*, a fear of thunder, lightning, howling winds, heavy rain, and other aspects of stormy weather; (4) *claustrophobia*, a fear of confinement or closed areas; (5) *cynophobia*, a fear of dogs; (6) *demophobia*, a fear of crowds; (7) *haptephobia*, a fear of being touched; (6) *hematophobia*, a fear of blood; (7) *hypnophobia*, a fear of sleep; (8) *monophobia*, a fear of being alone; (9) *mysophobia*, a fear of germs; (10) *nyctophobia*, a fear of darkness or the night; (11) *ochlophobia*, a fear of crowds; (12) *ophidiophobia*, a fear of reptiles; (13) *pathophobia*, a fear of disease; (14) *pyrophobia*, a fear of fire; and (15) *zoophobia*, a fear of animals.

It is possible to suffer from several phobias. One patient who has been the victim of multiple phobias commented, "I seem to suffer from a plague of phobias."

Phobias are common. They occur in children and adults of either sex. Although they are more frequently diagnosed in females, this may be due to bias in the evaluation and interpretation of symptoms. Many males, given cultural attitudes, are perhaps somewhat ashamed to confess that they suffer from one or several phobias. It is not unusual for people of either gender to be "closet phobics"—keeping their irrational fears to themselves and pretending to others that they are better than they actually feel.

Other signs and symptoms frequently associated with phobias are:

1. Avoidance of the feared situation or object
2. Great anxiety, or sometimes panic, if forced to deal with the feared situation or object
3. Realization that the fear is irrational
4. Disruption of life's normal course because of the need to find elaborate ways to cope with the phobia
5. Nightmares in which the individual is unable to escape from the feared situation or object
6. The nagging conviction that this is a threatening, extremely dangerous world
7. A chronic sense of morbid dread
8. Counterphobic behavior

Counterphobic behavior is paradoxical in that it is the logical opposite of the common-sense response to a fear. Instead of avoiding the feared situation or object, the individual displaying counterphobic behavior *seeks* contact—a person suffering from acrophobia might become a "human fly" and scale tall buildings as a way of mastering a fear of heights. Counterphobic behavior can be understood in terms of an ego defense mechanism called *reaction formation* in which a negative tendency (e.g., an irrational fear) is banished to the netherworld of the unconscious level of the personality by converting the tendency into a positive one at the conscious level.

Causes and Explanations

There are a number of causal factors associated with irrational fears. One or several of these may be involved in a particular case.

From the psychoanalytic point of view, phobias are the specific manifestations of an underlying *anxiety neurosis*. This is a way of saying that the roots of irrational fears reside in unresolved emotional conflicts. A fear situation or object is said to be an *externalization* of either an attitude or a fear that is held at an unconscious level. For an example of the externalization of an attitude, assume that Neil P., who was discussed in the first paragraph of this chapter, has a low opinion of people in general and has a strong tendency to laugh at others when they make errors. He represses some or all of his awareness of this tendency because it goes against his superego (i.e., his moral self), which is both decent and kind. However, the ego defense mechanism called *projection* is at work. Projection is characterized by a tendency to perceive the outer world in terms of repressed, or blocked, attitudes. Therefore, he tends to fear that others will laugh at him because at some secret level of his personality he wishes to laugh at others.

For an example of the externalization of a fear, it is instructive to cite the case of Little Hans, one of Freud's famous child cases. Hans, a preschooler, had an irrational fear of horses. A secondhand child analysis conducted by interviewing the boy's father suggested that Hans was really afraid of his father. The horse, like his father, was large and powerful and able to "bite" him (hurt him in an aggressive way). The horse symbolized the father, was a sort of "stand in" for him, because Hans was supposed to love and obey his father. By repressing his fear of his father, the horse became an object of fear.

The idea that the object of an irrational fear is a symbol for a fear in the unconscious has broad general applications. A person with acrophobia may be actually afraid of a repressed suicidal impulse associated with throwing oneself from a tall building or a bridge. A person with algophobia may be repressing self-destructive, self-defeating, masochistic tendencies. A person with claustrophobia may be actually afraid that an unhappy marriage or a hated job is a trap with no exit. Similar symbolic interpretations can be made of other phobias.

From the behavioristic point of view, irrational fears are conditioned emotional reactions. A classical experiment with a child known in the psychological literature as Little Albert provides a basic example. John Watson, the father of behaviorism, and his laboratory assistant Rosalie Raynor showed Albert, a toddler, a white rat. They established that Albert had no fear of the rat. Then they sounded a loud gong behind Albert when he was in the presence of the rat. The gong produced a startle response, and Albert began to cry. Upon repeated presentations of the rat, he began to cry and tried to avoid the rat. Albert had acquired a conditioned fear of the rat through association with the loud gong.

Applying what happened to Little Albert to common fears, it is reasonable that a bad experience with a situation or an object might make one excessively afraid of it. Thus, if a person has fallen from a ladder and been badly pained or injured, he or she is likely to be afraid of heights. If a person was laughed at as a child when giving a book report in junior high school, it is likely that he or she will be afraid to give a book report in college. If a person suffered through a lot of pain in a first operation, it is likely that he or she will dread a second one. The behavioristic explanation of irrational fears is straightforward and appeals to common sense.

However, the behavioristic viewpoint goes somewhat beyond what is obvious to common sense. Watson and Raynor showed Albert objects that were *similar* to the white rat. Examples of such objects include a Santa Claus mask with a white beard, a white rabbit, and a white terrycloth towel crumpled into a ball. All of these objects also produced fear in Albert. This is a phenomenon known in learning theory as *stimulus generalization*, a tendency to give conditioned, or learned, responses to stimuli (i.e., situations or objects) that are similar to the original stimulus (i.e., the white rat). This explains to some extent why a person with irrational fears is often afraid of something that was not actually harmful in his or her personal history.

Note that there are important parallels between the psychoanalytic concept of symbolism and the behavioristic concept of stimulus generalization. Both concepts say that a situation or object that is similar to an original source of fear can also produce fear. In the case of psychoanalysis, the source is buried in the unconscious. In the case of behaviorism, the source is in the objective world.

In connection with the behavioral viewpoint, it is possible to acquire fears by observational learning. Parents with irrational fears provide role models for children. Therefore, it is not at all unusual to find that the children of phobic parents have also been "infected" with the virus of dread and morbid anxiety.

An important factor in irrational fears is an active imagination. It is reasonable to hypothesize that highly creative people with good visual imagery may very well augment their natural anxieties with daydreams and fantasies in which they are the central figures in personal disasters. These are essentially waking nightmares. It is not at all unusual to find that the authors of novels have one or several phobias.

Finally, it should be pointed out that an innate temperament may play a part in irrational fears. This is particularly true of social phobias. Highly reserved, or introverted, people tend to have more preoccupation with their own thoughts and feelings than outgoing people. They tend to give their fears and their thoughts about their fears more status then they ought to. Carl Jung, a principal founder of the psychology of the unconscious, believed that the trait of introversion was primarily inborn. The trait can contribute to shyness and the social phobias in general. (For more on shyness, see Chapter 26.)

Coping

If it seems to you that you suffer excessively from irrational fears, you may find value in the following list of practical coping strategies.

· Make a list of your irrational fears. Name them and describe them. Doing this in writing helps to bring them under conscious, voluntary control.

· Examine your fears from a psychoanalytic perspective. Ask yourself what they might symbolize. You may discover that some of your manifest fears are just "ghosts" with no real substance. Instead, try to deal more realistically with actual emotional conflicts that may be at the roots of your fears.

· Look at your fears from a behavioristic perspective. Try to discover what actual situations or objects did you harm in the past. Perhaps you can jog your memory by talking over childhood experiences with a parent or a sibling. Also, identify ways in which you may be generalizing from one or several bad experiences in the past to situations and objects in the present that remind you of these bad experiences.

· In the case of a social phobia, use a cognitive-behavior modification technique called *stress-inoculation training*. This requires that you run a sort of mental movie in your head, a kind of preview of a situation before you are actually involved in it—if you are scheduled to give an oral report in a class, try to visualize yourself speaking before the group. Make the "movie" as detailed and vivid as you can, and be sure that you give the scene *desirable* outcomes. The images will invoke anxiety, but this is the idea. Each time you repeat the "movie," the anxiety will lessen, and you will find that you can go into the actual situation with less trepidation.

• If your parents were overly fearful people, work on *disidentifying* from them. It is natural to identify with parents, to imitate them and copy them to some extent. However, in cases where their behavior is counterproductive, it is useful to focus on that particular behavior and say to yourself, "I am not them. They are not me. I am I. They are they. If they had irrational fears, that was their problem. I don't have to be a copycat—I'm an individual in my own right."

• Examine your conscious thoughts. Most fears have ideas associated with them. These ideas can usually be elevated to the level of sentences. If you have an irrational fear of dogs, you might discover that, associated with this fear, is the conscious thought, "It's going to bite me." In addition, you might discover that this thought is there even if the dog is behind a fence or friendly. If so, you can challenge the thought and ask yourself, "How can a dog that is behind a fence bite me?"

• Learn to cope with your innate temperament. Even if you are overly reserved and introverted, and even if this contributes to your phobias, you can cope with your inborn disposition. You can lessen its influence on your emotions by the kinds of coping strategies described here and also with the help of professional treatment. One does not need to be ever the victim of oneself.

Professional Help

If you find that you cannot cope adequately with your irrational fears, there are a number of ways in which the professions of psychiatry and clinical psychology can help you.

Taking a behavioral approach, a therapist may employ *desensitization therapy*. The discovery and application of this approach is one of the outstanding success stories of the twentieth century. Pioneered by the psychiatrist Joseph Wolpe, desensitization therapy has been found to be highly effective for treating a wide range of phobic reactions. Desensitization is based on the principle of *counterconditioning*. Anxiety and fear are incompatible with relaxation. First, the patient is given suggestions that induce muscle relaxation. Then, the therapist induces a controlled fantasy through suggestion. The images in the fantasy are designed to induce anxiety. If the anxiety level rises too high, then relaxation suggestions are repeated. Gradually, the patient can tolerate more and more intense versions of the fantasy, and this, in turn, brings about a reduction of the irrational fear when actual situations and objects are encountered.

Desensitization can also be conducted *in vivo* (i.e., "in life"). A person who is afraid of snakes, for example, can look at pictures of snakes in various books until looking can be tolerated without much anxiety. Then, a tour can be taken of a museum with stuffed snakes. Finally, there can be a visit to see live snakes in a zoo. Sometimes, as a final test, the individual may handle harmless snakes. However, this final test need not be conducted. The purpose of the therapy is to reduce fear, not to replace it with bravado.

A rapid version of desensitization therapy pioneered by the therapist Thomas G. Stampfl is *implosive therapy*. The guided fantasy induced by the therapist brings anxiety to a high level very quickly; the individual is "flooded" with anxiety. If the client stays with the fantasy and does not open his or her eyes and break out of it, desensitization can be very rapid. Before a therapist uses this kind of therapy, an assessment is made to determine that the client has a robust sense of basic self-esteem and self-confidence. Not everyone can tolerate a big dose of anxiety all at once.

Taking a psychoanalytic approach, a therapist may help you to find the unconscious meaning of your phobia. This insight, or understanding, is not considered by a majority of therapists to be sufficient in and of itself to eliminate most irrational fears. However, it can be a helpful adjunct to desensitization therapy. Although the psychoanalytic approach is based on different theoretical assumptions than desensitization therapy is, in practice, the two can be quite compatible.

Taking a cognitive approach, a therapist may help you to see that you are thinking about your fears in an illogical, somewhat distorted way. Replacing illogical ideas with more logical ones can sometimes transform an intense, irrational fear into a mild apprehension. A person with an irrational fear of pain may go to a dentist's appointment thinking, "This is going to kill me." Upon examination, the thought is seen to be absurd. The pain experienced at the dentist will not "kill" the person. A new thought chain might be, "The pain is something I don't like. But I can tolerate *some* pain. And besides, most of the pain will be blurred by the shot the dentist gives me." This new chain will almost certainly lower the intensity of the fear.

Although there is no specific drug that can be taken to eliminate a well-defined irrational fear, it is also true that such fears are nurtured by underlying chronic anxiety. Therefore, in some cases, as a way of indirectly treating a phobia, a psychiatrist may prescribe an antianxiety drug (see the section "Professional Help" in Chapter 5).

Key Points to Remember

• A *phobia* in psychiatry and clinical psychology is defined as "an irrational fear or an obsessive dread."

• The three basic kinds of phobias are (1) agoraphobia, (2) social, and (3) simple.

• Examples of the other signs and symptoms frequently associated with phobias include avoidance of the feared situation or object, realization that the fear is irrational, nightmares associated with the feared situation or object, and counterphobic behavior.

• From the psychoanalytic point of view, phobias are the specific manifestations of an underlying anxiety neurosis.

• From the behavioristic point of view, irrational fears are conditioned emotional reactions.

• It is possible to acquire fears by observational learning.

• An important factor in irrational fears is an active imagination.

• An innate temperament may play a part in irrational fears. Specifically, this applies to persons who are highly reserved or introverted.

• Make a list of your irrational fears in order to bring them under better conscious, voluntary control.

• Examine your fears from a psychoanalytic perspective.

• Look at your fears from a behavioristic perspective.

• Taking a behavioral approach, a therapist may employ desensitization therapy.

• Taking a psychoanalytic approach, a therapist may help you to find the unconscious meaning of your phobia.

• Taking a cognitive approach, a therapist may help you to see how you are thinking about your fears in an illogical, somewhat distorted way.

• In some cases, a psychiatrist may prescribe an antianxiety drug as a way of indirectly treating a phobia.

Chapter 15

Loss of Pleasure: When Enjoyment Isn't Enjoyable

More than 2,000 years ago, the philosopher Aristotle suggested that the capacity to experience pleasure was one of the two key factors in happiness. (The other factor was the ability to exercise reason.) To Aristotle, pleasure was found primarily in the satisfaction of biological needs. Therefore, it is pleasurable to eat when you are hungry, drink when you are thirsty, and have an orgasm when you are sexually excited. Freud, by and large, agreed with Aristotle and said that biologically oriented pleasures are the primary ones.

Aristotle believed that pleasure and pain are the main motivational factors in human behavior. The concept is basic: one moves *toward* (i.e., seeks or looks for) situations and objects that provide pleasure and *away* from (i.e., escape from or avoid) situations and objects that inflict pain. This general motivational theory is called *hedonism*, and it makes a strong appeal to common sense.

Going somewhat beyond Aristotle and Freud, most people recognize that there are psychological pleasures. These may be inborn or learned. The pleasure someone gets from sightseeing is probably related to an inborn curiosity drive. There is probably an inborn tendency to seek ludic, or playful, behavior, and this is linked to the pleasure derived from watching a funny movie or playing a game. On the other hand, the pleasure associated with earning a large sum of money, winning a trophy, or receiving an A on an examination probably has a large component of social learning.

The above paragraphs identify normal psychological processes involved in the experience of pleasure. But what happens when the relationship to pleasure becomes *abnormal*, when it deviates from the expected course? The following excerpt from the journal of Blake K., a patient in psychotherapy, provides a description of the inner world of a person who has lost much of the capacity to experience pleasure:

> My food seems tasteless. A beautiful woman no longer excites me. Music no longer pleases me. I don't care if I ever go to a movie again. My friends all seem dull. I look forward to nothing. I don't want to die, but I don't care about living. I don't get a kick out of anything. . . .

Blake's experience is expressed in more than one literary work. *Nausea*, a novel by the philosopher Jean-Paul Sartre, describes the existence of a person who is disgusted with existence and unable to experience pleasure. The author Zane Grey's most uncharacteristic novel about the Old West was *Wanderer of the Wasteland*, and it follows the adventures of an individual who, for a large part of the book, is psychologically and emotionally numb. The poems *The Waste Land* and *The Hollow Men* by T. S. Eliot describe a joyless existence. To some extent, the cited literary works are reflections of the emotional state of each of the three authors at a particular time in his life.

The term used in psychiatry and clinical psychology for chronic, pathological loss of pleasure in existence is *anhedonia*. (The term *ahedonia* is also sometimes used.) Mental health professionals sometimes speak of an *anhedonic-apathetic syndrome* characterized by a combination of loss of pleasure and loss of interest in life. It is noteworthy that the film maker Woody Allen originally intended to assign the title *Ahedonia* to the movie *Annie Hall*. Central to the film is the portrayal of a protagonist who suffers to some extent from the anhedonic-apathetic syndrome.

Anhedonia is not in and of itself considered to be a specific mental disorder, but it is often associated with other mental disorders—schizophrenia and depression in particular. (For more on schizophrenia, see Chapter 7; for more on depression, see Chapter 8.) Therefore, the signs and symptoms associated with pathological loss of pleasure are similar to those listed in connection with both depression and schizophrenia. They also are very similar to those listed in connection with boredom. (For more on boredom, see Chapter 6.) Nonetheless, anhedonia merits a discussion in its own right. With the prior qualifications, the following signs and symptoms are frequently associated with the general symptom of loss of pleasure:

1. Loss of interest in eating, sex, and social interactions
2. Restricted range of emotional display
3. Speaking in a monotone
4. Lack of mobility in facial expression

5. Emotional insulation
6. Depression
7. Delusions
8. Egocentric thinking
9. Feeling "lifeless" and apathetic

Some of the items on the above list require expansion. A *restricted range of emotional display* refers to the fact that persons suffering from anhedonia only smile weakly when laughter would be the appropriate response, and they appear to have little concern when grief or mourning would be the appropriate response. *Emotional insulation* is a defense mechanism. Its purpose is to maintain ego integrity by blocking out feelings. The ego, the "I" of the personality, keeps from going to pieces under conditions of extreme personal stress by shutting down the capacity to feel, by going emotionally numb.

Delusions are false beliefs. They are cited as an indication of anhedonia because of the fact that the condition is often associated with schizophrenia. (For more on delusions, see Chapter 7.) *Egocentric thinking* is characterized by the attitude that the whole world revolves around oneself. The individual's automatic viewpoint is that it is *my* worries and *my* problems that occupy center stage—no one else's.

Causes and Explanations

From a psychodynamic point of view, a principal causal factor in chronic loss of pleasure in life is an overly strict superego. In classical psychoanalysis, the *superego* is the agent of society. It represents the internalization of a family's moral code. If one's upbringing is unusually strict and punitive and if this is combined, paradoxically, with an atmosphere of warmth and love, then a "tight," self-punishing superego may develop.

Under these conditions, it as if a little voice in the personality says, "That's foolish," "That's wasteful," "That's childish," and "That's sinful" whenever one is engaged in any pleasurable or semipleasurable activity. When one feels guilty for taking an extra helping of food, watching a movie, or engaging in sexual activity, how can there be any pleasure in life?

In connection with the psychodynamic explanation, there is the concept of a *life script*, an unconscious plan written by one's child self. The concept of a life script was proposed by the psychiatrist Eric Berne who pioneered an interpersonal approach to psychiatry and psychotherapy called *transactional analysis*. Claude Steiner, one of Berne's associates, wrote a book entitled *Scripts People Live*. According to Steiner, some children, around the age of six or seven, write for themselves a "No Joy script." This is essentially a set of personal instructions that say the days to come will be dull and devoid of any real pleasure. The children who tend to do this are the "good" little girls and boys who are perhaps overly conforming and too docile. They want badly to please their parents and to keep their love. Essentially, their No Joy script is a reflection of a parental injunction that says, "I will love you *only if* you are the kind of child I say you should be." This injunction contains information that identifies most normal pleasures as "bad" and "sinful."

The transactional analysis viewpoint overlaps with the behavioral viewpoint, which says that much of one's personality is due to observational, or social, learning. If one grows up in a family that laughs little and plays less, it is no wonder that the individual develops a sour, dour outlook on life. Too many "oughts" and "shoulds" interfere with the capacity to experience pleasure.

Going back to the interpersonal viewpoint, it is possible that one is a member of a couple in which a first person is hypercritical of a second person. Suppose that Stephen E., a husband, constantly finds fault with his wife's cooking, her clothes, her way of raising children, her housekeeping, her friends, her relatives, her choice of books, and so forth. Further suppose that Heather, his wife, is a traditional woman who reacts to his criticism by trying harder and harder to please. Heather may suffer and endure, but all sense of pleasure and joy takes flight from her life.

The causes and explanations that have been so far offered in this section overlap to some extent with the causes and explanations offered in connection with depression. (For more on depression, see Chapter 8.) This is as it should be because the anhedonic-apathetic syndrome has much in common with depression.

Biological factors in anhedonia should not be overlooked. The aging process may bring about a reduction in the intensity of some pleasures. It is common, for example, for elderly people to say that certain foods tasted better when they were children. They are likely to suggest that the quality and flavorings of food have declined. However, taste buds are neurons, living structures, and they age and die. Consequently, some elderly people may be relatively insensitive to basic taste sensations (i.e., sweet, bitter, salty, and sour). As another example, consider that the build-up of fatty deposits in the arteries that comes with aging can interfere with blood supply to the genital organs and reduce the capacity to experience sexual excitement. With aging, many experiences may be neither as intense nor as exciting as they once were.

One's general diet should not be overlooked as a factor in anhedonia.

Fatigue, apathy, and a general lassitude may be related to poor nutrition. Many people who believe they are eating well may in fact have an insufficient intake of proteins, complex carbohydrates, and essential vitamins and minerals. Hypoglycemia (i.e., chronic low blood sugar) is often linked to an overconsumption of refined carbohydrates.

A final contributing cause to anhedonia is the sense that one is living an empty, meaningless life. (For more on meaninglessness, see Chapter 16.)

Coping

If it seems to you that you suffer excessively from a loss of pleasure in life, you may find value in the following list of practical coping strategies.

• Fight against an overly strict superego. Recognize that a moralistic, "uptight" attitude toward life is just that, an *attitude*. It does not reflect reality. It arises from inner beliefs and perceptions that reflect a social self that is far too self-punishing. The little voice in your personality that says, "That's foolish," "That's wasteful," and so forth, is actually the "taped" voice of parents, teachers, or other caregivers in early childhood who did not allow sufficient pleasure and joy to a child.

• Learn to cope more effectively with hypercritical persons. If, for example, you have a hypercritical spouse, stop responding passively and apologetically from your child self. Learn to stand up for your rights. This does not mean you have to become hypercritical in return, but it does mean you must assert yourself and *be* yourself. You must speak to an overcontrolling partner from your adult self in a rational, steady manner. Otherwise, you are likely to feel used and abused. Anhedonia is one of the adverse outcomes of dysfunctional human relationships.

• Recognize that you may be obeying the orders of a "No Joy script." You wrote the script when you were a child. True, you may have written it in response to parental or family demands, but now you can rewrite the script from your adult self. Head a piece of paper "My No Joy Script," and write down all of the instructions that you think might go with such a script. Take a few days to do this. All of the ideas may not come to you at once, but they will generally pop into your head at odd times. Then on a second piece of paper write the heading "My Effective, Pleasure-in-Life Script," and write down all of the instructions that you think belong to such a script. Then, make a conscious decision to reject the "No Joy" instructions and follow the "Pleasure-in-Life" instructions.

• Keep in mind that pleasure in life does *not* mean you have to do wild, impulsive, irrational things. You will recall that Aristotle said that pleasure was one of the two key factors in happiness. The other factor was the ability to reason. You must temper desire for pleasure with reason. Only an approach in which you are both rational and reality-oriented will help you in the long run.

• If you are plagued by too many "oughts" and "shoulds," give yourself a time-out. Start by selecting one or two hours out of every week that is your private time. During this time, your only responsibility is to please yourself. Read a book, go see a movie, have lunch out, or do something else that has the potential to please you. Consciously say to yourself, "I have a right to this time. I have earned it. I don't feel guilty about it."

• Act on Henry David Thoreau's dictum that the simplest pleasures are the best. Examples include taking a walk in the woods or a park, gazing at the stars and the moon, going for a swim, or accompanying a child to see a re-release of a movie such as *Cinderella* or *Snow White and the Seven Dwarfs*.

• Give instead of take. It has been wisely observed that there is often great pleasure in giving. Call or visit someone you know to be sick or lonely, offer to run an errand for a friend, or help someone study for an examination. These small acts of giving can bring substantial psychological rewards.

• Be aware of a principle known as the *paradox of hedonism*. Both philosophers and psychologists have noted that in many cases pleasure cannot be pursued *directly*. Instead, pleasure often emerges as a side effect, when it is least expected, as you work toward general goals and lead a responsible life. Trying too hard to experience pleasure is often self-defeating.

• Avoid drugs that produce euphoria, such as cocaine. (See the section on stimulants in Chapter 9.) Drugs that produce intense temporary pleasure do not solve the problem of anhedonia. There is a "crash" and an emotional letdown that is the cost of the "high." In the long run, the abuse of stimulating drugs produces more psychological and emotional pain than pleasure.

Professional Help

If you find that you cannot cope adequately with anhedonia, there are a number of ways in which the professions of psychiatry and clinical psychology can help you.

Taking a psychodynamic approach, a therapist may help you to gain insight into the excessive demands and restrictions of a punitive superego. The roots of the moral self's overcontrol over your whole personality can be explored and discussed. Insight can be self-liberating, and practical ways can be sought to allow you more latitude in life as well as less guilt for experiencing certain pleasures.

Your therapist will possibly interpret some of your loss of pleasure in life as an ego defense mechanism designed to reduce psychological and emotional pain. As indicated earlier, this mechanism is called *emotional insulation*. When you run away from pain—refuse to cry or confront threatening situations—you also reduce your capacity to experience the opposite of pain, pleasure. The direct interpretation of a defense mechanism sometimes makes it possible to widen the range of an individual's emotional spectrum. If you can cry, you can laugh.

Taking a behavioral approach, a therapist is likely to encourage *actions* that will change your underlying mood. A classical theory of emotions known as the *James-Lange theory* states that actions can determine feelings. Therefore, if you *act* better, you are likely to *feel* better. A behavior therapist will give you homework assignments similar to some of the suggestions outlined in the "Coping" section (e.g., taking a walk in the woods, gazing at the stars and the moon, and so forth). The positive action can be willed *before* one "feels like" engaging in the action. The action tends to modify the feeling through a feedback process, and may, indeed, induce the formerly absent pleasure.

Taking a cognitive approach, a therapist will help you see how confused thinking is leading to loss of pleasure in life. Take a specific thought, such as, "My friends all seem dull." (Recall that this was a comment in Blake K.'s journal.) Cognitive therapy challenges you to ask yourself these questions: "Are *all* of my friends dull? Isn't this an overgeneralization? Are my friends objectively dull, or is this an unconscious projection of my current mood?" Cognitive therapy can help you think more clearly about your feelings.

Taking a humanistic approach, your therapist will discuss with you your basic outlook on life, your values, and your general self-image. The unconditional positive regard offered by the therapist in connection with humanistic therapy can boost your self-esteem and, in turn, your pleasure in living.

Taking an interpersonal approach, your therapist may encourage you to seek effective ways to cope with persons who are hypercritical of you. Assertiveness training skills can be taught and modeled by the therapist. You will learn how to activate your rational, adult self when you are communicating with someone who is overbearing. Frequently, the therapist will work with a couple instead of an individual. The assumption here is that it is the relationship that needs therapy as much as one person. When an important relationship improves, there is frequently an improvement in the capacity of one or both of its members to experience pleasure.

Although there is no drug that can give you the capacity to enjoy life, it is also true that anhedonia is linked to depression. In such cases, a psychiatrist is likely to prescribe antidepressant medication.

Key Points to Remember

• The general motivational theory that one seeks pleasure and avoids pain is called hedonism.

• The term used in psychiatry and clinical psychology for chronic, pathological loss of pleasure in existence is anhedonia.

• The anhedonic-apathetic syndrome is characterized by a combination of loss of pleasure and a loss of interest in life.

• Some of the signs and symptoms frequently associated with the general symptom of loss of pleasure in life include (1) loss of interest in eating, sex, and social interactions, (2) emotional insulation, and (3) ego-centric thinking.

• A "tight," punitive superego is a causal factor in inability to experience pleasure. Fight against an overly strict superego.

• Some people have written for themselves a life script known as a "No Joy script." It is possible to rewrite the script from the adult self.

• A sense of pleasure and joy takes flight from one's life when one lives in an atmosphere of overcriticism. Learn to cope more effectively with hypercritical persons.

• Act on Henry David Thoreau's dictum that the simplest pleasures are the best.

• Be aware of the principle known as the paradox of hedonism.

• Drugs that produce intense temporary pleasure do not solve the problem of anhedonia.

• Taking a psychodynamic approach, a therapist may help you to gain insight into the excessive demands and restrictions of a punitive superego.

• Taking a behavioral approach, a therapist is likely to encourage actions that will change your underlying mood.

• Taking a cognitive approach, a therapist will help you see how confused thinking is leading to loss of pleasure in life.

• Taking a humanistic approach, a therapist will discuss with you your basic outlook on life, your values, and your general self-image.

Chapter 16

Meaninglessness: Looking for the Purpose of Life

More than two decades ago, an Italian-made motion picture was released with the title *La Dolce Vita* (i.e., *The Sweet Life*). The title was intended to be ironic because the life it portrayed was anything but sweet. The film treated its viewers to a variety of dramatic scenes portraying a set of people who had "everything"—money, talent, fame, opportunity, leisure time, and so forth. However, this "smart set" lacked one thing, meaning in life. Consequently, they were, as a group, prone to suicide, promiscuous sexual activity, drug abuse, and other self-defeating and self-destructive behaviors. They did *not* have everything. They had nothing because their lives were empty.

There are many ways to portray a sense of meaninglessness in life. Some years ago the singer Peggy Lee made popular a song that repeated the question: "Is that all there is?" The implied answer was, "Yes, that's all. Life isn't much—it doesn't have any significant long-term rewards. We're all pretty much wasting our time. So about all we can do is keep dancing (i.e., continue our restless, pointless activity)." One of Shakespeare's plays has a character reflect and observe, "Life is a tale full of sound and fury, told by an idiot, signifying nothing." A poem by Percy Bysshe Shelley entitled "Ozymandias" tells of an ancient king who had great accomplishments during his lifetime. A modern traveler to the land once occupied by the forgotten empire sees only a broken statue of the king with the inscription on its base, "Look on my works, ye mighty, and despair." When the traveler looks all around, he sees only sand.

The idea that life is meaningless can be expressed in formal terms as a philosophical viewpoint called nihilism. *Nihilism* takes the position that nothing has any value and that, consequently, all human action is ultimately pointless. Nihilism is often identified with the writings of the philosopher Friedrich Nietzsche, who proclaimed, "God is Dead." However, Nietzsche was not a complete nihilist. He believed that old, outmoded values had to be replaced with new, more effective ones more in keeping with human nature. Nietzsche burned with passion to express his philosophy and convert people to his point of view. This is *not* absolute nihilism.

Absolute nihilism is a philosophy of utter despair. Persons who feel that their lives are totally devoid of meaning have taken the position, perhaps unwittingly, of absolute nihilism. Such a position is widely recognized by mental health professionals to be pathological. It is a very deep and pervasive sickness of the personality. The psychiatrist Viktor Frankl has termed this particular mental and emotional condition an *existential neurosis* in order to distinguish it from other kinds of neurotic reactions. In brief, an existential neurosis is characterized by chronic anxiety and despair in connection with the nature of existence itself.

In addition to its principal symptom, loss of meaning in life, an existential neurosis is associated with the following signs and symptoms:

1. An existential vacuum
2. Demoralization
3. Despair
4. Loss of interest in rearing children
5. Loss of interest in one's vocation
6. Inability to love
7. Seeing life as absurd

The above items merit comment. An *existential vacuum* is a term associated with the thought of Viktor Frankl. An existential vacuum exists when one's life is empty of meaning. It is as if existence has a large hole in it that cannot be filled. *Demoralization* is the conviction that life is worthless. It is obviously similar to depression. However, in depression, there is often the core thought, "I am worthless." In demoralization, the core thought is likely to be, "Life is worthless." And this includes all lives, not only one's own. The depressed person has a depleted psychological and emotional "bank account." The demoralized person is, so to speak, "emotionally bankrupt."

Despair is a condition of no hope. In *The Divine Comedy* by the Italian poet Dante Alighieri, the gate over the entrance to the Inferno (i.e., "Hell") has the sign, "Abandon all hope ye who enter here." The individual gripped by despair sees no pathway out of psychological hell to a better life. Loss of interest in both *rearing children* and in one's *vocation* reveals that the person suffering from an existential neurosis has lost faith in traditional values. The importance of being a parent and taking an interest in one's work are givens to most normal people.

The inability to love refers to the fact that a demoralized person cares very little for life itself. It is impossible to love a partner if each day seems to be a bowl of ashes. *Seeing life as absurd* suggests that persons with an existential neurosis tend to look on life as if it is a practical joke played on people by a cosmic wisecracker. Everything and all behavior is folly and in the end leads to nothing. Life itself is unnecessary and not needed in the general scheme of the universe.

Causes and Explanations

An important causal factor in an existential neurosis is human self-consciousness and the power to think. It is doubtful, for example, that animals, such as birds and dogs, are capable of suffering from a loss of meaning in life. Aristotle defined the human being as "the thinking animal." Humans look at life and ask of it hard questions: "Is there any sense to it? What is the purpose of life? Do I live on in some way after I die? Is there a God? What is and what is not worth doing?" If one cannot give oneself satisfactory answers to these questions, an existential neurosis may be the result.

It is certainly no coincidence that many highly intelligent people have fought the battle with loss of meaning in life. The author Oscar Wilde, often dispirited, wrote, "The cynic knows the price of everything and the value of nothing." He was probably writing about himself. The French philosopher and satirist Voltaire (the pen name of François Marie Arouet) said, "Life is a comedy to those who think, a tragedy to those who feel." He was saying that a highly conscious, overly analytical approach to life may make it seem, as already noted, absurd.

A contributing factor to an existential neurosis is a loss of belief in God. This is not to say that all atheists will fall into despair. Quite the contrary. There are ways to discover meaning in life—atheist or not. However, taking the position of atheism complicates the search for meaning. It appears clear from the writings of Viktor Frankl that the person who believes in the traditional Judeo-Christian God needs to *discover* values in order to make life meaningful. But these are God's values; they actually exist; and, in some cases, the suffering individual has only lost sight of them.

On the other hand, in *The Brothers Karamazov*, Dostoyevsky had one of the characters say, "If there is no God, then anything is permitted." This is almost certainly incorrect, but it is easy to see how a loss of faith may lead to such a superficial conclusion.

A terrible disaster resulting in the loss of, for example, loved ones, a way of life, or health may induce an existential neurosis. Frankl's book *Man's Search for Meaning* has the alternate title *From Death Camp to Existentialism*. He describes awful conditions in concentration camps in Nazi Germany during World War II and notes that many, perhaps most, camp residents lost their sense of meaning in life. (Frankl himself was one of the prisoners.) He also notes that those who were able to hold on to the idea that life is meaningful were more likely to survive.

An inability to make a choice among various goals in life can contribute to an existential neurosis. Without an important goal or goals, a person tends to be a kind of psychological drifter, an emotional vagrant. Sometimes, when there is too much opportunity, when many roads could be taken—but only one must be selected—a kind of mental dazzle befuddles the mind. Yet, existential choices must be made; otherwise, like a ship in an ocean without wind, one will be stalled, becalmed, and immobilized by life. (For more on indecisiveness, see Chapter 12.)

The somewhat nihilistic temper of the times contributes to loss of meaning. It has become "in" to question old-fashioned virtues such as courage, patience, consideration for others, sexual fidelity, and moderation. These traditional virtues also represent values. When values are repudiated or given up, often there is nothing to take their place. The emotional price is a slide downward into existential despair.

Frankl suggests that human beings have an inborn will to meaning. This will craves values as much as the hunger drive craves food. A person can no more live without life making sense than the body can live without calories. Values are the nutrition of the personality. If the will to meaning is frustrated, as it so often is by the situations and conditions already identified, it is no wonder that an existential neurosis is the result.

Coping

If you suffer from loss of meaning in your life, you may find value in the following list of practical coping strategies.

 • Learn to identify basic values. What are the essential values of life? There is really nothing that difficult about figuring out what they are. Traditionally, they have been associated with such behaviors as raising children, making the most of one's talents and aptitudes, respecting parents, finding a useful vocation, being faithful to a partner, and so forth. In brief, values for human beings are linked to what has been called *prosocial behavior*, behavior that furthers the welfare and interests of one's given reference group (e.g., the family, the tribe, the nation).

• Act as if you believe that values are real. Even if you doubt from a rational, skeptical position that values have any lasting, objective value, you can still act *as if* they do. This is the position of the existential philosopher Jean-Paul Sartre. He said that people can *create* values by their choices. If one *chooses*, by an act of will, a responsible pathway (i.e., a prosocial one) in life, then life will be filled with meaning. The novelist W. Somerset Maugham followed a line of reasoning similar to Sartre's. An atheist, Maugham decided in youth that there was value in making an orderly pattern of his life. This is explained in his autobiographical novel, and his acknowledged masterpiece, *Of Human Bondage*. Although Maugham felt barely nurtured emotionally and psychologically by his decision, it created enough value for him to live to a ripe old age.

• Look for the meaning *in* life, not *out* of it. There is a strong tendency to look upon life as instrumental, as having a purpose beyond itself. A common Western theological viewpoint sees this world's activities as a way to earn an eternal reward. However, if you are a person who believes that death is oblivion, then the problem of meaning in life is magnified. However, even if death is the cessation of all experience, you can enjoy *this* moment, *this* meal, *this* joyful experience, *this* contribution to the welfare of your children and others. Life itself is intrinsically meaningful from moment-to-moment. If there is something beyond biological life, that is just a bonus—an extra dividend.

• Turn the power to think upon itself. The philosopher Miguel de Unamuno suggested that the kind of self-consciousness possessed by human beings is the cause of all existential suffering. As already indicated, human beings ask questions of life that are very hard to answer. However, one can "fight fire with fire." If you dig your existential pit with the tool of consciousness, you can dig your way out with the same tool. If you have thought your way into an existential neurosis, it is only because your thinking is incomplete. You have only gone halfway. Think things through and you will see that you can both discover and create meaning.

• Refuse to be a victim of contemporary *nihilism*, the loss of traditional values associated with our rapidly changing times. If you have roots in a traditional religion or culture, learn about your roots. Read, study, do some research. Talk to older relatives about their attitudes and values. Stop looking at traditional values with skepticism. Have an open attitude, and approach them with respect. Perhaps you can rediscover something in your family's cultural foundations that will help you rebuild your house of meaning.

• Reexamine your ideas about God. As already indicated, a belief in the traditional Western God is not essential for you to find meaning in life. Nonetheless, such a belief is often helpful to many persons. You might familiarize yourself with the "proofs" in classical philosophy of God's existence. They are meant to appeal to the reasonable person. Thinkers of consequence ranging from Aristotle to René Descartes and from St. Thomas Aquinas to Albert Einstein have seen something of merit in arguments suggesting that God exists.

• Define your goals. A life that is aimless and without goals tends to also be a meaningless life. Set forth your goals in writing. Try to visualize them clearly. Goals act like a radio beam for an airplane. They guide you through the darkness of a psychological night. They help you find the way through the arbitrary temptations of life. And they add meaning to life.

• Accept the idea that reason points to the existence of meaning in life. In the same way that nature or God provides food for the hunger drive and water for thirst, it is logical to suppose that values, real ones, exist to satisfy the will to meaning.

Professional Help

If you believe that you suffer from loss of meaning in life, here are some of the ways that the professions of psychiatry and clinical psychology can help you.

The principal modes of therapy for an existential neurosis are existential therapy and humanistic therapy. *Existential therapy* is an outgrowth of an approach in Western European philosophy known as existentialism. Pioneered by such thinkers as Søren Kierkegaard, Martin Heidegger, and Jean-Paul Sartre, *existentialism* is the point of view that the starting place for understanding life is the *inner outlook*, life as it is actually lived and experienced, not as it is studied objectively by biology and academic psychology. Consequently, existential therapy is an application of existentialism that helps an individual examine and understand his or her relationship to life itself.

A specific kind of existential therapy is *logotherapy*, an approach developed by the psychiatrist Viktor Frankl, author of such books as *Man's Search for Meaning* (cited earlier in this chapter) and *The Doctor and the Soul*. A rough translation of *logotherapy* from its Greek roots is "meaning therapy." When asked the difference between psychoanalysis and logotherapy, Frankl once replied, "In psychoanalysis, a patient reclines on a couch, looks away from the therapist, and says things that are very hard to say. In logotherapy, a patient sits on a chair, looks at the therapist, and hears things that are very difficult to hear."

Existential therapists, including logotherapists, make the assumption that the patient has free will, that the power of choice is real. They suggest that people are responsible for their choices and that they are the architects of their own fates. The patient is encouraged to assert that values really exist in life and that they are within reach. The existential viewpoint in therapy glows with hope in contrast to the despair of the patient.

Another difference between existential therapy and traditional psychoanalysis is that existential therapy is future oriented. In psychoanalysis, an attempt is made to understand your problems in terms of your developmental history. In existential therapy, an attempt is made to help you escape from an existential vacuum by attending to alternatives open to you as you go forward in life.

In fairness to psychoanalysis, it should be noted that it is designed to deal with clinical neurotic disorders (e.g., obsessive compulsive disorder and phobic disorder) that may have their roots in childhood experiences. Existential therapy, on the other hand, deals with a different kind of neurosis. An existential neurosis arises from the collision of the individual's thinking and reflective powers with the hard, inherent uncertainties of life itself. An existential neurosis represents the dread and/or emptiness that arises when one tries to look forward into an uncertain future.

Humanistic therapy can also help you overcome loss of meaning in life. Any distinction between existential therapy and humanistic therapy is no more than academic. In practice, the two approaches overlap so much that formal distinctions blur. Nonetheless, for purposes of clarification, you will recall that existential therapy arose from European existentialism. It has its roots in the experiences of loss and desolation associated with both World War I and World War II. Its purpose is to salvage the individual and to make life bearable.

Humanistic therapy, on the other hand, derives much of its inspiration from American psychology. This kind of therapy tends to be optimistic, and says, "Life can be more than just bearable. It can be joyful." To be more specific, Abraham Maslow, a principal founder of humanistic psychology, noted that self-actualization is also a value to be fulfilled. He defined *self-actualization* as "an inborn need to make the most of talents and potentialities." When this need is frustrated, one of its effects can be loss of meaning in life. Humanistic therapy helps the individual to remove barriers to self-actualization.

An actual therapist is likely to use a combination of ideas and concepts in both existential therapy and humanistic therapy to help you discover the pathway leading in the direction of a more meaningful life.

Key Points to Remember

· *Nihilism* takes the position that nothing has any value and that, consequently, all human action is ultimately pointless. Refuse to be a victim of contemporary nihilism.

· An *existential neurosis* is characterized by chronic anxiety and despair in connection with the nature of existence itself.

· Some of the signs and symptoms of an existential neurosis include an existential vacuum, demoralization, despair, loss of interest in rearing children, loss of interest in one's vocation, inability to love, and seeing life as absurd.

· An important causal factor in an existential neurosis is human self-consciousness and the power to think. On the positive side, this power can be used to rediscover lost values and, in turn, meaning in life.

· A contributing factor to an existential neurosis is a loss of belief in God. Reexamine your ideas about God.

· A terrible disaster resulting in the loss of, for example, loved ones, a way of life, or health may induce an existential neurosis.

· An inability to make a choice among various goals in life can contribute to an existential neurosis. Define your goals.

· If the will to meaning is frustrated, an existential neurosis can be the result.

· Learn to identify the basic, essential values of life.

· Act as if you believe that values are real.

· Look for meaning *in* life, not *out* of it.

· The principal modes of therapy for an existential neurosis are existential therapy and humanistic therapy.

· *Logotherapy*, developed by the psychiatrist Viktor Frankl, is a specific kind of existential therapy.

· *Humanistic therapy*, deriving much of its inspiration from American psychology, tends to be optimistic.

Chapter 17

Memory Problems: More Than Ordinary Forgetfulness

In the motion picture *Heaven Can Wait*, the protagonist (played by Warren Beatty) dies and goes to Heaven. Mr. Jordon, an agent of the Higher Powers, discovers that a mistake has been made and that the hero has died before his time. His first body was cremated. Arrangements are made to return him to Earth in a second body until a third, and final, body is found. In this last incarnation, he supposedly will live out his allotted days on Earth. The story has a happy ending when he is reunited with his soul mate.

However, how happy *is* the ending? The Beatty character has lost the memory of his first life. He only vaguely recognizes his beloved. Has he kept his life if he has lost its continuity? Probably not. You are not you if you do not remember your parents, your childhood, your friends, and both your sad and joyful moments. If you lose the thread of personal memories, then *you* are gone.

Oliver Sacks, the neurologist who wrote *Awakenings*, describes a sad case of memory impairment in his book *The Man Who Mistook His Wife for a Hat*. A particular patient received a severe head injury in World War II. He lives in an eternal present. He has some long-term memory of childhood and adolescence, but it stops with the date of his injury. For many years, he has not remembered yesterday or any of his yesterdays. If someone visits him, he remembers the visit for only a few hours. Obviously, his life is very limited, and he lives in an institution.

It was for good reason that the novelist Vladimir Nabakov, author of *Lolita*, gave his autobiography the title *Speak, Memory!* He recognized that his memory was his life.

Everyone has problems with memory some of the time. Who has not been unable to recall a familiar name or fact? The experience is distressing.

• 126 •

The person is likely to mutter something such as, "I'm losing it," or "What's wrong with me?"

This chapter concerns itself with memory problems—not the ordinary lapses everyone experiences, but significant disruptions in memory. These need to be looked at seriously, and sometimes they are pathological.

Before examining memory gone wrong, let's look at it as a normal process. Early psychology, influenced by classical philosophy, tended to look on memory as a "power of the mind," an inborn mental faculty. Consequently, some people had "good memories" and others had "bad memories." Furthermore, the memory could be trained and improved something like a muscle.

More recently, psychologists have tended to look on memory as a process involving the encoding, storage, and retrieval of cognitive information. *Encoding* refers to the fact that memories are stored as images, words, or numerals that represent outer reality. *Storage* refers to the idea that memories are "filed" as if in a mental cabinet. Of course, this "cabinet"—the memory cortex in the brain—is alive and subject to a host of disturbances. *Retrieval* refers primarily to the mental processes of recognition and recall. Of the two, recall is by far the more demanding. It is much more difficult to recall and use a person's name than to passively recognize it.

If someone's processes of encoding, storage, and retrieval begin to operate in an abnormal manner, then that person has the appearance of memory problems. These, as the subtitle of this chapter suggests, are more than ordinary forgetfulness. Some of the principal signs and symptoms associated with memory problems are listed below.

1. Confabulation
2. Short attention span
3. Impairment of short-term memory
4. Appearance of the tip-of-the-tongue phenomenon
5. Hyperesthetic (i.e., oversensitive) memory
6. Bewilderment
7. Loss of self-esteem
8. Loss of identity

The above items merit comment and explanation. *Confabulation* is characterized by making up information to fill in memory blanks. A person born in 1920 might say, for example, that he or she was born in 1940. The aim is *not* to lie or mislead, but to appear competent. A person with a *short attention span* is easily distracted and unable to concentrate. The condition is characterized by an inability to fix the attention on a small number of elements or facts for a prolonged period of time. The trait is normal in toddlers and preschoolers, abnormal in adults.

Short-term memory is also called "working memory." It is characterized by the ability to remember facts and ideas that one needs to use in the present. Examples include remembering a telephone number until it is dialed, a waiter or waitress remembering that a customer wants dry toast, and a parent remembering that a child is visiting a friend until 4:00 P.M. If short-term memory is impaired, then life—just ordinary activities—take on an incredible complexity.

The *tip-of-the-tongue phenomenon* is the frustrating experience of knowing that at some level one *knows*, but cannot *recall*. A familiar name, a key fact, a date, or a definition cannot be dredged up from the storage level to full consciousness. Everyone experiences the phenomenon from time to time, but it may appear with dismaying frequency when there are other memory problems.

Hyperesthetic memory (i.e., oversensitive memory) is a peculiar problem in that it is characterized by involuntary recollections. An example is recalling in detail an incident in which one was slighted or insulted by a partner or friend. Freud once remarked that neurotic persons suffer from "reminiscences"—involuntary memory fragments. (It should be noted, however, that in psychoanalytic theory it is also hypothesized that neurotic persons suffer from the repression of painful early memories. So, it would be more accurate to say that neurotic persons suffer from two kinds of memory disturbances—repressions and reminiscences.)

Bewilderment suggests that an individual is confused by conflicting memories or the absence of key ones. The result is sometimes an inability to function in the most basic ways. In diseases that bring about severe memory difficulties due to organic deterioration, the person may not remember something as simple as the fact that a toaster has to be plugged in before it will function. In less severe cases, common behaviors such as adding numbers, spelling words, or using the telephone may be somewhat impaired.

The person with memory problems often suffers a loss of *self-esteem*. One's basic sense of self-worth, tied to competence, is damaged when one cannot effectively carry out common behaviors that depend on a well-functioning memory.

In extreme cases, memory impairment can lead to a *loss of identity*. The two clinical conditions that are usually identified with this state are psychogenic amnesia and psychogenic fugue. In *psychogenic amnesia*, the person no longer knows his or her own name, place of residence, social security number—any information that will reveal identity. Other facts, as well as vocational skills, are often intact. In *psychogenic fugue*, the person combines the symptoms of psychogenic amnesia with a flight from home, often arriving in a strange city. (The word *fugue* is related to the word *fugitive*.) Both conditions described are thought to have roots in psychological and emotional conflicts.

Causes and Explanations

Broadly speaking, causes of memory difficulties fall into two categories: (1) organic and (2) psychological. *Organic causes* have a biological basis. There may be a blood chemistry problem or damage to the brain and nervous system. *Psychological causes* suggest that there is no gross impairment at the biological level (i.e., the "equipment" is not damaged). Nonetheless, the *functioning* of the organism is abnormal because of emotional conflicts, anxiety, depression, or something similar.

Some of the principal organic mental disorders associated with an impairment of memory include Alzheimer's disease, general paresis, and alcohol amnestic disorder. *Alzheimer's disease* is characterized by not only memory loss but also such signs and symptoms as bewilderment, lack of trust, useless activity, and agitation. Postmortem examinations of patients with the disease reveal that many neurons have died in the frontal portion of the brain. Also, the axons leading from neurons are tangled, somewhat like the threads in a knotted ball of yarn. The basic causes of Alzheimer's disease are somewhat obscure. One strong possibility is a genetic predisposition. A few researchers suggest that overexposure to products containing aluminum is a factor. Alzheimer's disease is classified as a *senile dementia*, meaning it affects mainly elderly persons. However, it can strike middle-aged individuals.

General paresis is associated with syphilis, one of the sexually transmitted diseases. In addition to memory impairment, general paresis is characterized by motor-coordination difficulties, paralysis, and a decline in functional intelligence. Paresis is caused by destruction to the brain and nervous system by the syphilis spirochete, a type of bacterium shaped like a corkscrew.

Alcohol amnestic disorder is characterized by a gradual loss of memory abilities and a deterioration of the personality. Its older name was *Korsakoff's psychosis* in honor of the Russian neurologist who studied the disorder approximately 100 years ago. The basic cause is chronic abuse of alcohol. (For more on alcohol abuse, see Chapter 2.)

An important organic factor in memory problems is atherosclerosis, a condition associated with blockage of the arteries. With age, arteries tend to become clogged with plaque, and blood flow is restricted. Less oxygen is supplied to the brain. Neurons deprived of oxygen do not function as effectively as those that are adequately supplied. In more severe cases, atherosclerosis plays an important role in cerebrovascular accidents (i.e., strokes).

Hypoglycemia, or chronic low blood sugar, will also impair memory. If glucose levels fall below normal, then neurons are starved for food and cannot operate as effectively as they should.

Some of the principal disorders associated with psychological factors are psychogenic amnesia and psychogenic fugue (already cited). The principal psychological process used to explain these disorders, as well as many other memory difficulties, is repression. In psychoanalytic theory, *repression* is an ego defense mechanism that protects the conscious level of the personality against threats to its integrity. In extreme cases, an individual can maintain self-esteem by wholesale repression of an identity. (This is what appears to be happening in cases of psychological amnesia and fugue.) Similarly, others might not remember certain painful child memories.

What Freud called "the psychopathologies of everyday life" can also be explained by repression. When one blocks and cannot recall a familiar name, it is possible that this represents hostility or the forbidden wish, "I would like it better if you weren't here." The repression of the "not nice" wish carries the name along with it into the psychological netherland of the unconscious level of the personality. A name sometimes applied to the process described in this paragraph is *motivated forgetting.*

A cause of difficulty in recall, not pathological in nature, is failing to effectively encode new information in the first place. Suppose that a child in the eighth grade is asked to learn the names of the Great Lakes. The child may try to memorize by rote, relying primarily on mechanical repetition. When two of the five lakes cannot be recalled while taking a subsequent examination, the child shrugs the lapse off because the experience is so common. However, if the child had looked for a *pattern* in the information, recall would have been greatly facilitated. (The pattern usually used to help remember the Great Lakes is that the first letters form the word *HOMES.* When presented with a recall task, the child could then think, "H-O-M-E-S: H—Huron, O—Ontario, M—Michigan, E—Erie, and S—Superior.") The failure to encode effectively accounts for many lapses in recall ability.

A memory failure can be a key element in a passive-aggressive syndrome. In this case, *passive-aggressive* refers to the expression of hostility in a safe, unconscious way. For example, "forgetting" to do a chore or run an errand for someone else may be a nonverbal way of saying, "I do not want to do it. Leave me alone." The lapse may be, at a conscious level, quite innocent. The resistance to the requested behavior can be traced to repressed hostility.

Coping

If you suffer from memory problems, you may find value in the following list of coping strategies.

- Do not abuse alcohol. Any memory problems you have will be aggravated by such abuse. The same is true of "recreational" drugs in general (e.g., cocaine, amphetamines, and marijuana).
- Do whatever you can that you believe to be practical to avoid contracting syphilis. If you believe you have been infected and are in an early stage, seek immediate medical attention. In most cases, antibiotic treatment will bring about a complete cure.
- Consider restricting excessive exposure to aluminum products (e.g., some cans, foil, some underarm deodorants, and certain cooking utensils). The link between aluminum and Alzheimer's disease is problematical and questioned by most researchers. Nonetheless, you might want to take the safest possible road if it imposes no great hardship.
- Restrict saturated fats in your diet. These are fats that are solid at room temperature. By the way, this includes hydrogenated vegetable oils. These kinds of fats possibly contribute to atherosclerosis in the way that animal fats do.
- If you have a tendency to hypoglycemia, avoid foods high in refined sugar (e.g., some soft drinks, candy bars, jams, syrup, cakes, and pies). Taking in excessive dietary sugar may cause the glucose level in the blood to rise too high too rapidly. This produces a rebound effect and, in turn, low blood sugar.
- Be sure to get a regular and adequate amount of moderate aerobic exercise. At the minimum, this should be brisk walking for 20 minutes three times a week, or the equivalent. Aerobic exercise, exercise that works the heart and the lungs, helps to keep the arteries in good condition and has a positive impact on the supply of oxygen to the brain's neurons.
- Ask yourself *why* you are unable to remember a name or a fact. Psychoanalytic theory suggests that repression might be at work. Explore reasons you are possibly unconsciously motivated to forget something you consciously want to recall. It is feasible that finding the hidden motive will relieve some of the tendency to repress. And the "mental block" is likely to move out of memory's pathway.
- Learn to encode information effectively. It is often helpful to use *mnemonic devices*, conscious memory strategies, to help you remember. (The use of the word *HOMES* to remember the Great Lakes is an example of such a device.) The key to such devices is this: *make an association with*

something that is already familiar to you. If, for example, you are introduced to someone who has the name *James*, think of someone you know
who already has the name. Or you can think of a famous person with the
name. Then visualize the less familiar person acting like, or doing something commonly done by, the more familiar person (e.g., smoking a pipe
or talking in a characteristic manner). Although all of this sounds complex,
in practice, it is fairly easy and will in fact help you to remember names.
For another example of a memory strategy, suppose that you are familiar
already with English and are learning Spanish as a second language. You
see on a vocabulary list that the Spanish word *libro* means "book." You can
memorize this by mechanical repetition, of course, but your task is greatly
eased if you note that books are in libraries and that the Spanish word has
the same root as the word *library*. Pay attention to *how* you encode information, and you will greatly facilitate recall.

    • Ask yourself if you are using forgetting as a passive-aggressive trait.
Are you employing memory lapses as a way of "punishing" someone else?
If you think that you are, then define your own behavior as childish and
irresponsible. Look for more effective ways in which to respond and
behave.

Professional Help

If you suffer from significant memory problems, here are some of the ways
in which the professions of psychiatry and clinical psychology can help
you.

    Taking a biological, or organic, approach, a therapist may help you find
ways in which to improve the general health of your neurons. A basic
recommendation is to avoid or restrict the use of drugs such as nicotine,
alcohol, cocaine, amphetamines, and marijuana. Other recommendations
include the restriction of refined sugar and saturated fats in the diet. You
will also be encouraged to obtain moderate aerobic exercise. These recommendations imply life-style changes and patients are often resistant to such
changes. The behavioral approach can be combined effectively with the
biological approach.

    Taking a behavioral approach, a therapist will employ behavior modifi-
cation strategies that make it possible to give up maladaptive habits and
replace them with adaptive ones. A behavioral approach can also be used
to help you develop more effective ways to use your memory. One practical
avenue is to develop a set of personal mnemonic devices, or memory
strategies. Behavior therapy is particularly valuable in this regard because
it is inspired by learning theory. The principles of learning theory go hand
in hand with strategies that improve memory.

Taking a psychodynamic approach, a therapist is likely to employ *free association*, a basic technique used in psychoanalysis. The patient is encouraged to talk about anything and everything that comes to mind without regard for such considerations as logical order or guilt feelings. The seemingly pointless verbal rambling is only "free" on the surface. The associations are determined by forbidden wishes and repressed memories. In this manner, it is often possible to uncover buried memories. These buried, or repressed, memories may in various ways be interfering with the effective functioning of memory in general.

In some cases, repressed memories can be uncovered with more powerful techniques. Hypnosis is one such technique. A patient in a deep trance can often remember events that are not accessible to the conscious will. The trance acts like a sharp knife and cuts through the repressive barrier. A similar technique is the administration of the drug sodium Pentothal (thiopental sodium). When this drug is used to recover and explore repressed memories, the procedure is known as *narcoanalysis*. Both hypnosis and narcoanalysis can be useful in the treatment of psychogenic amnesia and fugue. In some cases, a tape recording, audio or video, is made of the patient's responses. Later, the tape is played for the patient so that an externalized look at his or her behavior can be obtained. The methods described in this paragraph are very powerful and are not used by a responsible therapist unless there is ample reason to believe that the patient has the ego strength to integrate the discovered information in the buried memories.

You will recall that in some cases lapses in memory can be expressions of passive-aggressive behavior. Taking an interpersonal approach, a therapist is likely to help a client develop insight into how a "bad" memory can be a way of punishing another person and moving against him or her. The therapist will help the client to find more effective ways to relate to significant-other people.

Key Points to Remember

• Memory is a process involving the encoding, storage, and retrieval of cognitive information.

• Some of the principal signs and symptoms associated with memory problems include confabulation, short attention span, impairment of short-term memory, and bewilderment.

• Psychogenic amnesia and psychogenic fugue both involve some loss of personal identity. In some cases, hypnosis and narcoanalysis can be useful in the treatment of these conditions.

• Broadly speaking, causes of memory difficulties fall into two categories: (1) organic and (2) psychological.

• Some of the principal organic mental disorders associated with an impairment of memory include Alzheimer's disease, general paresis, and alcohol amnestic disorder.

• An important organic factor in memory problems is atherosclerosis, a condition associated with blockage of the arteries. Restrict saturated fats in your diet. Be sure to get adequate amounts of moderate aerobic exercise.

• *Hypoglycemia*, or chronic low blood sugar, will impair memory. Avoid foods high in refined sugar.

• *Repression* is an ego defense mechanism that protects the conscious level of the personality against threats to its integrity. What Freud called "the psychopathologies of everyday life" can be explained by repression.

• A cause of difficulty in recall, not pathological in nature, is failing to effectively encode new information in the first place. Learn to encode information effectively.

• Lapses in memory can be a passive-aggressive trait. Taking an interpersonal approach, a therapist can help a client find more effective ways to relate to significant other people.

• Behavior therapy, employing behavior modification techniques, can help a person make important life-style changes that have a beneficial impact on memory functioning.

• *Free association*, a basic technique used in psychoanalysis, can help a patient uncover buried memories.

Chapter 18

Mood Fluctuations: The Storms of Temperament

Are you a victim of your moods?

To some extent, each person is at the mercy of the shifting winds of individual temperament. Approximately 2,400 years ago, the Greek playwright Euripedes said, "There is no harbor of peace from the changing waves of joy and despair." And about 400 years ago, the French author Michel de Montaigne wrote in his *Essays,* "If health and a fair day smile on me, I am a very good fellow; if a corn trouble my toe, I am sullen, out of humor, and inaccessible." In short, to be human is to have emotional ups and downs. Within reasonable limits, this must be accepted.

However, there are people who experience wild, uncontrollable mood swings. These unhappy individuals are like ships at sea trying to keep from sinking in a storm—in this case, a storm of temperament. The subject of this chapter is pathological fluctuations in mood—mood swings that leave the individual emotionally drained and that interfere with the normal functioning of everyday life.

Before defining the word *mood*, it is useful to look at ways in which the word is used in speech. You might hear such statements as, "I'm not in the mood to watch a movie tonight," "I'm in a mood for pizza," "I'm in a bad mood," "I'm in the mood to take a ride," and so forth. "I'm in the Mood for Love" is the title of a song that was popular some years ago. All uses of the word *mood* suggest that it is a vagrant psychological event. *Mood* can be defined as follows: "a transient, involuntary emotional state."

Associated with the primary psychological symptom of pathological fluctuations in mood are the following signs and symptoms:

1. Episodic mania or hypomania
2. Episodic depression

3. Erratic, unpredictable behavior
4. Alternations in both approaching and avoiding others
5. Extreme fluctuations in weight
6. Wide variations in the need for sleep
7. A chaotic, ragged emotional life

The items identified above merit comment. *Mania* is characterized by euphoria, elation, agitation, and hurried speech. When mania is extreme, the individual will appear to others as "mad" or "crazy." For lower levels of mania intensity, it is appropriate to use the term *hypomania*. (The root *hypo* means "below." Consequently, *hypomania* is "a low-grade mania.") The individual displaying hypomania will seem neither mad nor crazy, but will appear to be inappropriately elated and excited. When there are pathological fluctuations in mood, either mania or hypomania will alternate with depression. (For a discussion of depression, see Chapter 8.)

Examples of *erratic, unpredictable behavior* include picking a fight with a loved one for no good reason, making too many impulsive purchases, signing contracts without sufficient reflection, failing to meet family obligations, and so forth.

People suffering from extreme mood swings often manifest *alternations in both approaching and avoiding others*. First, they will be too friendly and "all over" other persons. Then, they will become reclusive, withdrawn, and unresponsive. Sometimes, they will move against a friend or loved one in a hostile, aggressive way. This will be followed by contrition and an effort to make amends.

Extreme fluctuations in weight are associated with mood swings. During episodes of mania, the person may seek to be "perfect" and superthin. During episodes of depression, a pattern of either steady compulsive eating or episodic binge eating may manifest itself.

Wide variations in the need for sleep are linked to mood. In general, persons in a state of mania seem to need little sleep or suffer from insomnia. Depressed persons, on the other hand, may sleep 10 or 12 hours per day. They appear to use sleep as a way to escape from reality.

A ragged, chaotic emotional life suggests that the individual is living as if acting in a soap opera. There are great successes and great failures. There are histrionic displays. Every event is overdramatized. The person is riding a car on an emotional roller coaster.

Bipolar disorder is the diagnostic term used in psychiatry and clinical psychology when mood fluctuations are severe and extremely disruptive. The former name of this disorder was *manic-depressive psychosis*, which suggests that alternations of mania and depression were so severe that the individual had lost touch with reality. A less intense, not as disabling condition, is identified with the more or less exchangeable terms *cyclothymia, cyclothymic disorder*, and *cyclothymic neurosis.* In this condition, there tends to be hypomania, not mania, and good reality contact is maintained.

Causes and Explanations

A general underlying cause of extreme mood fluctuations may be a genetic tendency or an inborn temperament. Studies suggest that close relatives are more likely to suffer from the problem than are people in general. Research in personality strongly indicates that emotional stability is a basic, or source, trait of personality. Such a trait arises not from learning but from biological causes.

A psychological factor can readily interact with an inborn tendency. If, for example, a person who is a natural extravert is forced by life circumstances to lead a reserved, inhibited life, then an "emotional breakout" may occur. This will be identified as a mania. Once the mania runs its course, the person may submit to social pressure, retreat, and manifest depression. The mood swings under these circumstances can be interpreted as a kind of protest by the natural personality against the imposed social one.

Mood fluctuations are possibly related to the body's *circadian rhythms*, biological processes that "travel in circles in one day." The wake-sleep cycle is the prime example. Consequently, disturbances in the wake-sleep cycle can be disruptive. This is particularly true if the individual relies on barbiturates to induce sleep and on amphetamines to provide stimulation during the day.

Although it is not technically a circadian rhythm, because it does not take place in a 24-hour period, the menstrual cycle is, nonetheless, a biological rhythm. If a female suffers from the *premenstrual syndrome (PMS)*, a cluster of symptoms including cramps, headaches, illogical thinking, and excitability, this may have an adverse effect on momentary emotional disposition. (PMS should not be confused with *premenstrual tension*, a common condition that possibly affects most women to some degree. PMS is a clinical condition and is believed to affect 1 to 2 percent of the female population.) In general, it can be said that anything that interferes with the body's regular patterns of functioning can induce oscillations of mood.

Recent studies suggest that a large-scale biological rhythm is induced by the seasons. In summer, there is more sunlight, and, in winter, less. This is particularly true of Northern latitudes. Light appears to affect the production of *melanin*, a dark pigment that is evident when the skin tans. Melanin production, in turn, has an effect on the *pineal gland* in the brain, a gland that appears to be involved in the regulation of biological rhythms. It has been suggested that some individuals suffer from a clinical condition called *seasonal affective disorder (SAD),* alternations of mood such that there is emotional elevation in the summer and depression in the winter.

One of the ego defense mechanisms identified by psychoanalysis is *reaction formation*, a tendency for a negative element at the repressed unconscious level to make an appearance at the conscious level as its psychological opposite. What this means in the case of mood swings is that a mania can be a defense against depression. The individual denies the reality of depression by acting elated, devil-may-care, and confident. That these are all false and forms of psychological posturing can be seen from the fact that they manifest themselves in both excessive and compulsive ways. Reaction formations are brittle shells. When the shells crack, the negative element asserts itself, and the person is plunged back into depression. If the reaction formation is eventually rebuilt, the cycle of mania and depression repeats itself.

Wendell Johnson, author of *People in Quandaries*, described a psychological pattern called the *idealization-frustration-demoralization (I-F-D) syndrome*. The first step in the pattern, idealization, suggests that a specific event in the real world leads to unrealistic expectations. Suppose Jeffrey meets Eileen, falls in love, and decides, "She's the most wonderful woman in the world." He daydreams that she will someday be the perfect wife and mother. He is in a state called *limerance*. Limerance is characterized by elevated mood and the conviction that a partner, or potential partner, will satisfy all of one's psychological and emotional needs. The second stage in the pattern, frustration, emerges when it becomes evident that the other person is *not* perfect, that he or she will not live up to all expectations. Jeffrey finds out that Eileen has some attitudes that he deplores, that she is late for dates, and that she is not very interested in having children. Demoralization, the third and last step in the pattern, is a psychological low point. It is an emotional state in which life does not seem worth living and everything has turned "to ashes." Jeffrey has given up hope of having a long-lasting relationship with Eileen. And, perhaps more importantly, he is convinced that he will *never* meet the woman for him.

As a last causal factor, it should be noted that one of the cognitive distortions imbedded in the I-F-D syndrome is *either-or thinking*. Either Eileen is "wonderful" or she is "awful." Similarly, life is either "terrific" or it is "stupid." A new car is either "fantastic" or it is "a lemon." One's career is a "success" or a "failure."

Coping

If you believe that you suffer from pathological, excessive fluctuations in mood, you may find value in the following list of practical coping strategies.

• Become familiar with the concept of emotional modulation. *Emotional modulation* is a self-control process that helps you reduce the intensity and range of mood swings. It is the aim of the coping strategies identified and described in this section to help you achieve emotional modulation. The goal is to put *you* in control of your own emotional life. However, emotional modulation does not seek to eliminate mood swings. Instead, it seeks to bring highs and lows within a normal range. Say to yourself, "I will *modulate*, not eliminate, my emotional fluctuations." Under these conditions, anger becomes irritation, anxiety becomes mild apprehension, and depression becomes disappointment.

• Apply the concept of emotional modulation to the idea that the presence or absence of emotional stability is a source trait of personality. Even if you have a genetic tendency or an inborn temperament that is volatile, you can do something about it. You can apply to yourself some of the measures discussed in this chapter and become less of a victim of your own temperament.

• Find ways to assert your natural personality traits. This will help you to avoid emotional breakouts. If you repress your "true self," you will feel as if you are in a psychological prison. And when you are in prison what do you want to do? The answer is: "Break out." If you find ways to keep yourself out of that prison in the first place, you will not need to break out. And, in turn, you will undermine tendencies toward either mania or hypomania.

• Lead an orderly life. Develop regular habits of sleep, eating, work, and recreation. This will help to stabilize circadian, and other, biological rhythms.

• If you are a female and suffer from either premenstrual tension or premenstrual syndrome (PMS), seek effective ways to reduce your life demands and responsibilities during the days before your menses. Plan ahead and lighten your load if at all possible. Look for ways to relax and reduce anxiety. (For more on anxiety, see Chapter 5.) You can only cope with so much. Do all you can to avoid the feeling that you are overwhelmed.

• If you suffer from depression during the winter, it may be that you need more natural sunlight. Whenever possible during the short days of the year, take walks for 15 or 20 minutes during the middle of the day when the sun is overhead and the Earth is bathed in maximum light. If it is not too cold, expose at least some skin (e.g., hands, face, and neck) to the sunlight. This will allow changes in melanin to have a beneficial effect on your mood.

• Be aware of the tendency to use reaction formation as a defense mechanism. When you find that you are becoming either manic or hypomanic, ask yourself, "Am I defending against disappointment, depression, or demoralization? What am I running from? How can I stand my ground, face reality, and do something effective about my problems?"

• Avoid idealizing another person, possession, or opportunity. In this way, you will undercut the idealization-frustration-demoralization syndrome. Try to see, for example, others in the light of reality, "warts" and all. Do not project your own fantasies and wishes on them.

• Challenge your own ideas when you perceive that you are engaging in either-or thinking. Say to yourself, "I'm oversimplifying. I'm turning a *range* of possibilities into only two categories." Recognize that between the extremes of a blind optimistic outlook and a bleak pessimistic outlook is the balanced, *realistic* outlook.

Professional Help

If you find that you are unable to cope with extreme, pathological fluctuations of mood, here are some of the ways in which the professions of psychiatry and clinical psychology can help you.

Taking a life-centered, humanistic approach, a therapist can help you to recognize the nature of your own temperament. You will learn to know yourself better in order to live at greater peace with yourself. Self-acceptance is an important part of self-esteem. This is a principal theme in humanistic therapy. The humanistic therapist is an active listener who provides unconditional positive regard. This helps you to see yourself not only in a realistic light, but in a self-accepting one.

Humanistic therapy will also encourage you to *be* yourself—to act on your own self-actualizing tendencies. Therefore, if you are a natural extravert who is suppressing your own outgoing nature until it bursts forth in a mania, therapy will help you be the self-expressive person you are meant to be. This will help you to modulate episodes of excitement.

Taking an organic approach, a therapist will help you recognize that your life style may be disrupting the body's biological rhythms. You will be encouraged to develop regular habits of living. Behavior therapy can be of particular value in this regard. A therapist may employ techniques such as the management of reinforcers (i.e., psychological "payoffs"), the management of cues that trigger habits, desensitization, and counter-conditioning to help you modify behaviors.

A psychiatrist may prescribe light therapy if you suffer from seasonal affective disorder. In light therapy, you are exposed to special lamps that produce all of the wavelengths of sunlight.

Taking a psychodynamic approach, a therapist may help you to develop insight into how you use reaction formation as a defense against depression to generate a mania. Also, as your self-esteem builds in therapy, you will have less need to depend on a psychological crutch such as reaction formation.

Taking a cognitive approach, a therapist will help you to recognize that self-defeating behavioral patterns such as the idealization-frustration-demoralization syndrome arise because of cognitive distortions (e.g., either-or thinking). The therapist will listen to your statements and encourage you to challenge their logic. You may be given psychological exercises and homework assignments that help you to see and understand your own thoughts more clearly. Then cognitive-behavior modification can be introduced in order to induce greater emotional stability.

If your fluctuations of mood do not respond well to any of the previously described modes of therapy, a psychiatrist may prescribe lithium carbonate. This is the drug of choice when the diagnosis is bipolar disorder (manic-depressive disorder). Lithium carbonate is marketed under various trade names such as Eskalith, Lithane, and Lithotabs. Research evidence suggests that lithium carbonate may improve biochemical irregularities in the brains's neural impulses, particularly those associated with mood. Because of possible adverse side effects, it is often recommended that a patient's blood be tested on a regular basis to determine lithium levels.

Key Points to Remember

· The subject of this chapter was mood swings that leave the individual emotionally drained and that interfere with the normal functioning of everyday life. These are *pathological fluctuations* in mood.

· A mood is a transient, involuntary emotional state.

· Some of the signs and symptoms associated with pathological fluctuations in mood are episodic mania or hypomania, episodic depression, erratic behavior, wide variations in the need for sleep, and a chaotic emotional life.

· *Bipolar disorder* is the diagnostic term used in psychiatry and clinical psychology when mood fluctuations are severe and extremely disruptive. A less intense, not as disabling condition is *cyclothymic disorder*.

• A general underlying cause of extreme mood fluctuations may be a genetic tendency or an inborn temperament. However, even if you have a genetic tendency or an inborn temperament that is volatile, you can do something about it.

• A psychological factor can readily interact with an inborn tendency. Find ways to assert your natural personality traits. This will help you to avoid emotional breakouts.

• Mood fluctuations are possibly related to the body's circadian rhythms and other biological cycles. Lead an orderly life with regular habits of sleep, eating, work, and recreation.

• In females, both premenstrual tension and premenstrual syndrome can have an adverse effect on mood and its fluctuations. Seek effective ways to reduce your life demands and responsibilities during the days before your menses.

• Deprivation of sunlight during the winter may be associated with a condition called *seasonal affective disorder*. If practical, obtain more sunlight by going for walks. A psychiatrist may prescribe light therapy.

• Mania can be a reaction formation, a kind of ego defense mechanism. In this case, the defense is against depression. Ask yourself the kinds of key questions suggested earlier in the chapter. These will help you to obtain some freedom from the defense mechanism.

• The idealization-frustration demoralization (I-F-D) syndrome can be a contributing factor to excessive mood swings. Learn to avoid either-or thinking, a cognitive distortion associated with the I-F-D syndrome.

• Become familiar with the concept of *emotional modulation.*

• Taking a life-centered, humanistic approach, a therapist can help you to recognize the nature of your own temperament.

• Behavior therapy can help you develop regular habits of living.

• Taking a psychodynamic approach, a therapist may help you to develop insight into how you use reaction formation as a defense against depression to generate a mania.

• Cognitive-behavior modification can be used in therapy in order to induce greater emotional stability.

• A psychiatrist may prescribe lithium carbonate if fluctuations of mood do not respond well to other modes of therapy. This is the drug of choice when the diagnosis is bipolar disorder.

Chapter 19

Obsessions and Compulsions: Of Persistent Ideas and Magic Rituals

Shortly after awakening on a Tuesday morning about six months ago, Richard J., a married man with three children, had the unbidden thought, "*Today is the day I will die.*" He felt a chill go through his body, and he tried to counter the frightening idea by thinking, "That's silly. I'm in perfect health. I don't do dangerous work. I'm a careful driver." However, in a short time, the unbidden thought returned. He was shaving, and he watched his hand tremble as he rinsed his razor in warm water. "Today is the day I will die." His heart began to pound, and he broke out in a cold sweat. Then he voluntarily thought, "Superman, Batman, and Tarzan protect me." He felt an almost immediate decrease in his anxiety. Three more times that day he had the unbidden thought that he would die, and each time he controlled his anxiety by invoking the names of the three superheros. As indicated above, this happened six months ago, and it has repeated itself two to seven times a day every day since.

What is Richard's problem? Does it have a name? What causes the problem? Is this sort of problem common? These and similar questions will be discussed and answered in this chapter.

Richard's strange thought is an *obsession*, a persistent, invasive idea that is perceived to be illogical by either the subject who holds the thought or an outside observer. (This assumes that the subject is willing to discuss the thought with someone else, which is often not the case.) Obsessions are common mental phenomena in both neurotic disorders and in schizophrenia. This chapter will focus on the neurotic process. (For more on schizophrenia, associated with a psychotic process, see Chapter 7.) An additional feature of obsessions in neurotic conditions is that they have a content suggesting the possibility of some danger, loss, or risk. Consequently, they induce anxiety.

Other than Richard's obsession, here are some additional examples. "I'm going to lose all of my friends." "I have a wart on my nose that's getting bigger and bigger." "Every man wants to rape me." "I'm ugly." "You can get AIDS and other diseases by touching contaminated objects such as doorknobs." "Maybe I forgot to lock the door and unplug the iron." "My partner secretly hates me." "An earthquake will destroy our house next week."

A *compulsion* is a ritual, tinged with either an irrational or a magical quality, designed to reduce the anxiety associated with an obsession. In Richard's case, invoking the names of the three favorite superheros of his late childhood and early adolescence gave him a temporary sense of security. He recognized the silliness of both his obsession and his compulsion, but he was powerless to prevent the thought and to resist the compulsion. A compulsion can express itself in the form of either thought or action. Richard's took the shape of thought. Washing one's hands after touching a "contaminated" doorknob is an example of a ritual that expresses itself in action. Other examples of such rituals are avoiding cracks on the sidewalk, tapping with either the hands or feet and counting to a predetermined number, always entering rooms with a particular foot first, and humming a "protective" tune. Notice that in some cases action rituals, like thoughts, can be concealed from others. It should also be noted that action rituals usually have a shred of logic behind them. A hand-washing compulsion is the prime example because it is true that washing is a hygienic procedure. However, washing one's hands 30 or 40 times a day is a gross distortion of normal hand washing.

If a person suffers from one or several obsessions and compulsions over several months, and if these ideas and rituals create both personal suffering and significant problems in living, the pathological condition may be diagnosed as an *obsessive compulsive disorder*. This is also called *obsessive compulsive neurosis*.

An obsessive compulsive disorder should be distinguished from obsessive compulsive *tendencies*. It is possible to have one or two obsessions with related compulsions that come and go. Such a state of affairs is not all that pathological and is on the borderline of what is normal. A *disorder,* or neurosis, should not be diagnosed unless the pathology is long-lasting and severe.

It is also important to make a distinction between obsessive compulsive disorder and *obsessive compulsive personality disorder*. The second condition is associated with perfectionism and is the subject of Chapter 20.

Signs and symptoms frequently associated with obsessive compulsive tendencies or obsessive compulsive disorder include the following:

1. Episodic anxiety
2. Episodic depression
3. Magical thinking
4. Secretive behavior
5. Inability of the will to control behavior
6. Taking "forever" to get things done
7. Personal superstitions

The above items merit comment. *Episodic anxiety* is caused by an obsession that seems to point to danger. *Episodic depression* is caused by the fact that a victim of obsessions and compulsions feels helpless in the face of hostile psychological powers. *Magical thinking* is a part of most rituals. Often the sufferer has lost faith in medicine or traditional religious teachings. Consequently, the individual feels unprotected. Under such conditions, one falls back on the most primitive effort of humankind to take control of events: magic.

The troubled person is ashamed of obsessions and compulsions because they are recognized to be childish, irrational, and silly. *Secretive behavior* arises that is designed to present a better face to the world than is actually felt. Health of the personality becomes a social mask, and one feels like an imposter.

One of the most distressing aspects of obsessions and compulsions is *inability of the will to control behavior*. Most victims try to push obsessions out of consciousness; they also try to resist acting on their compulsions. Both efforts fail, and there is the pervasive sensation that one's life is completely out of control.

Sometimes, because of compulsions, it can *take "forever" to get things done*. It may be necessary to check the back door seven times before leaving the house, to get in and out of the car three times before starting it, to put on and take off the blue blouse before putting on any other blouse, to walk backwards into a room, to touch all of the drawer knobs in the bathroom before washing, and so forth.

To some extent, compulsions can be looked upon as *personal superstitions*. Instead of general superstitions that are well known in folklore, such as not crossing the path of a black cat, not walking under a ladder, carrying a rabbit's foot, and avoiding objects with the number 13, one's own idiosyncratic behavior patterns are substituted. Note that superstitious behavior, like compulsive behavior, is both irrational and magical. Also, superstitions are designed to ward off danger. Consequently, superstitions and compulsions are, fundamentally, expressions of the same basic psychological process: the need to control events and reduce anxiety when one feels helpless.

It is estimated that about two to three percent of the U.S. population, or four to five million persons, suffer from obsessive compulsive disorder. More than this suffer from less disabling obsessive compulsive tendencies.

Causes and Explanations

Classical psychoanalytic theory suggests that obsessions come from repressed id impulses. The *id* is the primitive, wishing, fantasy-oriented agent of the personality. These impulses are more likely to be present in persons (1) who suffered emotional wounds in early childhood and (2) who are socialized and lead a conforming, morally conventional life. Put differently, the *superego*, the moral agent of the personality, does not allow the expression of the id impulses in either consciousness or action. Richard J., referred to at the beginning of this chapter, is trapped in a loveless marriage. Being a traditional man dedicated to the social conventions of his family and culture, the thought of leaving his wife is morally unacceptable. As a solution, his id wishes to simply do away with his wife and children—the obvious obstacles to his happiness and to the possibility of a loving relationship. As farfetched as this sounds to most people, it must be remembered that there are married partners—both male and female—who actually act out such impulses and kill a spouse as well as children. In state mental hospitals, there are numerous individuals called "criminally insane" who have inflicted either death or great bodily injury on their partners or children.

In Richard's case, it must be remembered that it is not Richard, represented by his whole personality, who wants to inflict injury on his loved one. Rather, it is his id, a primitive part of his personality. He is nowhere near acting out his hostile impulses. Instead, they are blocked—repressed into the unconscious realm. However, his *ego*, the conscious agent of the personality, senses danger to his loved ones. This danger signal is converted, for the purposes of censorship and protection against the id's wishes, into hostility directed against the self. In other words, the unconscious logic is, "There is danger to my wife and children. The source of this danger is me. Therefore, I must die for their safety." The conscious obsession is, "Today is the day I will die." And the unconscious mental processes are blocked from view.

The purpose of the compulsion, or ritual, is straightforward. It reduces the anxiety associated with the obsession via the power of magic. If the underlying conflict remains, the obsessions and compulsions repeat themselves.

Of course, other factors play a role in obsessive compulsive behavior. Learning theory says that reinforced behavior tends to acquire habit strength. Each time an obeyed compulsion reduces anxiety, the tendency to engage in the compulsion is reinforced. In this manner, it can be seen that compulsions fall within a class known as *pathological conditioned emotional reactions.* Therefore, as will be seen, the treatment of compulsions includes extinction procedures derived from studies of the learning process.

An aggravating factor in obsessive compulsive behavior is lack of religious belief. *Existential anxiety,* the natural anxiety one feels about threats associated with existence itself, is to some extent reduced when one has faith in traditional teachings about God and life. The person without such a faith is thrown on his or her own resources. Obsessions and compulsions become a kind of surrogate religion—an unsatisfactory one. Magic rituals, recognized to be weak shields against hostile forces, become substitutes for religious rituals grounded in one's general culture.

Another aggravating factor in obsessive compulsive behavior is an active imagination. Highly creative people are somewhat more likely than others to be plagued with persistent images of what might go wrong, of how they can be hurt, of how a minor error (e.g., leaving an appliance plugged in) can turn into a major disaster (e.g., the house burning down). Imaginative persons can *see* future catastrophes as if motion pictures are running in their minds.

Finally, there is the possibility that a brain dysfunction plays a role in at least some cases of obsessive compulsive disorder. Physician and researcher Judith L. Rapoport, Chief of the Child Psychiatry Branch at the National Institute of Mental Health, cites evidence suggesting that obsessive compulsive behavior is a first cousin to other disorders such as uncontrollable tics and Parkinson's disease. One hypothesis is that there are communication difficulties between the brain's frontal lobes and the basal ganglia buried deep in the "lower" parts of the brain. This creates problems in integrating sensory, motor, and cognitive processes. These problems may manifest themselves as persistent, unwanted thoughts and involuntary actions.

Coping

If you believe that you suffer from either obsessive compulsive tendencies or from obsessive compulsive disorder, you may find value in the following list of coping strategies.

• Keep a journal of your thoughts and reflections. Write down your obsessions, and then, in writing, make an analysis of what they might mean. Taking a clue from psychoanalysis, obsessions often are distorted representations of forbidden wishes—often of a hostile or a sexual nature. Insight, even partial insight, into your unconscious motives might provide a degree of relief. Blind forces operating in the unconscious netherworld have the power to control you. You are much less likely to be their victim if you subject them to the clear, cool light of reason. If you just think about your problems, your thinking is likely to remain obsessional and go in circles. The act of writing helps you to bring order and direction to mental chaos.

• Do not try to fight obsessions and compulsions with brute will power. It is as if they have a will of their own. This energy, arising from the unconscious realm, will usually overwhelm the resistance provided by your conscious will. The result of this engagement will be increased feelings of failure and helplessness. This does not mean the will cannot be employed to defeat obsessions and compulsions, but it must be done in a skillful, indirect way. That is the approach built into the coping strategies and other information in this chapter.

• Use negative practice. *Negative practice* was first introduced into the literature of habit modification by the psychologist Knight Dunlap. Negative practice is also known as the *beta method of extinction*. It is a sound technique based on well-established principles of learning and unlearning and has been used with success to treat a range of personal problems, including stuttering. (Note that stuttering, like many compulsions, is an involuntary motor behavior.) Negative practice calls for the individual to consciously and voluntarily produce the "error," or unwanted behavior. This is to be done at times when the individual is *not* compelled to act, is temporarily free of the nuisance. At first, this may seem odd; but a moment's reflection makes evident that *voluntary control* over nuisance behavior is exactly what the troubled person does not have. This is a new experience, and it helps the individual gain eventual control over a problem. In the case of obsessions and compulsions, you can "practice" either one at times when you have no urge whatsoever to do so. Repeated voluntary practice of this kind gradually weakens the involuntary power of the obsessions and compulsions.

• Do some creative writing. As already indicated, persons who suffer from obsessions and compulsions often have very active imaginations. Write, for example, a story involving one of your obsessions. Use your imagination to exaggerate the outcomes. This may involve elements of fantasy or horror. Keep in mind that the story is your own private property and need not be shown to others or offered for publication. In this way, you will let your imagination roam free. Note that this method bears some resemblance to negative practice. You control the negative aspects of the story. You are the author—the "authority." This introduces important elements of voluntary control. Also, production of mental images associated with either obsessions or compulsions helps you desensitize to them.

• Reacquaint yourself with your religious traditions. If you have drifted away from your spiritual roots or if you have actively rejected them, you may find some degree of comfort in reading the *Bible*, the Old Testament or the New Testament, or other literature associated with your particular background. Even Freud, who professed to be an atheist, was well acquainted with the Judaic teachings. It can be argued that even if the conscious mind rejects religious teachings on a cold, rational basis, the subconscious mind—because of both emotional needs and suggestibility—will accept them to some extent. Keep in mind that an obsessive compulsive disorder is a kind of private religion based on superstition and primitive magic. A traditional outlook is fabricated from stronger philosophical and theological thread, and is likely to provide better emotional support.

• Attend to your own biochemistry. If, to some extent, obsessions and compulsions are based on a brain dysfunction, anything you can do to normalize the firing of neurons as well as the transmission of messages along nerve pathways will act in favor of reducing the intensity of your symptoms. Some lines of research indicate that the amino acid tryptophan and the mineral calcium may have a tranquilizing effect on the brain's activity. Milk is a good source of both substances and may act as a natural sedative. Two minerals other than calcium that appear to be of particular importance in the regulation of nerve impulses are magnesium and potassium. Whole grains, green vegetables, and milk are good sources of magnesium. Fruits, whole grains, vegetable, potatoes, and bananas are good sources of potassium. (A warning should be issued about getting vitamins and minerals from a source other than food, that is, tablets or some other supplemental form. Excessive amounts of some vitamins and minerals can be toxic. That is why food, a well-balanced healthful diet, is your best source.)

• Do not be too self-critical. Do not pound on yourself and tell yourself that you are a fool or stupid for having obsessions and compulsions. This will only make matters worse by lowering your self-esteem. Ask, instead, what you can effectively do to *manage* your obsessive compulsive behavior.

• Do not despair. Although you cannot count on it, obsessive compulsive tendencies are sometimes self-terminating. They may burn out on their own and build up a resistance to their own repetition. This does happen. If it does not, you can still cope and work around your irrational tendencies. Finally, professional treatment is often effective.

Professional Help

If you find that you cannot cope with either obsessive compulsive tendencies or an obsessive compulsive disorder, here are some of the ways in which the professions of psychiatry and clinical psychology can help you.

Taking a psychodynamic approach, a therapist can help you attain deeper understanding of an obsession than you can attain on your own. An obsession is structured somewhat like a dream. Its manifest content often masks a latent content (i.e., a forbidden wish). The manifest content must be decoded in order for its meaning to be revealed, and you might be resisting this decoding because of the danger inherent in the forbidden wish. A therapist can help you overcome your resistance by methods such as free associations on your part to various aspects of the obsession. If you can obtain significant insight into the roots of an obsession, you can bring it under conscious control. The need to engage in a compulsive ritual will also diminish because the principal purpose of such a ritual is to reduce anxiety associated with the obsession.

Taking a behavioral approach, a therapist can show you how to effectively apply Dunlap's method of extinction, negative practice, described in the "Coping" section. Often it takes a therapist's assistance to make the method work because patients frequently question that it can be of any real value. Using social learning theory, the therapist can role play with the patient and demonstrate verbally how an obsession can be voluntarily produced and controlled. Observational learning on the patient's part facilitates the actual production by the patient of negative practice. Homework assignments can be given toward the conclusion of one session and their application discussed at the next session.

Another behavioral approach that can sometimes be used with obsessive compulsive disorder is *implosive therapy*. In this kind of therapy, a controlled fantasy is induced and the worst features of the obsession are described (e.g., dying, being sexually abused, or the destruction of one's home by an earthquake). This will bring anxiety to a very high level. If this can be tolerated, anxiety will reach a peak and then diminish. In this manner, the strength of the obsession will be weakened. Implosive therapy can be used only on persons with a high level of ego strength who are willing to tolerate and "ride out" the worst induced anxiety. If the patient's eyes open and the fantasy is arbitrarily broken off, the patient may become hypersensitized, instead of desensitized, to the obsession.

Taking a cognitive approach, a therapist may help you to see just how unrealistic and absurd are the assumptions that reside below an obsession. It can be argued that you already recognize the obsession as silly and irrational, which is true. However, cognitive therapy can reveal to you the precise cognitive distortions that you are employing. Your thoughts, perceptions, and wishes interplay to produce a given obsession. An obsession, like a chain, is only as strong as its weakest link. Understanding the weakness of the obsession's psychological links can weaken its power.

Taking a humanistic approach, a therapist may offer you emotional support. This mode of therapy will help you stop judging yourself too harshly if you have "bad" or "evil" obsessions. Unconditional positive regard offered by the therapist will help you to realize that punitive self-judgment is a one-way street into depression. By learning to judge your *behavior*, not your whole personality, you can be helped to find a way out of the trap of your obsessions.

If all of the interventions previously described prove to be inadequate, then a psychiatrist may recommend drug therapy for an obsessive compulsive disorder. A commonly prescribed drug is imipramine, marketed under brand names such as Janimine Filmtab, SK-Pramine, and Tofranil. Imipramine is a member of a larger class of drugs called tricyclic agents, usually used to treat depression. The drug appears to act by normalizing levels of two of the brain's chemical messengers, norepinephrine and serotonin. Like most prescription drugs, there is a possibility that taking imipramine may produce adverse side effects.

Key Points to Remember

• An *obsession* is a persistent, invasive idea that is perceived to be illogical by either the subject who holds the thought or an outside observer.

• A *compulsion* is a ritual, tinged with either an irrational or a magical quality, designed to reduce the anxiety associated with an obsession.

• If a person suffers from one or several obsessions and compulsions over several months and if these ideas and rituals create both personal suffering and significant problems in living, the pathological condition may be diagnosed as an *obsessive compulsive disorder*. This is also called *obsessive compulsive neurosis*.

• Signs and symptoms frequently associated with obsessive compulsive tendencies or obsessive compulsive disorder include episodic anxiety, episodic depression, magical thinking, inability of the will to control behavior, and personal superstitions.

• Classical psychoanalytic theory suggests that obsessions come from repressed id impulses.

• Each time an obeyed compulsion reduces anxiety, the tendency to engage in the compulsion is reinforced.

• An aggravating factor in obsessive compulsive behavior is an active imagination.

• There is the possibility that a brain dysfunction plays a role in at least some cases of obsessive compulsive disorder.

• Keep a journal of your thoughts and reflections. Make an analysis of what your obsessions might mean.

• Do not try to fight obsessions and compulsions with brute will power.

• Use *negative practice*, also known as the *beta method of extinction*.

• Taking a psychodynamic approach, a therapist can help you attain deeper understanding of an obsession than you can attain on your own.

• Taking a cognitive approach, a therapist may help you to see just how unrealistic and absurd are the assumptions that reside below an obsession.

• A psychiatrist may recommend drug therapy for an obsessive compulsive disorder.

Chapter 20

Perfectionism: The Flaw of Flawlessness

Amelia G. is single, 33 years of age, has never been married, and teaches English composition and literature in a community college. She is an admirer of Edna Ferber, who wrote such novels as *So Big*, *Showboat*, and *Giant*. As a homework assignment, Amelia's therapist asked her to write a few words about her perfectionistic tendencies, and this is what she wrote:

> I used to think well of my perfectionism and looked down on others because they didn't strive to do their best at all times. I admired Michelangelo's statement, "Trifles make perfection, and perfection is no trifle." I also admired Edna Ferber's admission in her autobiography that she had no shortage of beaus in her younger days. However, those men who pursued her were not attractive to her. And those to whom she was attracted were not interested in her. Therefore, she rejected all suitors. This attitude seemed fine when I was in my twenties. Now I'm afraid that I'll never marry. I know I'm setting my standards too high, and I'll probably be a lonely older woman without children as a result.
>
> I have been working on the same novel for seven years and have revised it extensively at least ten times. I won't send it to a publisher until it is flawless, and I don't know when that will be. I'm beginning to think that my perfectionism is one of the major obstacles to having a better life and reaching my goals. And the worst part of it is that it is self-imposed.

Amelia wrote more, but the excerpt from her assignment gives a vivid picture of the shortcomings of perfectionism. *Perfectionism* can be defined as a personality trait characterized by a compulsive effort to eliminate all flaws and blemishes from one's behavior and the products of that behavior.

If perfectionism is chronic and excessive, as it appears to be in Amelia's case, then the individual is said to suffer from an *obsessive compulsive personality disorder*. This is not to be confused with an *obsessive compulsive disorder*. (For more on obsessive compulsive disorder, see Chapter 19.) The two disorders are different. In the personality disorder, there are neither blatant irrational ideas nor magic rituals. It might have been better if the personality disorder had been called *perfectionistic personality disorder*. This is accurate, and this chapter will refer informally to persons with a "perfectionistic personality."

It should be stressed that *some* perfectionistic tendencies are not enough to warrant a clinical diagnosis of obsessive compulsive personality disorder. Nevertheless, perfectionistic tendencies can be distressing, self-defeating, and carry the individual to the edge of an actual disorder.

Signs and symptoms associated with perfectionistic tendencies or an obsessive compulsive personality disorder include:

1. Emotional isolation
2. Inflexibility and rigidity
3. A tense, "uptight" attitude toward life
4. Excessive attention to minor details
5. Miserliness
6. Abandonment of personal projects
7. A desire for complete personal effectiveness and competence

The above items merit comment. When people are perfectionistic about their own behavior, they also tend to set excessively high standards for others. They may express their disappointment in sharp, hostile ways. This tends to drive others away and, in turn, drives the perfectionistic person into *emotional isolation*, a condition characterized by loneliness and a sense that there is no real human contact with others—including partners and children.

Inflexibility and rigidity express themselves in various ways. The individual may insist, for example, that everything be "just so" and become very irritated if a kitchen utensil or household tool is occasionally misplaced or not returned to its proper drawer. Magazines on a coffee table may be found in chronological order and in highly formalized arrangements. Clothing may be precisely arranged in a closet.

The perfectionistic person has a *tense, "uptight" attitude toward life*. The individual does not have such thoughts as these: "Oh, well, things go wrong sometimes." "That's the way the cookie crumbles." "What will be will be." Instead the individual thinks such thoughts as these: "Why does everything happen to me?" "It's always Murphy's Law—if something can go wrong it will." "This damn flat tire ruined my whole day." In other words, there is the demand that the day's course of events be perfect.

Perfectionism may manifest itself in *excessive attention to minor details*. A report cannot be turned in because its author is not sure that a particular comma is in the right place. A new car cannot be enjoyed because of a particular squeak. A new dress is "awful" because it does not hang quite the way one imagines that it should.

Miserliness is characterized not only by a tendency to be stingy with money. It is also characterized by a tendency to be stingy with one's affection, time, and personal thoughts about various subjects. There is too much withholding of anything of value, subjective or objective.

A demand for perfection often leads the individual to *abandon personal projects*. These personal projects can be anything from an oil painting in progress to recovering a sofa, from writing a book to completing an education. Flaws are magnified, and the whole project seems worthless.

A self-imposed *desire for complete personal effectiveness and competence* can greatly interfere with practical aspects of living. The individual is bitterly disappointed in himself or herself if a job interview seems to go a little wrong, if a B instead of an A is earned on an examination, if a manuscript is rejected by a publisher, and so forth. There is always the internal cry, "What's wrong with *me*? Why can't I do *anything* right?" Keep in mind that the trait under discussion is present in persons who by most objective standards, and in the eyes of others, are quite effective and competent.

Causes and Explanations

To some degree, perfectionism may be built on a foundation of an innate disposition. Carl Jung, one of the early pioneers in psychotherapy, asserted that some individuals are basically *thinking-sensation types*. They base their decisions and actions on precise, highly logical grounds and do not trust their emotions or intuitions. Having a thinking-sensation orientation is not, of course, in itself a pathology. However, this disposition, combined with developmental experiences that reinforce it, may produce the personality trait of perfectionism.

Classical psychoanalysis offers the possibility that punitive experiences in early childhood, particularly around the time that the individual was a toddler, create distortions of psychosexual energy, known as *libido*, such that the individual develops the traits already described in connection with the perfectionistic personality. The character type in question is identified as *anal-retentive*. (The name arises from the fact that toddlerhood is usually the age during which toilet training takes place, and some of the described traits—such as stinginess or a need for neatness—may arise in connection with learning how to gain control of bowel functions.) Research has given some, but not complete, support to the psychoanalytic formulation.

In connection with the psychoanalytic viewpoint, it is of some merit to identify a causal factor arising from Adlerian theory. (Alfred Adler, principal founder of a personality theory and system of therapy called *individual psychology*, was one of Freud's early associates.) Adler proposes that each person has an inborn *will to power*, a striving tendency to become competent and effective. If a child is made to feel incompetent and ineffective, the child may compensate by striving to "be perfect" and to "do better" in order to achieve the mastery that seems to be absent. Therefore, in broad general terms, *perfectionism* can be seen as a version of the ego defense mechanism that Adler called *compensation*, an effort to counterbalance real or imagined feelings of inferiority.

A parental style characterized by authoritarianism combined with conditional love may contribute to the formation of perfectionism during one's developmental years. The *authoritarian parent* tends to be bossy, overcontrolling, and highly judgmental. *Conditional love* is love that must be earned. Thus, the child may come to believe, "I am not really worthy of love for myself. I am worthy of love only if I earn straight A's in school, keep my room as neat as a pin, and am always polite to my elders." The person may carry the tendencies over into later years, and the adult may be vainly striving to "be loved" by "being perfect."

Perfectionism can be a way to control anxiety. A "perfect" world, controlled and ordered by the individual, is also a "safe" world. Nothing is left to chance. There is no room for error. Everything is so carefully attended to that absolutely nothing can go wrong. This is all, of course, fantasy. If things do go wrong, the unwelcome turn of events can be devastating to a perfectionistic person.

An important source of perfectionism is the judging self. (In transactional analysis, this is called the *Parent ego state*. The concept is very similar to the concept of the *superego* in psychoanalysis.) The judging self is a reservoir of unexamined values, often reflecting the standards and opinions of one's parents. This judging self scrutinizes our behavior and says, "You should have done it differently" or "You ought to try harder." Note that the theme consists of *oughts* and *shoulds*. If you have a particularly strict judging self, you will tend to be overly dissatisfied with your own performance in life.

The toddler and preschooler look at the world in *egocentric terms*. This is in accordance with the research of Jean Piaget, a pioneer in the study of cognitive development in children. Egocentric thinking implies that the world is perceived as revolving around oneself. One's own ego is the hub of the universe. This is natural in childhood. However, if it carries over into adulthood, it is obviously the basis for a very immature attitude. Adults with an egocentric viewpoint tend to exaggerate the importance of both their own behavior and their personal projects. And this fuels the flames of perfectionism.

Coping

If you believe that you are too perfectionistic or suffer from an obsessive compulsive personality disorder, you may find value in the following list of coping strategies.

• Be satisfied with a 95-percent, rather than a 100-percent, standard of accomplishment. There are self-demanding students who are disappointed if they do not earn a score of 100 percent on an examination. Even though a score of 95 percent will still earn them an A, they will say, "I botched up the test." When the author George Orwell completed, after much toil and trouble, his famous novel *1984*, he said that it was a good idea but he had made a muddle of it. The world's opinion is that it is one of the finest novels ever written. In everything you do, decide that a "score" of 95 percent is quite adequate.

• Recognize that perfection is not attainable. The philosopher Plato made a distinction between this world and the Ideal World. He suggested that this world, the domain of the senses, is a *shadow world*, an *imperfect* reflection of a transcendental, eternal realm. If there is anything at all to Plato's viewpoint, one can hardly expect to find perfection on this plane of existence. Even the annual Miss America does not have a perfect face and figure. She is the one who, in the mind of the judges, comes closest to a platonic ideal. But she herself is not that ideal, only an approximation of it.

• Challenge unexamined self-criticisms coming from your judging self. Use your thinking self to ask, "Is it really true that I ought to try harder? Or is this just an excessive demand imposed by my judging self?" "Is it true that I should have done this job differently?" Use your thinking self to ferret out arbitrary *oughts* and *shoulds*.

• Meet others halfway. Do not expect perfection from your partner, children, or other significant people in your life. Tom G. gets furious because his wife leaves a wet towel on the bathroom floor. Loretta O. screams at her seven-year-old son because he did not hang up his jacket when he came home from school. Professor K. is tense and irritated because the academic performance of his students does not match his own high standards. All of these people are imposing their own perfectionism on others. The fact of the matter is that no one is perfect, including yourself. Consequently, why should you expect it of others?

• Do not expect to be a superparent. Most people are parents or will be some day. One of the prime causes of parental suffering is expecting that as a parent you can be effective and competent in every way. If your child is sickly, unpopular, brings home poor grades, or fails in any manner at all, you blame yourself. "I could have done more." "Where did I go wrong?" You need to recognize that no parent is perfect. Bruno Bettelheim, a psychoanalyst and authority on child development, used the term "the good-enough parent" to describe a relatively adequate parent. He believed that parents who do what they can within their own limits and capacities will do a fair job of child rearing. As uninspiring as this sounds to a person with perfectionistic tendencies, it is realistic.

• Remember that you cannot please everyone, cannot be all things to all people. You cannot live up to all of the expectations of your parents, your partner, your children, your siblings, your coworkers, and so forth. No matter what, you are bound to learn or to recognize that you have disappointed someone in some way. Abraham Lincoln made a famous statement about a politician's ability to fool the people. The statement can be modified to the purposes of this chapter as follows: "You can please some of the people you know all of the time, and all of the people you know some of the time, but you cannot please all of the people you know all of the time."

• Decenter. Remove your ego from the center of the universe. Stop thinking that everything revolves around you, that things *must* go your way. Here is a psychological exercise: Imagine yourself floating hundreds of feet in the air in the basket of a hot-air balloon. Now look down and "see" yourself in your house or at work as if you were looking from a great distance at someone else. Perceive that you are just one out of many. Shrink your problems and your life down to their proper size. Let go of the excessive intensity that comes with egocentrism.

Professional Help

If you find that you cannot cope adequately with your perfectionistic tendencies, or if you suffer from an obsessive compulsive personality disorder, there are a number of ways in which the professions of psychiatry and clinical psychology can help you.

Taking a psychodynamic approach, a therapist will help you explore events in early childhood that may have contributed to perfectionism and the traits that go with it, such as miserliness and the withholding of affection. You may discover that some of your adult tendencies are traceable to punitive or abusive experiences when you were a toddler or preschooler. Discharging emotions associated with these experiences by crying and expressing rage can often be therapeutic. (This process is called an *abreaction* in classical psychoanalysis.) Free association and hypnotherapy are techniques commonly employed in therapy to encourage a temporary regression of the ego to an earlier level of development.

Continuing with a psychodynamic approach, a therapist can focus on the possibility that in your developmental years you had to earn love by being a "little angel." You may feel today that you are not deserving of love unless you are perfect yourself and meet all of someone else's expectations. Introducing a cognitive modality, your therapist will make it clear to you that no one is loved only because he or she is perfect. People have flaws, yet they are loved *in spite of* the flaws if love is real. It is important to recognize that in perfectionistic persons the dropping of the role of Perfect Person may automatically induce anxiety because of the fear of loss of love.

Staying with a cognitive modality, a therapist will help you to see how certain *cognitive distortions*, illogical ways of thinking, can contribute to perfectionism. An example of such a distortion, already given, is egocentrism. Another often identified cognitive distortion is *magnification*. This is a tendency to enlarge in personal perception events that are small in the perception of others. A minor flaw in a construction project makes it "worthless." A grade of B on an examination means, "I'll never become a nurse." A lie told by a child means, "I'm an ineffective parent." These kinds of self-oriented statements are evaluated and revealed to be, from a rational level, magnifications. A cognitive approach in therapy teaches you how to introduce an element of reason into your evaluations.

Taking an Adlerian approach, a therapist will assist you to see how the ego defense mechanism of compensation contributes to perfectionism. As indicated earlier, Alfred Adler was one of the Freud's early associates. An Adlerian approach is psychodynamic in nature. However, in therapy, it tends to focus more on the present and today's choices than does classical psychoanalysis. Adler postulated that some adults suffer from an *inferiority complex*, meaning they feel extremely ineffective or inadequate to cope with certain of life's challenges (e.g., succeeding as a student, making friends, functioning as a parent, or pleasing a sex partner).

One way to compensate for inferiority feelings is to repress them to an unconscious level. At the conscious level, one becomes "perfect." Such persons may act superior to others, but their "superiority complex" is really a pose. It is a compensation for an inferiority complex. Applying an Adlerian outlook, the patient and therapist can work together and analyze the way in which the defense mechanism of compensation works. The denied ideas and feelings become available to the rational mind. At this level, the conscious one, the ideas and feelings can be dealt with in a practical and reality-oriented manner.

Taking a behavioral approach, a therapist can help perfectionistic persons to learn assertiveness skills. Often, such individuals are too aggressive in their personal relations. Assertiveness training is not just for passive individuals who allow themselves to be used and abused. It is of equal value for hostile, abusive persons. These traits, often associated with perfectionism, can be significantly modified with assertiveness training.

There is little or no place for drug therapy in the treatment of obsessive compulsive personality disorder. (This is not the case in the treatment of obsessive compulsive disorder; see Chapter 19.) It is true that the disorder in question may be accompanied by either anxiety or depression, as is the case with most behavioral disorders. If a drug is prescribed, it is prescribed for these symptoms as such, not for perfectionism itself. Perfectionism is a personality trait and is best dealt with by the kinds of modalities in psychotherapy already identified.

Key Points to Remember

• *Perfectionism* is a personality trait characterized by a compulsive effort to eliminate all flaws and blemishes from one's behavior and the products of that behavior.

• If perfectionism is chronic and excessive, then the individual is said to suffer from an *obsessive compulsive personality disorder*.

• Some of the signs and symptoms associated with perfectionistic tendencies or an obsessive compulsive personality disorder include emotional isolation, a tense, "uptight" attitude toward life, and a desire for complete personal effectiveness and competence.

• *Thinking-sensation types* may be more prone than others to develop the personality trait of perfectionism.

• According to classical psychoanalysis, punitive experiences in early childhood, particularly around the time that the individual was a toddler, are significant causal factors in the formation of a perfectionistic personality.

• A parental style characterized by authoritarianism combined with conditional love may contribute to the formation of perfectionism during one's developmental years.

• Be satisfied with a 95-percent, rather than a 100-percent, standard of accomplishment.

• Challenge unexamined self-criticisms coming from your judging self.

• Do not expect perfection from others.

- Remember that you cannot please everyone.

- Decenter. Stop thinking that everything revolves around you, that things *must* go your way.

- Taking a psychodynamic approach, a therapist will help you to explore events in early childhood that may have contributed to perfectionism and to explore the traits that go with it, such as miserliness and the withholding of affection.

- Taking a cognitive approach, a therapist will help you to see how certain *cognitive distortions*, illogical ways of thinking, can contribute to perfectionism.

- Taking a behavioral approach, a therapist can help perfectionistic persons to learn assertiveness skills.

Chapter 21

Physical Complaints: Aches, Pains, and Fatigue

The nineteenth century biologist Charles Darwin, author of *The Origin of Species*, suffered from multiple physical complaints for most of his adult years. A relatively wealthy man, the entire household revolved around his varying states of health. Appointments were made to accommodate his "frail condition." He often complained of numb fingertips, digestive problems, and insomnia. Many evenings, he vomited shortly after dinner. He saw himself as a semi-invalid. In his later years, many of his symptoms subsided. He lived to the age of 73, and there appears to have been no organic basis for his various complaints.

There are two general sources for physical complaints: (1) the organic, or biological, domain and (2) the psychological, or behavioral, domain. Physical complaints arising from the psychological domain are presumed to be due to mental and emotional conflicts or maladaptive habits and are said to be *psychogenic*. Another term applied to such complaints is *functional*. Complaints of this variety are the subject of this chapter.

Signs and symptoms associated with physical complaints of a functional nature include the following:

1. The conviction that one is frail and suffers from poor overall health
2. Stomach and digestive disturbances
3. Various aches and pains
4. Disturbances in the sense of touch
5. Irregular heartbeat
6. Irrational worry about one's health
7. Imaginary disorders

8. Fatigue
9. Sexual difficulties

The above items merit comment. *The conviction that one is frail and suffers from poor overall health* is a concept, an idea in the mind, in the case of psychogenic complaints. There will be more about this particular point later in the chapter. *Stomach and digestive disturbances* include the conviction that one has too much gas, that flatulence cannot be controlled, that one is constipated, frequent nausea, and so forth. *Various aches and pains* in the muscles and joints are often associated with the notion that one has a muscle-wasting disease or rheumatoid arthritis. It is important to stress here that the aches and pains are real to the sufferer. They are actually felt and cause perceived discomfort.

Examples of *disturbances in the sense of touch* include tingling, numbness, or heat in the fingers or toes. The clinical name for this condition is *paresthesia*. You will recall that Darwin suffered from this symptom. *Irregular heartbeat* includes palpitations and tachycardia (i.e., rapid heartbeat). Such symptoms can and do occur in the absence of underlying heart disease.

It is common in persons who suffer from psychogenic complaints to develop excessive worry about their health. This is known as *hypochondria*. The person who suffers from hypochondria takes a small sign or symptom and magnifies it. A headache suggests the possibility of brain cancer. Blurred vision foreshadows blindness. Victims of hypochondriasis recognize that their fears are irrational, but they feel helpless to control them.

Imaginary disorders often show up as false neurological impairments. These frequently involve problems in vision, hearing, the sense of touch, and movement (e.g., the ability to walk). Complete blindness, deafness, or paralysis is not at all unusual. The traditional name for this condition is *hysteria*. It is considered outdated today because the term was originally applied to women only. (*Hyster* is the Greek word for *uterus*, and the original idea was that hysteria involved some sort of pathology of the uterus.) The contemporary name for the condition described in this paragraph is *conversion disorder*, the idea here being that anxiety has been converted into a bodily symptom.

Fatigue is one of the most common symptoms associated with psychogenic physical complaints. The individual says, "I have no energy— no get up and go. I drag myself through the day. I seem to always be exhausted. It's all I can do to meet my minimum responsibilities."

Sexual difficulties include problems such as inability to become excited, inability to reach an orgasm even if excited, inability in males to maintain an erection adequate for intercourse, and painful intercourse. (For more on sexual difficulties, see Chapter 25.)

A few comments concerning terminology are appropriate here. The constellation of signs and symptoms that have been described are traditionally identified with the name *neurasthenia*. This term, meaning "weak nerves," was introduced by George Miller Beard, an American psychiatrist, about 130 years ago. Contemporary terms suggested by the American Psychiatric Association to cover physical complaints without organic basis include *dysthymia* (depressive neurosis) and *somatization disorder*. It is clear today that the concern is *not* weak nerves at all. Therefore, the term *neurasthenia* is considered to be obsolete. It has no formal diagnostic status in American psychiatry. (However, it is still used in the *International Classification of Diseases* published by the World Health Organization.)

It is, of course, still possible to speak of a *neurasthenic syndrome* in a loose, informal way, recognizing that there is a certain lack of precision. Consequently, for the sake of both convenience and shorthand communication, this syndrome may be mentioned from time to time in this chapter. In brief, a neurasthenic syndrome refers to the constellation of signs and symptoms listed earlier. This includes the implication that the signs and symptoms are without organic basis.

A neurasthenic syndrome is *not* due to an organic factor, such as a viral infection or a biochemical imbalance. And there is no *neuropathy*, pathology of the nerves. If these statements are correct, to what is a neurasthenic syndrome due?

Causes and Explanations

As already indicated, the causal factors in a neurasthenic syndrome, by definition, are *not* organic. There is no infection, or neuropathy, or disease at a biological level. However, before proceeding, it *is* important to note that, of course, physical complaints may suggest a medical problem. The assumption in this section is that this has been realistically ruled out by competent medical opinions.

According to psychoanalytic theory, psychogenic physical complaints may arise from an unmet need for nurturing. It is possible that in early childhood the patient was neglected or emotionally abandoned by his or her parents. If needs for love and recognition were unmet during the developmental years, the individual may seek to have these needs met, particularly during times of excessive stress, by playing the role of Sick Person. It is important to understand that the roots of such a role are unconscious. The individual has not consciously decided to play the sick role. Nor is he or she malingering. The physical complaints are real to the patient.

A reference was made above to times of excessive stress. The reference is to acute stress associated with significant life changes. Research conducted by the psychiatrists T. H. Holmes and R. H. Rahe has ranked these changes and assigned weighted values to them. These values are referred to as *Life Change Units* (LCUs) in the literature of behavioral science. If a person accumulates too many LCUs in a defined time span, he or she is somewhat more likely than others to develop an actual physical illness. The important point here is that life changes can also trigger a latent neurasthenic syndrome. A person who seems for a time otherwise well may display symptoms upon the death of a spouse; a promotion to a position with new, demanding responsibilities; a move to a different part of the country; loss of an important friendship; and so forth. Charles Darwin's symptoms flared up when he married.

A causal factor in neurasthenic symptoms is underlying depression. A depressed person lacks interest in life. Formerly valued goals seem unimportant. There is a lack of energy and a pervasive apathy. The conscious mind reasons that this lack of energy is due to an organic sickness. "Maybe I have iron-poor blood." "Maybe I have a malabsorption factor and do not get full advantage from the vitamins and minerals in my food." "Maybe I have a sluggish thyroid gland." "Maybe I'm suffering from the residual effects of mononucleosis."

In regard to the last statement quoted above, the reference is to the possibility that the Epstein-Barr virus, the virus that causes infectious mononucleosis, has long-term residual effects on health. This has been suggested to be one cause of *chronic fatigue syndrome*. The clinical picture is confusing because perhaps 80 to 90 percent of adults test positive to antibodies for the Epstein-Barr virus. This means that they were exposed at one time to the virus and that they are presumably immune to its effects. A positive test result is sometimes taken as evidence that the virus is at work in a low-grade way. Other organic factors ranging from those already named (i.e., iron-poor blood, and so on) to others such as hypoglycemia (i.e., low blood sugar) have been suspected to be important in chronic fatigue syndrome.

The question arises: Are chronic fatigue syndrome and neurasthenic syndrome two names for the same thing? The answer is *probably not*. The convention is to use the first term when the suspected causal factors are organic. Thus, chronic fatigue syndrome is seen as primarily a *medical* problem and may include physical signs and symptoms such as swollen lymph glands. The second term is reserved for cases in which the suspected causal factors are *psychological* in nature. Thus, the neurasthenic syndrome is seen primarily as a problem in the domain of psychiatry or clinical psychology. It is, of course, often difficult to distinguish the two syndromes in actual work with patients. One syndrome can easily mask itself as the other.

A genetic tendency may be a predisposing factor in neurasthenic distress. Case histories and research on temperament combine to suggest that some toddlers and preschoolers are more "sensitive" than others. These children are said to be *vulnerable*, and traumatic early experiences, including patterns of neglect and lack of affection, may make a greater impression on them than on children who are said to be *invulnerable*, who keep their mental health over a wider spectrum of parental mistreatment.

One way to look at chronic complaining about aches and pains when there is no organic pathology is to identify the behavior as a maladaptive habit. Learning theory suggests that such behavior is maintained by reinforcers that are readily obtained by playing the role of Sick Person. (It is a convention to capitalize a social role played for ulterior purposes.) The frail person has a certain amount of control over the behavior of others. This person, for example, may refuse to entertain, go on a trip, or participate in an outing because of fatigue, a headache, an upset stomach, or a similar complaint. The need for power, an important need in everyone, can be readily exerted in this manner. When the need for power is neurotic, as it is when it arises from low self-esteem or the conviction that one is unloved, then the maladaptive complaining habit can be a manipulative tool.

Note also that playing the sick role can be a way to express aggression, to move against another person in a "hidden" way. This is known as *passive-aggression*. Another possibility is that the sick role may allow the individual to escape from responsibilities.

Finally, it is important to note that a neurasthenic pattern is aggravated by chronic underlying anxiety. This is why heart disturbances, such as palpitations and tachycardia (i.e., rapid heart beat), may be present in the absence of underlying heart disease. It is a commonplace observation that anxiety can induce these symptoms. (For more about anxiety, see Chapter 5.)

Coping

If you believe that you suffer from physical complaints of psychological origin or have neurasthenic tendencies, you may find value in the following list of coping strategies.

• Believe your physicians. Note that I have used the plural form *physicians*, not *physician*. Many people with hypochondriacal or neurasthenic tendencies go from doctor to doctor hoping to find one who will agree that their problem has an organic basis. You should seek a second, and even a third, opinion before you are satisfied with a diagnosis. But there is a logical limit.

• Do whatever you can to manage stress. Beard, who you recall first introduced the term *neurasthenia*, believed that the condition was induced by overwork. Today, this appears to be an oversimplification. It is probable that an underlying neurotic process is at work. Nonetheless, there is some value to Beard's formulation. Overwork, life changes, difficult interpersonal relations, and so forth, can all act as triggers that precipitate a rash of complaints. Sources of stress, if they are not eliminated, can also aggravate the distress associated with complaints. Try to become an expert at "stress management." Learn effective ways to control, or at least to diminish, the impact of stress-inducing events in your personal world.

• Challenge the idea that you are frail and sickly. George Kelly, a pioneer figure in personality theory and psychotherapy, introduced the concept of a personal construct. A *personal construct* is an idea that one holds about oneself. It may or may not reflect objective reality. However, it is treated *as if* it is real by the individual holding it. Consequently, it determines behavior and forms the basis of a self-fulfilling prophecy. Thus, if you have ideas such as, "I am frail" or "I am sickly," you will certainly act like a frail and sickly person. And by your own behavior, you will create the very state of affairs you wish to avoid.

• Refuse to play the role of Sick Person. It is important to recognize that this role is a kind of *choice* or *decision* that you make and that you have other options. The decision to play the sick role is made by your emotional self. It is seeking reinforcers such as attention, tokens of love, power over others, and so forth. You need to find more effective ways to meet your emotional needs. Use your thinking self to make a rational decision to give up the short-term satisfactions of the sick role and to seek the long-term satisfactions of mature behavior.

• Reflect on your early childhood. Keep a journal with dated entries and try to explore the roots of any feelings you have of being unloved and underappreciated. Try to ask and answer questions such as this one: "Did I feel emotionally abandoned as a child?" Developing insight into the origins of today's emotional needs can give a certain amount of conscious control over these needs. It is one way to loosen the grip of a neurotic process.

• Develop a stoical attitude toward minor aches and pains. *Stoicism*, an ancient philosophical viewpoint, teaches that it is possible, within rational limits, to develop an attitude of cool, calm indifference toward suffering. Such an attitude has at least two advantages. First, you will extract less expressions of pity from others, and this will help to extinguish complaining as a maladaptive habit. Second, you may find it possible to reduce the amount of pain medication you take. The Greek dramatist Aeschylus expressed almost 2,500 years ago this thought in his play *Agamemnon*: "Who, except the gods, can live time through forever without any pain?"

• Seek effective ways to deal with anxiety and depression. Both of these emotional states, if chronic, magnify the symptoms common in a neurasthenic syndrome. (For more about anxiety and depression, see Chapters 5 and 8, respectively.)

Professional Help

If you find that you cannot cope adequately with physical complaints of psychological origin, there are a number of ways in which the professions of psychiatry and clinical psychology can help you.

Before proceeding, it should be established that you will *not* receive a formal diagnosis of neurasthenia. As earlier indicated, this is a traditional term, but it is considered to be too all-inclusive to be used for a formal diagnosis. Instead, if a formal diagnosis is required for insurance or statistical purposes, it is likely to be either somatization disorder or dysthymia (depressive neurosis). Both of these diagnoses include psychogenic complaints of either pain, fatigue, or other bodily expressions.

For a number of years, the principal modalities used to treat a neurasthenic syndrome were either psychoanalysis or therapy arising from psychoanalytic assumptions (i.e., psychodynamic psychotherapy). The psychodynamic approach still tends to be a dominant one in treating physical complaints that do not have a well-defined organic basis.

Taking a psychodynamic approach, a therapist will use techniques such as free association or hypnotherapy to help you explore childhood events. You are likely to discover that the roots of your distress can be found in lingering feelings of neglect or abandonment associated with your developmental years. The actual events that produced the feelings may have been traumatic in an objective sense, or they might have been slight to a neutral observer, but of great magnitude to you. Remember that the person prone to a neurasthenic syndrome was probably a sensitive, vulnerable child. Becoming consciously acquainted with long-repressed feelings of neglect and abandonment allows them to enter the domain of voluntary control.

In the case of "hysteria," or conversion disorder, a technique known as the *amobarbital (Amytal) interview*, based on psychodynamic principles, can be helpful. (See the opening pages of this chapter for a discussion of *conversion disorder*.) Acting very much like a deep trance in hypnotherapy, the injection of the drug amobarbital allows both the psychiatrist and the patient access to repressed memories associated with both old and recent emotional wounds. An *abreaction*, or emotional release, can be obtained, and severe symptoms can rapidly diminish in intensity. Although useful in bringing about temporary relief from the worst symptoms of a conversion disorder, it is important to realize that the amobarbital interview and its associated abreaction is not a cure. Follow-up therapy is required in order to bring about permanent improvement.

Taking a behavioral approach, a therapist can help a person with nonorganic physical complaints to define the way in which chronic complaining is an instrumental behavior that brings into the troubled person's world such immediate gratifications as attention, recognition, and sympathy—the tokens of love. Behavior therapy can be useful in mapping out more effective and satisfying strategies than chronic complaining to obtain these important social reinforcers. A *functional analysis*, a technique often used in behavior therapy, can break down a general pattern of behavior into a set of specific habits. Cues that trigger maladaptive habits and their specific psychological payoffs can be identified. Then the specific habits can be modified one by one.

As earlier indicated, a personal construct such as "I am sickly" may aggravate a neurasthenic syndrome. Taking a cognitive approach, a therapist can help you to examine your personal constructs in the light of logic. Familiar with the array of cognitive distortions that lead to many emotional disturbances, the therapist can provide you with the rational tools you need to reframe your personal constructs.

Drug therapy may play an adjunct role in the treatment of a neurasthenic syndrome. Over-the-counter as well as prescription pain medications may be used as temporary palliatives to help the troubled person through a crisis. However, the basic goal should be to give up the pain medication or to greatly reduce its use. In treatment, this can best be accomplished by the psychotherapeutic modalities already outlined. Because both anxiety and depression are associated with nonorganic physical complaints, either an antianxiety agent or an antidepressant may be prescribed by a psychiatrist as a component of a treatment program.

Key Points to Remember

• There are two general sources for physical complaints: (1) the organic, or biological, domain and (2) the psychological, or behavioral, domain.

• Signs and symptoms associated with physical complaints of a functional, or nonorganic, nature include the conviction that one is frail and suffers from poor overall health, stomach and digestive disturbances, irregular heartbeat, and irrational worry about one's health.

• The term *neurasthenia* is a traditional one and is considered obsolete for formal diagnostic purposes. Contemporary terms include *dysthymia* (depressive neurosis) and *somatization disorder*.

- According to psychoanalytic theory, psychogenic physical complaints may arise from an unmet need for nurturing.

- The excessive stress associated with significant life changes may trigger a latent neurasthenic syndrome.

- The convention is for the terms *chronic fatigue syndrome* and *neurasthenic syndrome* to name different disorders.

- Chronic complaining about aches and pains in the absence of organic pathology may be identified as a maladaptive habit.

- Do whatever you can to effectively manage stress.

- Challenge the idea that you are frail and sickly.

- Refuse to play the role of Sick Person.

- Develop a stoical attitude toward minor aches and pains.

- The psychodynamic approach still tends to be a dominant one in treating physical complaints that do not have a well-defined organic basis.

- The *amobarbital (Amytal) interview* can be useful in the treatment of cases of "hysteria," or conversion disorder.

- Behavior therapy can be useful in mapping out more effective and satisfying strategies than chronic complaining to obtain important social reinforcers such as attention, recognition, and sympathy—the tokens of love.

- Taking a cognitive approach, a therapist can help you examine a personal construct such as "I am sickly" in the light of logic.

Chapter 22

Procrastination: The Tomorrow Syndrome

In the musical play *Annie*, the young heroine sings that she loves tomorrow because "it's only a day away." To Annie, tomorrow is a metaphor for her future—and she hopes that it will be brighter and better than today's dismal circumstances. In this sense, tomorrow is a kind of friend to troubled persons and those in adverse circumstances. However, tomorrow becomes a kind of enemy—perhaps disguised as a friend—to those who procrastinate on a regular and frequent basis. Dreams vanish. Goals are not attained. Tasks and projects are finished badly or not completed on schedule. As Edward Young, an English poet and playwright of the eighteenth century, said, "Procrastination is the thief of time."

Procrastination is defined as postponing the actions required to complete a task, attain a goal, or rise to the challenge of an opportunity. The required actions may be postponed to a time later than the present or to a time that never arrives. Often, important tasks go completely undone. At other times, opportunity knocks and it goes begging.

Everyone procrastinates occasionally. It has been said that to err is human. It could be just as well said that to *procrastinate* is human. However, the kind of procrastination under discussion is not of the infrequent, occasional kind. No, the procrastination of present concern is a disturbing personality trait that interferes with individual satisfaction and undermines the quality of human relationships. This kind of procrastination can be referred to as *chronic procrastination,* or "the tomorrow syndrome."

Frequently associated with chronic procrastination are the following signs and symptoms:

1. Working rapidly at the "last minute"
2. Not enjoying recreational activities
3. Time-wasting behavior
4. Feeling overwhelmed by responsibilities

5. Inability to reach important goals in life
6. Daydreaming and wishing instead of doing
7. Talking without acting

The above items merit comment. Persons who suffer from chronic procrastination frequently find themselves *working rapidly at the "last minute."* Ernest A., for example, is a student in a college history class. He has had three months to do the research for and accomplish the writing of an important term paper. He has waited to start until three days before the due date. Now he is in a panic and finds himself spending long hours in the library and working at his word processor until 4 A.M.

When one is postponing an important task, it becomes very difficult to *enjoy recreational activities.* One is socializing with friends or watching a film, and there is the nagging thought, "I should be working." A dark cloud of guilt hangs over the person's head and dampens any pleasure he or she might be extracting from the distractions of the moment.

Time-wasting behavior is one of the ploys used by the person who is procrastinating. Often, the behavior is relevant to the task, but only in an indirect way. The image of the would-be author comes to mind. Willa E. is such a person. She has set aside a two-hour time block to work on a story. She sharpens pencils, arranges papers, dusts her desk, rereads a favorite article on the craft of storytelling, and so forth. She does some actual writing in the last 20 minutes available.

It is common for persons suffering from the tomorrow syndrome to feel *overwhelmed by responsibilities.* They have put off so many things that now there are bills to pay, a lawn to mow, a present to buy for a relative's birthday, telephone calls to make, and a car to get repaired. As one individual put it, "I feel as if I'm in a vise. Everything is closing in. I have the sensation that I'm being crushed by all sorts of things I do not want to do— and now I have to do them all at once."

One of the worst aspects of serious procrastination is the *inability to reach important goals in life.* By not getting things done in a reasonably timely manner, or not done at all, precious opportunities may be lost. Hopes for higher degrees and the possibility of a profession may go begging because of procrastination as a student. A business that might have been a success is never started. A relationship with an attractive person does not materialize because a first step is not taken, or taken too late.

Daydreaming and wishing instead of doing may seem harmless enough. After all, it is often said that great accomplishments are often preceded by fantasies. And a strong wish provides the motive power that impels action. All true. Nonetheless, the victim of chronic procrastination never gets beyond these opening mental states. He or she remains stuck, does nothing, and stays an idle dreamer with a head full of unrealized plans.

The person who displays the trait of chronic procrastination often is very good at *talking without acting*. This is obviously closely related to day-dreaming and wishing instead of doing. However, in talking, there is the difference that one is *sharing* ideas with others. Frequently, a substantial amount of attention and recognition—important social reinforcers—can be obtained from this kind of behavior. But it is all a kind of psychological froth.

Causes and Explanations

In terms of early childhood experiences, clinical practice and case histories suggest that chronic procrastination is related to an authoritarian parental style. Parents who are overcontrolling and too bossy fail to inspire a sense of cooperation in their children. A pattern of resistance to parental demands often forms. This is one way that a very young child can express a sense of autonomy—a declaration that says in effect, "I am the owner of my life, not you." Procrastination, in this case a kind of passive-aggressive behavior, is one way among others that some degree of autonomy can be both preserved and expressed. True, it is in a negative form. But the need for self-direction is so important that at all ages that people will frequently make the choice of a negative expression if that seems to be the only option.

Although chronic procrastination is not in and of itself a behavioral disorder, it is not a surprise to find that it is one of the signs of a *passive-aggressive personality disorder* in some adults. To some extent, this may be a carryover from childhood. Of course, a pattern of procrastination is not enough in itself to make a diagnosis of the identified personality disorder. Other traits must be present such as sulkiness, irritability, working slowly, "forgetting" obligations, disliking the suggestions of others, and making a mockery of authority figures.

One of the principal causal factors underlying frequent procrastination is a need to reduce anxiety. Often the task or project at hand is threatening to one's self-concept. If an individual feels inadequate to meet a challenge, there is a great potential threat to self-esteem. The path of least resistance is to avoid the potentially damaging situation. This is particularly true of persons with creative talent. They frequently avoid writing poems or stories, composing music, or going to auditions and interviews. The self-image is more easily maintained with daydreams of success than by objective failure experiences.

Related to the above is a causal factor that is the mirror opposite of the fear of failure. It is the *fear of success*, and it too plays a role in chronic procrastination. Success can be as threatening as failure. If the manuscript for a novel sells to a publisher, the sale may in turn require trips, interviews, a disruption of relationships, and so forth. If a person is agoraphobic or overly self-conscious, the "success" opens a Pandora's box of anxiety-arousing possibilities. This is perhaps one reason why Emily Dickinson kept most of her poems locked in drawers for many years. She feared recognition and the impossible demands on her introverted personality that would go with it.

According to Abraham Maslow, a principal founder of humanistic psychology, each person has an inborn need for *self-actualization*, a desire to make the most of talents and potentialities. There is probably a great deal of truth to this idea. But what is often missed is that many persons *resist* their own need for self-actualization. The self-actualization process involves growth and change, and this can often "upset the apple cart" of long-standing adjustments. Again, this can be very threatening.

A common practice among those who procrastinate excessively is to set an overly high level of aspiration. Alfred G. entered a community college at the age of 23. He had earned a C average in high school. He was married, had two children, and worked 25 hours a week as a shipping clerk for a stationery company. A counselor asked him what he wanted to become in terms of a trade or profession. He replied, "A brain surgeon." He was not joking. Against all advice, he signed up for a full load of classes including difficult courses in anatomy and chemistry. When he dropped out of college with poor grades after one semester, his comment was, "Well, at least I shot for the moon. But I've got too many responsibilities, and I'm too old to make it now." Alfred had a *high need to avoid failure*, and that is why he set his level of aspiration so high. This seems odd. A high need to avoid failure? Here's the logic: by setting an unrealistic level of aspiration he guaranteed failure in *objective terms*. But he assured the avoidance of failure in *subjective terms*. He could easily rationalize his objective failure and maintain his self-esteem. He, in his own eyes, was a man who wanted to be a brain surgeon, who "shot for the moon," but who could not accomplish these lofty goals because of his responsibilities and his age. As a consequence, he procrastinates—postpones indefinitely—any realistic plans to better his life because these imply the risk of real failure.

Finally, it may be asserted that no complex or profound explanations need be proposed for procrastination. Common sense says that some tasks are unpleasant—that they are burdens to be avoided. True. It has already been noted that to procrastinate is human. However, the common-sense explanation at best explains only occasional, or situational, procrastination.

For chronic procrastination, one needs to look at the causes and explanations already discussed.

Coping

If you suffer from chronic procrastination, you may find value in the following list of coping strategies.

• Take a task-oriented, not a time-oriented, approach. Say to yourself, "I will fix three sprinklers and mow the lawn this morning," not "I'll work in the yard from 8:00 A.M. until 12:00 P.M." Say to yourself, "I will wash a batch of white clothes and vacuum the living room and dining room," not "I'll do housework for two hours." The aspiring author should think, "I'll write two pages per day," not "I'll write an hour per day." The student is advised to think, "I'll study 10 pages in the textbook," not "I'll study for an hour." When one frames a task in terms of time, one feels boxed in, becomes a clock watcher, making the *pace* of the work unimportant. When one frames a task in terms of the task itself, he or she feels in control. The pace of the work determines when it will be finished and the worker will be "free." Consequently, the work is done efficiently and effectively without the worker feeling trapped.

• Use Premack's principle. *Premack's principle*, stated in formal terms, may be expressed as follows: if a high-probability action is made contingent on a low-probability action, the high-probability action will act as a reinforcer on the low-probability one. (The principle was first clearly defined and expressed by the research psychologist David Premack. And it was based on experimental work with both animals and human beings.) In informal terms, Premack's principle can be stated in advice form: Put unpleasant tasks or "work" before pleasant tasks or "play." When behavior modification is applied to children, it is usually a good idea to ask them to study before they watch television, clean a room before they call a friend, and do a chore before they go outside to play. Similarly, wash clothes before you watch television, study before you visit with a friend, write (if you are an author) before reading a novel. In Premack's terms, the probability of performing the difficult, challenging behavior will go up. And the probability of performing the less important, possibly more pleasant, behavior will go down.

• Avoid talking too much before acting. This behavior, or sign associated with chronic procrastination, often robs one of psychological energy. This advice is of particular value to persons with creative aspirations. If you want to invent something, write a story or a book, or design new patterns for sweaters, then *invent*, *write*, or *design*. Do not drain off energy by telling your friends and relatives at great length about all of your ideas. By the time you are finished telling your ideas to everybody you know, odds are that you will not feel like doing anything about your ideas.

   • Set subgoals. Do not try to reach your highest goal in one great leap. If, for example, you aspire to eventually earn a Ph.D. in some subject, earn an A.A. degree from a community college first. This normally takes two years of class work and will bring you closure and satisfaction. Then raise your sights to a B.A. Then work toward an M.A. Finally, work toward the Ph.D. Your subgoals are within your immediate reach. Achieving them is realistic. Even if it takes eight or ten years to reach your ultimate goal, there will be interim satisfactions. Think of your progress as a series of manageable steps. This general line of logic goes for reaching any important long-range goal.

   • Action overcomes anxiety. Suppose you are facing a task that induces anxiety—a threat to your self-esteem. Examples include preparing for a talk, asking someone attractive for a date, working on a term paper, applying for a job, and so forth. Common sense says that you must first conquer the anxiety, and then you can act. Common sense may be wrong here. A well-regarded theory of emotions in traditional psychology is the *James-Lange theory*, which says that it is quite reasonable to assert that behavior induces and modifies emotion. If, for example, you try to run from a crowded theatre when someone yells, "Fire," you may experience panic. The act of running itself induces fear and increased arousal. It makes the heart beat faster and increases the flow of hormones from the adrenal glands. Conversely, if you force yourself to walk at a moderate pace, you will dampen arousal and control anxiety. By the same logic, if you will *start working at a task before you feel like it*, you will find that the very act of working will reduce anxiety and build self-confidence.

   • Sometimes act first and think later. The behavioral psychologist B. F. Skinner wrote an article for would-be authors called, "On Finding Out What You Have to Say." The key point of the article was that you learn what you think about a subject by the act of writing itself. You cannot think everything through and know what you have to say before you write. After you write, you can modify and revise. The same advice can be applied in many areas of living. You can find out what you are good at—what you can do effectively, what your talents are—simply by *doing*. You learn "on the job," and the outcomes of behavior turn into a process of self-discovery. Much of the art of living is the willingness to engage in the process of trial and error as opposed to constantly avoiding this process. Chronic procrastination involves preparing and preparing and preparing—getting ready. It may seem like odd advice, but often it really is a good idea to start doing before you are ready.

• Remember Mr. Meant-To. He was the subject of a short poem by an anonymous author:

> Mr. Meant-To has a comrade,
>   And his name is Didn't-Do.
> Have you ever chanced to meet them?
>   Did they ever call on you?
>
> These two fellows live together
>   In the house of Never-Win,
> And I'm told that it is haunted
>   By the ghost of Might-Have-Been.

Memorize the poem or carry a copy of it with you. When you want to resist the temptation to procrastinate, mentally recite or read the poem. Then ask yourself, "Do I want to be like Mr. Meant-To? Do I want to live in the house of Never-Win?"

Professional Help

If you suffer from chronic procrastination, there are several ways in which the professions of psychiatry and clinical psychology can help you.

Taking a psychodynamic approach, your therapist can help you explore and understand the deeper motives—such as anxiety and hostility—that create resistance to taking effective action in the present. Bringing these motives out of the unconscious realm into the conscious one can help you gain greater voluntary control over your own behavior.

Still applying a psychodynamic approach, a therapist will help you to understand more clearly how you use rationalization as a defense mechanism. When you *rationalize*, you give yourself good-sounding (i.e., "rational") reasons for your own behavior. If you think about it, the whole idea that "I can always do it tomorrow" is one big rationalization. A therapist will help you see that the only person you are kidding is yourself.

Taking a behavioral approach, a therapist can help you to find ways to apply Premack's principle. Together, you can make a functional analysis of your behavior, breaking down the trait of procrastination into specific behavioral units. Then these units can be dealt with one by one. Sam B., for example, hated to pay bills. He had the money but resisted sitting at a desk and writing out checks. He enjoyed working crossword puzzles. He and the therapist made a behavioral contract as follows: Sam could earn the right to work on a crossword puzzle if he first paid five bills. Keep in mind that not paying bills is just one example of Sam's procrastination tendencies. After changing his bill-paying habit, he was able to modify other habits of procrastination.

Taking a cognitive approach, a therapist can help you discover how certain distortions can contribute to the tomorrow syndrome. One such distortion is *self-labeling*. You may say to yourself that you are a procrastinator. This is of dubious value. It is as if your entire being is procrastination, which is, of course, not true. It also implies that you always procrastinate in all situations, which again is not true. A label tends to create a helpless feeling. You will note that throughout this chapter I have spoken of chronic procrastination as a personality trait, not of *the* procrastinator. A therapist will help you avoid the label and instead look at the trait. In turn, this will help you discover effective ways to improve your actual behavior.

Cognitive therapy tends to focus somewhat more on the present and the future than it does the past. Consequently, a cognitive approach can be of particular value in therapy when procrastination is a problem because it will help you evaluate realistically where you are going in life and why you are going there. You will be encouraged to make those choices that lead to the best long-run personal consequences.

Finally, taking an interpersonal approach, a therapist will help you assess the possibility that you are using procrastination as a passive way to express aggression toward a significant-other person in your life. If you are using procrastination in this way, a therapist may help you acquire some *assertiveness skills*, communication techniques that allow you to express your autonomy in constructive ways. Also, a therapist may approach an interpersonal problem by the application of either couple therapy or family therapy.

Key Points to Remember

• *Procrastination* is defined as postponing the actions required to complete a task, attain a goal, or rise to the challenge of an opportunity.

• *Chronic procrastination*, or "the tomorrow syndrome," is a disturbing personality trait that interferes with individual satisfaction and undermines the quality of human relationships.

• Signs and symptoms frequently associated with chronic procrastination include working rapidly at the "last minute," time-wasting behavior, inability to reach important goals in life, and daydreaming and wishing instead of doing.

• Parents who are overcontrolling and too bossy fail to inspire a sense of cooperation in their children. Procrastination in childhood or adolescence can be a way to express a sense of autonomy.

• One of the principal causal factors underlying frequent procrastination is a need to reduce anxiety.

• The *fear of success* often plays a role in chronic procrastination.

• Take a task-oriented, not a time-oriented, approach to tasks and projects.

• Use *Premack's principle* as a way to reinforce your own responsible behavior.

• Avoid talking too much before acting.

• Often, action helps you to overcome anxiety.

• A therapist can help you explore and understand the deeper motives that create resistance to taking effective action in the present.

• You and your therapist can make a functional analysis of your behavior, breaking down the trait of procrastination into specific behavioral units.

• A therapist can help you discover how certain cognitive distortions can contribute to the tomorrow syndrome.

• A therapist will help you assess the possibility that you are using procrastination as a passive way to express aggression toward a significant-other person in your life.

Chapter 23

Risk-Taking: Getting High on Danger

Phil V. is an enthusiastic hot-air balloonist. One of his best friends died in a fiery crash three months ago. Nonetheless, Phil particularly relishes going up in a balloon in a rain storm. Shannon C. flies hang gliders. Although it is illegal, she often glides near dangerous power lines and runs the risk of electrocution. Ray D. cuts recklessly in and out of traffic on the freeway and exceeds the speed limit by more than 20 miles per hour whenever he believes he can elude highway patrol officers.

Most people know what it is to take an unnecessary risk. Introductory psychology students were asked this question: "How many of you have taken a risk, such as driving your car as fast as it will go for no particular reason late at night on a stretch of lonely road or a nearly deserted freeway?" Usually more than one-half of the hands go up. Ordinary people with no pathology will go for a roller-coaster ride. Nonetheless, the average person is not addicted to unnecessary risks.

All of the individuals referred to in the opening paragraph have in common the trait of actively seeking risks that are both unnecessary and irrational by almost any set of standards. The subject of this chapter is that kind of risk-taking behavior—particularly the kind in which there is a real danger of loss of life or limb.

Some of the signs and symptoms associated with the trait of taking irrational risks include the following:

1. A happy-go-lucky pose
2. An unrealistic appraisal of probabilities
3. An underactive imagination
4. Little apparent concern for loss of life or limb
5. Lack of insight into one's own motives
6. The "cyborg complex"
7. The charmed-life fallacy

The above items merit comment. A *happy-go-lucky pose* is a social mask of "toughness." Often, the individual initiates quite a bit of banter and wisecracking. These are strategies that keep others at an arm's-length psychological distance. Instead of closeness to others, there is emotional isolation.

The individual addicted to taking excessive risks often makes an *unrealistic appraisal of probabilities*. He or she says, "I'm not a daredevil. I use good equipment and make sure it is working right. I take only calculated risks." Unfortunately, each risk taken without injury tends to raise the stakes. Jay G., for example, who initially always went skydiving with a backup chute now disdains a second chute. Also, he waits longer than he once did before pulling the rip cord.

It is common to find that those who regularly take irrational risks suffer from an *underactive imagination*. It is, in part, because they do not find excitement in the vicarious experiences in films and novels that they are forced to go to excessive lengths to put excitement into their lives. They have a difficult time extracting much satisfaction from a fantasy. They must *do* instead of dream. In this regard, they are quite different from individuals who are phobic or who suffer from an anxiety neurosis. In contrast, the individual who runs irrational risks tends to be stolid and unmoved by threats that have little or no objective basis.

Those who take irrational risks seem to have *little apparent concern for loss of life or limb*. These individuals tend to be foolhardy. They do not seem to fully appreciate that they are creatures of flesh and bone—that they can break and bleed. They may greatly resent using such safety equipment as a motorcycle helmet, for example. It often requires an actual injury for reality to hit.

Lack of insight into one's own motives is common. Individuals with a daredevil mentality seldom ask themselves *why* they do what they do. They tend to be extroverted and unreflective. Acting impulsively without self-analysis tends to be the rule.

The *cyborg complex* is the tendency to make a subconscious identification of the ego with a machine or device (e.g., a car, a hang glider, or a motorcycle). (*Cyborg* is a contraction of two words, *cybernetic* and *organism*.) William James, a key figure in the history of American psychology, said that the self is anything that one calls one's own. One's partner, one's children, and one's property are all extensions of the self. Richard T. owned a red sports car on which he lavished much care. He drove it at breakneck speeds between 2 A.M. and 3 A.M. on California freeways. He did not worry about hurting himself, but he did worry about damaging his car. In an interview, he admitted that he would much rather be injured himself than to see his car mangled.

The *charmed-life fallacy* is the unconscious assumption that an aura of luck follows the individual into all situations. Persons in the grips of this fallacy think that they are magically protected from injury, that they are in some way "special," that they can always beat the odds.

Causes and Explanations

Classical psychoanalytic theory assumed that the taking of irrational risks was an expression of Thanatos—the death instinct. The energy of this instinct, called *destrudo*, was turned in on the individual. This may to some extent be true in some cases (see the discussion of self-destructiveness in Chapter 24), but it does *not* appear to be true in the case of the trait presently under discussion.

The aim of behavior that tempts fate is a *flirtation* with death. It is not death itself that is sought, but the *excitement* that comes with a close look at the abyss of oblivion.

There must be an element of chance in order for this flirtation to work. Russian roulette was invented by bored cavalry officers holed up for weeks and months in bunkers covered with snow during long winters. Note that they placed only *one* bullet in the gun's chamber. If they had been seriously suicidal, they would not have played a game. They would have loaded the gun with six bullets or placed a single bullet in a position to be fired. It is clear that the main aim of the game was to overcome deep boredom, not really to die—although this was often enough the tragic outcome.

An important psychological factor in irrational risk taking is a neurotic need for power. The person who stands at the edge of disaster and escapes with his or her life feels briefly omnipotent. Persons who have a strong need to prove their competence to themselves and others may seek dangerous ways to make their point. This might be called the "Captain Nemo syndrome." Captain Nemo, alienated antihero of Jules Verne's *Twenty Thousand Leagues under the Sea*, believed himself to be above and beyond ordinary mortals. He was the master of his undersea world. He flirted with disaster and lost in the end. But while he was winning, he was described as feeling like a living god.

As a personality type, the individual who plays with the fire of death is an *unstable extrovert*. The individual is extroverted because his or her libido (i.e., psychological energy) turns to the outer world for gratification. The inner world of thought, memory, fantasy, and imagination brings very limited pleasure. It is the world of fast cars, boats, and airplanes that is exciting. It is the sea and sky that provide attractive landscapes for one's being. The individual is unstable because he or she tends to display such personality traits as excessive touchiness, restlessness, aggressiveness, excitability, changeability, and impulsiveness.

There is a childish, immature quality to excessive risk taking. Everyone is familiar with the image of the child who walks, like a tightrope artist, on a picket fence in order to impress a small audience of more timid children. Much of the same psychology is at work in the adult who walks the razor's edge of existence. He or she is showing off—playing to a real or imagined audience of awe-struck admirers.

An important ego defense mechanism that plays a part in some compulsive risk taking is *reaction formation*. Reaction formation is characterized by a tendency to convert an impulse at the unconscious level into its opposite at the conscious level. Consequently, a person with a deeply repressed fear of heights might become a "human fly" and scale the sides of buildings. A person with a fear of dismemberment might seek to become a human cannonball with a circus. This kind of behavior is described with the adjective *counterphobic*, and such behavior is designed to add additional force to the repression of a fear. If the explanation sounds a little farfetched, keep in mind that the behavior under question is also farfetched. When behavior is irrational, it is plausible to suggest that there are equally irrational psychodynamics behind it.

Another defense mechanism that is called into play in irrational risk taking is *denial of reality*, a tendency to avoid unpleasant facts. This is evident in the charmed-life fallacy identified earlier. Accident statistics and other data mean nothing. They are like water on a duck's back. Rational information is not used in the decision-making process. Consequently, a sort of bliss and indifference surrounds the person like an invisible aura as he or she ventures forth into the jaws of a dangerous destiny.

Coping

If you suffer from a tendency to take irrational risks involving danger to life and limb, you may find value in the following list of practical coping strategies.

• Stimulate your active imagination. The imagination can be trained and improved in the same way that the memory can be improved. Learn to derive satisfaction from motion pictures and novels—particularly novels. The mass-media specialist and social philosopher H. Marshall McLuhan made a distinction between "cool" and "hot" media. Films and television are "cool" because you can receive the information passively; note that these media require very little imaginative effort. In contrast, novels are "hot" because the information can only be obtained actively. You can receive a measure of excitement by reading the kinds of fiction that involve action and adventure. Novels like those in the series by Robert B. Parker about the private investigator Spenser might provide a starting point. Keep in mind that, as you age, you may be forced to get much of your excitement secondhand by the exercise of imagination. Now is a good time to start.

• Do some creative work as an avocation. This is a second way to stimulate your active imagination. Try to make a painting or drawing, to write a story or poem, or to compose a song. The quality of your work is not the key issue. It is the *creative process* that will enhance your imaginative abilities.

• Change jobs or careers. Studies suggest that a certain amount of irrational risk taking is induced by a need to overcome the boredom of life. This is particularly true of those who perceive their vocations as tedious and devoid of challenge. If you have burned out in this regard, consider possibilities for making a switch. If this is not possible, look for effective ways to introduce elements of novelty into your work.

• Take psychological risks. These risks can be as exciting as physical ones. Take an evening course in public speaking, for example. It has been said that the number one fear in America is the fear of talking to a group. When you stand and begin your presentation, you are likely to find that your heart is pounding, your palms are sweating, and your muscles are tense. You are "on alert," and there is a "rush" of adrenal hormones. You have activated the primitive fight-or-flight mechanism in the same way that you would by skydiving. Other possibilities include introducing yourself to an attractive stranger and sending a manuscript to a publisher. In both cases, you must run the risk of rejection.

• Make a distinction between having courage and being foolhardy. If you are employed in a mental hospital and must cope with an aggressive, dangerous patient, you have *courage*. If you bait someone else and pick a fight for no reason, you are *foolhardy*. Or, if you drive an ambulance in a combat zone, you have courage. If you drive 90 miles per hour and cut in and out of traffic on a freeway, you are being foolhardy. Courage implies taking calculated risks for an intelligent social purpose. Reject foolhardy behavior in favor of the more quiet, and more desirable, trait of courage.

• Challenge your personal constructs. *Personal constructs* are ideas about the self that may or may not reflect reality. An example of such a construct is, "I lead a charmed life." An honest analysis of this construct reveals that it arises from the ego defense mechanism earlier identified as denial of reality. Replace the construct with one that provides a better fit with the facts. The Spanish philosopher Miguel de Unamuno, author of *The Tragic Sense of Life*, said, "We are persons of flesh and bone." You can be hurt. Your bones can break, and you can bleed. These are hard facts to face, but they can perhaps save you from a premature death.

• Avoid drugs. One way to increase physiological arousal—and consequently to raise the level of excitement—is to take stimulant drugs, such as amphetamines or cocaine. Some people turn to these drugs as a way to replace the search for dangerous action. Unfortunately, the drugs in question have significant, long-range, adverse side effects; and the potency of a particular dose decreases quickly over time (the person taking the drug builds up a tolerance to it). Consequently, the drugs have to be taken in ever-increasing doses to give the taker a "high." They are a dead end.

Professional Help

If you find that you cannot cope effectively with a tendency to take irrational physical risks, there are several ways in which the professions of psychiatry and clinical psychology can help you.

Taking a psychodynamic approach, a therapist will help you explore the defensive aspects of your thoughts and behavior. You can obtain a clearer understanding of how denial of reality contributes to the charmed-life fallacy. You will obtain insight into ways that counterphobic behavior—acting fearless or like a daredevil—may in fact be devices you use to repress your fears of death and dismemberment. A psychodynamic approach will reveal the way in which you are a victim of your own unconscious motives.

Taking a behavioral approach, a therapist will assist you in identifying the psychological payoffs you derive from flirting with the loss of your life. The excitement, the sense of competence and power, may be gratifications you can obtain in more constructive, meaningful ways. This requires an objective analysis of the habits of your life. And behavior modification is an avenue that is particularly helpful in this regard.

In the framework of a behavioral approach, a therapist may use a variation of implosive therapy (see the "Professional Help" section of Chapter 14). Implosive therapy is sometimes used to treat phobic disorders. Its purpose is to bring about rapid desensitization by flooding the patient with anxiety. However, if an intense, anxiety-arousing, guided fantasy is *interrupted* (if closure is not permitted), then the result may be not desensitization but *hypersensitization*. This is, of course, not a desirable result in the treatment of phobias. However, it may be a desirable result in the treatment of a person who frequently takes irrational risks. It helps the patient to realize that he or she is a creature of flesh and bone.

Applying a cognitive approach, a therapist will encourage you to challenge illogical ideas associated with your risk-taking behavior. Paul E., for example, expressed the thought, "I'd rather live dangerously than die of a heart attack like my dad did." The therapist was able to assist Paul to see that he was setting up a false either-or situation. He had more choices in life than the two that preoccupied him. A common idea among those who live dangerously is one that states, "I would hate to be an old, frail person in my second childhood." Those who seek danger would, unconsciously, rather die young than live to be old. Facing the reality of aging by getting to know older people who have both integrity and wisdom, who are vital and alive, can reduce some of the fear of aging.

Finally, it is possible to use an interpersonal approach in the treatment of those who take irrational risks. It is possible that one partner may be using dangerous behavior as a way of demanding from the other partner such personal gratifications as attention and admiration. In therapy with an interpersonal orientation, the first partner is likely to learn that his or her efforts are backfiring. Instead of accomplishing its aims, the risk-taking behavior may be perceived by the second person as childish bravado and an immature way of showing off. An exchange of ideas with the assistance of the therapist may reveal ways for the first partner to obtain emotional satisfaction from the second one in more mature ways.

Key Points to Remember

• The subject of this chapter is irrational risk-taking behavior—particularly the kind in which there is a real danger of loss of life or limb.

• Some of the signs and symptoms associated with the trait of taking irrational risks include a happy-go-lucky pose, an underactive imagination, lack of insight into one's own motives, the "cyborg complex," and the charmed-life fallacy.

• Classical psychoanalytic theory assumed that the taking of irrational risks was an expression of Thanatos—the death instinct.

• The aim of behavior that tempts fate is a *flirtation* with death. It is not death itself that is sought, but the *excitement* that comes with a close look at the abyss of oblivion.

• An important psychological factor in irrational risk-taking is a neurotic need for power.

• As a personality type, the individual who plays with the fire of death is an *unstable extrovert*.

• Stimulate your active imagination. Learn to derive satisfaction from vicarious experiences.

• If your work bores you, consider a job or career change.

• Take psychological risks. These risks can be as exciting as physical ones.

• Make a distinction between having courage and being foolhardy.

• Taking a psychodynamic approach, a therapist may help you explore the defensive aspects of your thoughts and behavior.

• Taking a behavioral approach, a therapist will assist you in identifying the psychological payoffs you derive from flirting with the loss of your life.

• Applying a cognitive approach, a therapist will encourage you to challenge illogical ideas associated with your risk-taking behavior.

• Taking an interpersonal approach in therapy, an individual may see how he or she is using dangerous behavior as a way of demanding from another person such personal gratifications as attention and admiration.

Chapter 24

Self-Destructiveness: When the Personality Attacks Itself

The ultimate act of self-destruction is suicide.

However, for every person who directly destroys himself or herself, there must be 10 or 20 who do it indirectly. Making themselves victims of a slow process of self-defeat and self-torture, they hasten their deaths by years.

An autoimmune disorder in medicine is one in which a disorder of the immune system causes that system to attack the organs or tissues of one's own body. In the case of self-destructiveness, it is as if some persons have a psychological autoimmune disorder, one in which the personality attacks itself.

In the 1930s, the psychiatrist Karl A. Menninger, author of *Man Against Himself*, called the process of gradual self-destruction *chronic suicide*, in contrast to *acute suicide*. The second kind is characterized by direct and quickly lethal acts of self-destruction. Another, more recently coined term for chronic suicide is *indirect self-destructive behavior*. Both terms have the same meaning and will be used interchangeably in the present discussion.

The focus of this chapter is on chronic suicide. The psychology of both acute and chronic suicide is similar, but not identical. One factor that distinguishes the two is that in acute suicide, there is no denial of the wish for death. In chronic suicide, there is denial of such a wish. It is a repressed wish. On the surface, the individual seeks pleasure, an immediate gratification, a sense of control, or some other psychological payoff. Death or disability are recognized, naturally, as unfortunate consequences of one's actions, but that is usually as far as insight penetrates. The understanding of one's own motives is, consequently, shallow.

Some of the signs and symptoms frequently associated with self-destructive behavior are listed below. Not all of these will necessarily be evident in a particular case.

1. Substance abuse
2. Refusal to comply with a physician's instructions
3. Food abuse
4. Seeking unnecessary surgery
5. Accident proneness
6. Self-absorption
7. A need for self-abasement
8. Asceticism
9. Masochism
10. Denial of reality

The above items merit comment. *Substance abuse* includes the imprudent use of alcohol and drugs such as cocaine and amphetamines. (For more on alcohol abuse and drug abuse, see Chapters 2 and 9, respectively.) It is usually clear to the individual that he or she is inflicting long-term damage on the body.

It is quite common among those who display indirect self-destructive behavior to *refuse to comply with a physician's instructions*. Nick L., for example, has Buerger's disease, a condition in which there is restriction of blood flow through peripheral blood vessels. Often, persons with the disease lose fingers, toes, or a limb. It is well known that smoking greatly affects the disease in a pathological way. In spite of his physician's warnings, Nick continues to smoke heavily. Another example is May C., who has diabetes. She has been given instructions telling her to avoid foods containing refined sugar. She continues to eat candy bars and ice cream and drink soft drinks sweetened with sucrose. She knows she is damaging the retinas of her eyes and may lose her vision.

Overlapping somewhat with resistance to a physician's advice is *food abuse*. Two related expressions of self-destructiveness are anorexia and morbid obesity. In anorexia, the risk of death is increased via the route of self-imposed starvation. In the case of morbid obesity, the risk of death from such afflictions as a heart attack or kidney failure is increased; and, as indicated above, diabetes is aggravated. (For more about food abuse, see Chapter 10.)

Persons with self-destructive tendencies often *seek unnecessary surgery*. The patient presents complaints and pseudosymptoms so convincingly that it is often difficult to evaluate the reality of the organic condition. This may be particularly true in the case of such conditions as backaches and gastric distress. The complaining person often has an underlying fantasy in which surgery is associated with scarring and mutilation.

Accident proneness is indicated when an individual has a series of injuries in which either standard safety precautions are disregarded or there is an element of carelessness. The individual protests that he or she is unlucky—there is no pattern; these are "just" accidents.

Persons who display self-destructiveness tend to be *self-absorbed*. They display *narcissism*, a preoccupation with one's own self and one's personal needs. They are *egocentric*, and, as children do, perceive the world—including the social world of friends and family—as revolving around them. They are very aware of their own pain and suffering but have little or no real feeling for the tribulations of others.

A *need for self-abasement* is a need to be "dumped on" by others. An example is becoming a skid row wino. Another example is becoming a prostitute on the streets. In both cases, the individual invites the abuse of others. Eric Berne, father of transactional analysis, said that some people seem to carry an invisible sign that says, "Kick me."

Asceticism is a tendency to impose harsh, difficult conditions on one's life. Trying to live on bread and water, fasting for long periods, sleeping on a hard bed, refusing to use a furnace in the winter or an air conditioner in the summer are all examples of ascetic behavior. Without objective reason, the individual acts very much like a religious martyr.

Masochism is obviously connected with behaviors identified earlier such as seeking unnecessary surgery and asceticism. Masochism is a behavioral trait in which a person seeks either physical or psychological pain. There is an element of paradox in masochism because the person appears to extract pleasure from pain.

Individuals with self-destructive tendencies rely heavily on the ego defense mechanism of *denial of reality*. There is no admission that damage to the body is being actively sought. Instead, the conscious perception is that one is a victim of external causes outside of one's control.

Causes and Explanations

In classical psychoanalytic theory, there are two master principles that determine the course of all human lives. These are *Eros* and *Thanatos*, the life instincts and the death instinct. (Note that there is more than one life instinct; examples include hunger, thirst, and sex. But there is only one death instinct.) The energy of the life instincts is called *libido* and the energy of the death instinct is called *destrudo*.

According to Freud, when a person is relatively normal and well adjusted these two energies are in a healthy balance. In youth, Eros is dominant. In old age, Thanatos is dominant and eventually succeeds in bringing about the biological death of the individual. It should be noted that the German word *Trieb*, the one that Freud used to indicate the presence of an instinct, has a meaning approximately the same as the term *biological drive* in American psychology. Freud did not mean by the word *instinct* "a complex behavioral chain," the meaning usually assigned to it in the United States. He meant, as already suggested, a general directive force.

In persons with self-destructive tendencies, Eros and Thanatos are out of balance, and Thanatos is in the dominant position. This point of view was articulated and formalized in Menninger's *Man Against Himself*. The image of Thanatos, the Greek god of death, riding in the driver's seat of one's life is a terrifying one. It is a useful image because it places the individual on alert and helps him or her to more deeply appreciate that indirect self-destructive behavior can be a compelling theme in one's general style of life.

Nonetheless, the Freudian picture is incomplete. The question arises: What throws Eros and Thanatos into a state of imbalance? A number of causal factors can be important, and they can interact with each other, magnifying their independent effects.

An important factor is self-hate arising out of guilt. In the Pulitzer Prize-winning novel *Ironweed* by William Kennedy, the protagonist has a strong need to abase and punish himself for an error he committed as a young husband. He inadvertently dropped his infant son on the floor, and the child died of the consequent injury. The central character never forgives himself and spends years as an alcoholic who sleeps in alleys. Another example is Sally E., who has had two abortions. She was raised as a Roman Catholic. She feels very much like a murderer and believes that she deserves punishment. She allows her sadistic lover to beat and slap her. It is one of the few ways in which she feels she can atone for her perceived crimes.

There are times when self-destructiveness can be a way to punish someone else. When Nancy G. married her prominent-attorney husband, she was slim and pretty, the winner two years before of a beauty pageant. Her husband was her senior by 20 years. It quickly became evident to Nancy that he had "purchased" a sex object. He acted as if he owned her, and he was dictatorial. Also, he was sexually overbearing, caring little or nothing for Nancy's gratification. Nancy is both a passive and a traditional woman. She felt locked into the marriage. Her way of punishing her husband was to become obese. She has destroyed the body and the beauty that he thought he owned. Her self-destructiveness is really an attempt to both damage her husband's ego and to deny him sexual pleasure.

A complicating factor in self-destructiveness is the "too much, too soon" phenomenon. When wealth, success, or fame is attained too early in life, it often throws the recipient into a psychological tailspin. A vivid description of this pattern is presented in such autobiographical books as *Too Much, Too Soon* by Diana Barrymore and *My Wicked, Wicked Ways* by Errol Flynn.

The conviction that life is meaningless and that there is no point in living can be an underlying theme in some instances of self-destructiveness. (For more about loss of meaning in life, see Chapter 16.) In connection with this point, persons who are attacking themselves often entertain the fantasy of destruction and rebirth. It is an item of folklore that something must be torn down before rebuilding can take place. One expression of this idea is the image of the phoenix, a legendary Arabian bird, rising from its own ashes. Loosely associated with the phoenix myth is the idea that biological death will bring a second life, or a second chance, at a higher and better spiritual level.

Asceticism can be explained in part by returning to the factor of self-hate arising out of guilt. The imposition of harsh conditions on one's life may be for some persons a way of "cleansing" the soul, a means of purifying the self. It is another way of paying for real or imagined "crimes."

Finally, it should be noted that self-destructiveness can be a response to feeling helpless in the face of a chronic illness such as diabetes, heart disease, or Buerger's disease. Paradoxically, persons who feel overwhelmed by health problems may regain a sense of power and a modicum of control over their own lives by resisting, instead of cooperating with, a physician's instructions. It is a self-defeating declaration of autonomy.

Coping

If you recognize that to some extent you are engaging in indirect self-destructive behavior, you may find value in the following list of coping strategies.

• Reinforce the life forces. Assume for the moment that Eros and Thanatos, the life instincts and the death instinct, are in a state of imbalance. Add whatever psychological weight you can to the side of the scale of life occupied by Eros. Make a list *in writing* of reasons why life is worth living. Include your blessings and your talents. Name the things that bring you pleasure in life. Start the list, carry it with you, and add to it as ideas occur to you. You may start out by thinking that there is little or nothing you can list; but you may find, to your surprise, that the list will grow fairly long.

• Recognize the ambivalent nature of your behavior. It is *not* true that you simply want to hasten your death, that you do not believe that life is worth living. If this were so, you would find a way to simply kill yourself quickly and effectively. The fact that you engage in indirect self-destructive behavior shows in itself that you are of two minds. Within this very fact resides hope. You are not a complete enemy to yourself. Somewhere within your personality you are also a friend to yourself. Learn to work *with*, not against, this friend.

Coping

- Intensify your reality orientation. The very fact that you are recognizing within yourself some of the symptoms of self-destructive behavior suggests that your denial of reality is far from complete. Build on this. Say to yourself, "I am going to face the long-term consequences of my behavior." Ask yourself, "What will become of me if I persist in my present pattern?" Tell yourself, "I am a creature of flesh and bone like all human beings. I need tender loving care, not abuse—certainly not abuse at my own hands."

- Find ways to decenter. Decentering is a technique that reduces high levels of self-absorption. This is particularly true in the case of persons who suffer from the "too much, too soon" phenomenon. They often display narcissism. In decentering, one takes *active* steps to engage oneself in helping others. There are many ways to do this. Volunteer work in hospitals or the tutoring of children with learning disabilities provide two examples.

- Reevaluate your guilt feelings. It is possible that your guilt feelings are excessive, that your self-hate is an overreaction. This is frequently the case in persons who have had a very traditional upbringing and who have, in Freudian terms, a punitive superego (i.e., the moral agent of the personality). Ask yourself, "Am I in fact as guilty as I feel, or am I the victim of an overly moralistic attitude that I acquired in childhood from authoritarian parents?" Your own answer to this question may come as something of a surprise, and possibly will relieve you of some of your burden of guilt.

- Search for the meaning in life. Perhaps you are in a state of despair and demoralization because you see no real point or purpose in living. Start searching for meaning by reading and reflection. The search itself will help to restore a degree of sense and purpose to existence. (For more about restoring meaning to life, see Chapter 16.)

- Look for long-term gratifications. Instead of the short-term gratifications that can be found in alcohol, other drugs, food, and masochistic behavior, lift your eyes to a more distant horizon. Look down the road of your life. First, imagine as vividly as you can your future if you continue on your present course. Then imagine your future and its gratifications if you give up the dubious "pleasures" associated with self-destructive behavior. Return frequently to the images associated with delay of gratification.

- Ask yourself, "Who am I really punishing?" It is possible that your self-destructive behavior is a way of punishing someone else. If you answer the suggested question honestly, you are likely to discover that you are punishing yourself *much more* than you are punishing the other person. If the cost of your maladaptive behavior is clearly seen as outweighing its benefits, you might find that you are able to give it up. Say to yourself, "I want to stop being a victim of myself."

- Declare your autonomy in positive ways. Refusing to follow a physician's instructions when you have a chronic illness is a way of declaring your autonomy, but it is a negative way. It is the mode of the toddler. The "terrible twos" is characterized by the child frequently saying, "No." Refusal to obey instructions is a way of saying, crudely, "I am my own person." Reject childish ways. Remind yourself that you are not two years old, but an adult. Find ways to be your own person by building, by doing creative things, by acting in constructive ways.

Professional Help

If you find that you cannot cope adequately with your own self-destructive tendencies, there are several ways in which the professions of psychiatry and clinical psychology can help you.

Taking a psychodynamic approach, a therapist will help you to understand how you turn around natural aggressive tendencies that should be directed toward the challenges and obstacles of life and instead uselessly direct them toward yourself. You will attain a deeper understanding of this self-defeating process and learn ways to change it. A psychodynamic mode in therapy makes it possible for you to comprehend ways in which such paradoxical behaviors as accident proneness have unconscious motives behind them. As these unconscious motives surface, you will be better able to bring them under conscious control. Examples of such unconscious motives include a need to escape from a given vocation, a desire to punish oneself, and the fantasy that injury will lead to consequent death and rebirth.

A psychodynamic approach can help you gain insight into how you use denial of reality as a defense mechanism. You will be encouraged to face facts because only by doing so can you effectively free yourself from self-destructive traits. In connection with this, you will explore narcissism, a common defensive stance in persons who display indirect self-destructive behavior. You will find out how you use self-absorption as a way of avoiding deeper emotional involvement with others.

A psychodynamic mode is of particular value in the treatment of masochistic tendencies, that is, the extraction of pleasure from pain. A therapist will help you understand how unresolved guilt feelings often play a role in masochism. Therapy will help you develop constructive ways of discharging your guilt feelings and also ways of changing masochistic behavior.

As is evident from the preceding paragraphs, a psychodynamic approach has much to offer in the treatment of self-destructive behavior. It has, in fact, been the principal modality used in the psychotherapy of this particular kind of pathology. This is not to say, however, that other modalities cannot make a contribution to treatment.

Taking a behavioral approach, a therapist can help you pinpoint ways in which the momentary gratifications associated with self-destructive behavior continuously reinforce it. Examples of such transient gratifications are the pleasure of an alcoholic drink or other drug, the taste of sugar for someone who suffers from diabetes, or injury for someone who has masochistic tendencies. Making a detailed functional analysis of behavior, the therapist can assist you in finding other ways to obtain substitute gratifications without unfortunate harmful consequences.

Taking a cognitive approach, a therapist will help you identify ideas that reside behind self-destructive behavior. These ideas come and go in consciousness and must be captured "on the fly." Trapped in the net of therapy, they can be scrutinized for their irrational content. In the case of a cigarette smoker who has Buerger's disease, high blood pressure, or emphysema, an example of such an idea might be, "I'm going to die anyway. Why not enjoy my 'coffin nails'?" Cognitive therapy will reveal the illogical aspect of this line of thought—not only will the cigarette hasten death, it will also reduce the *quality* of life for the person with one of the named chronic diseases. The overall level of suffering is increased by the moment's pleasure, not decreased.

Taking an interpersonal approach, a therapist can help you discover that you may be using self-destructive behavior to punish someone else, such as a partner. It may be that you are playing a game, casting yourself in the social role of Persecutor and your partner in the role of Victim. Perhaps you felt that in the past you were victimized by him or her and now it is the partner's turn to be victimized. An interpersonal mode, often with both members of a couple present, will reveal ways to deal more effectively with each other. The goal is to develop constructive autonomy in a relationship and not to express the need for autonomy in self-destructive ways.

Finally, a humanistic approach has great value in the psychotherapeutic treatment of self-destructive behavior. Using insights derived from existential philosophy and the logotherapy of psychiatrist Viktor Frankl (see the "Professional Help" section of Chapter 16), your therapist will act as a guide into the wilderness of confused feelings about the value of life and the meaning of existence. With the right kind of guidance, you can come out of this forest of confusion with a clearer vision about the direction you want life to take. In consequence, your self-destructive tendencies will diminish.

Key Points to Remember

• *Chronic suicide* is a gradual self-destructive process in contrast to *acute suicide*. Another term for chronic suicide is *indirect self-destructive behavior*.

· Some of the signs and symptoms frequently associated with self-destructive behavior include substance abuse, refusal to comply with a physician's instructions, food abuse, accident proneness, a need for self-abasement, and denial of reality.

· According to classical psychoanalysis, in persons with self-destructive tendencies, Eros and Thanatos are out of balance.

· An important factor in self-destructive behavior is self-hate arising out of guilt.

· There are times when self-destructiveness can be a way to punish someone else.

· A complicating factor in self-destructiveness is the "too much, too soon" phenomenon.

· Self-destructiveness can be a response to feeling helpless in the face of a chronic illness.

· Reinforce the life forces by adding whatever psychological weight you can to the side of the scale of life occupied by Eros.

· Recognize the ambivalent nature of your behavior.

· Intensify your reality orientation by learning to face the long-term consequences of your behavior.

· Declare your autonomy in positive ways. Find ways to be your own person by building, by doing creative things, by acting in constructive ways.

· A psychodynamic approach in therapy will help you bring unconscious motives under better conscious control

· A psychodynamic mode is of particular value in the treatment of masochistic tendencies.

· Taking a behavioral approach, a therapist can help you pinpoint ways in which the momentary gratifications associated with self-destructive behavior continuously reinforce it.

· Taking a humanistic approach, your therapist will act as a guide into the wilderness of the confused feelings you may have about the value of life and the meaning of existence.

Chapter 25

Sexual Difficulties: "Now That You've Opened This Medusa's Box . . ."

In therapy, Alice W. talked about anything and everything to do with her unhappy marriage except her sex life. Finally, the therapist decided to prod her a bit and said, "You haven't talked about your sexual relationship at all. Is everything O.K. there? Is there anything you want to discuss?" Alice, usually voluble, stopped short and stared at the therapist. Her eyes became moist, and, after a substantial delay, she said, "Now that you've opened this Medusa's box, there's quite a bit I want to talk about."

The therapist noted, without comment at the time, that Alice had made a Freudian slip, classical in its form. There is no Medusa's box in mythology. There *is* a Pandora's box. And it contained a number of evils. There is a Medusa's head, a head with serpents for hair, and the serpent is a common phallic symbol. Alice had unconsciously combined the two images into one, a process called *condensation* in psychoanalysis. As the therapist interpreted the slip, Alice was disclosing that she perceived sex as an ugly, dangerous, and perhaps "evil" thing. The slip did, in fact, foreshadow information that came out subsequently: Alice thought of sex as dirty and associated it with the behavior of barnyard animals; she had been married several years and had had only two orgasms.

Suppose what Alice inadvertently called the "Medusa's box" of sex is opened and the contents are examined, that is, the kinds of difficulties that people experience in this very important arena of life. The discussion will revolve around *sexual dysfunctions*, problems in the area of sexual response characterized by such experiences as lack of excitement, inability to attain an orgasm, or painful intercourse.

In order to enhance the appreciation of abnormal patterns, it will be instructive to briefly review the normal pattern. The sexual response cycle, as studied and defined by the researchers William H. Masters and Virginia E. Johnson, consists of four stages: (1) excitement, (2) plateau, (3) orgasm, and (4) resolution. *Excitement* is characterized by increased arousal, such as an increase in the rates of both heartbeat and respiration. At the *plateau* stage, the increased arousal remains "flat," or stable. In females, the clitoris retracts. In males, the penis maintains an erectile state. During the *orgasm*, there is the subjective response of great pleasure. From the physiological point of view, in the female, there are involuntary wavelike contractions of the *pubococcygeus (PC) muscle* surrounding the vaginal channel. In the male, there are involuntary contractions of the penis and the ejaculation of semen. During *resolution*, there is a loss of excitement and a lack of responsiveness to erotic stimuli. (It should be noted that in persons who experience multiple orgasms, after each orgasm, there will be a return to the plateau stage, not the resolution stage. Multiple orgasms, although not experienced by a majority of persons, are considered to be a part of a normal response pattern. This kind of response is more common in women than in men.)

There can be disturbances of the sexual-response cycle at any of its various stages or, as will be described, even before the cycle is given an opportunity to start. The principal sexual dysfunctions are listed below.

1. Hypoactive sexual desire disorder
2. Sexual aversion disorder
3. Female sexual arousal disorder
4. Male erectile disorder
5. Vaginismus
6. Premature ejaculation
7. Inhibited female orgasm
8. Inhibited male orgasm
9. Dyspareunia

The above dysfunctions merit both description and comment.

Hypoactive sexual desire disorder is logically identified with a time period *prior* to the four-stage cycle. The Greek root *hypo* means "below." Consequently, if one suffers from a hypoactive desire, one in fact has little or no desire for sexual relations. Psychiatry and clinical psychology sometimes use the terms *low libido* or *loss of libido* in connection with this disorder. This usage is from classical psychoanalysis in which the word *libido* is Freud's term for combined psychological and sexual energy.

Consciously, the individual is indifferent toward sexual contact and does not look for it.

Sexual aversion disorder has a stronger emotional tone than the first disorder listed. The individual with this second disorder may be, for example, actively disgusted by the idea of sexual contact. Images of participating in sexual activity are likely to induce anxiety, nausea, or a headache. Males or females can suffer from either of the first two disorders.

Female sexual arousal disorder is associated with the excitement stage of the sexual-response cycle. Although willing to participate in sexual relations, the female in question does not in fact become excited by kissing, stroking, the language of love, music, or any of the other stimuli that often are associated with erotic arousal. The traditional term for this condition is *frigidity*, and it appears frequently in the older literature of psychoanalysis. The term is considered obsolete in clinical language because it is too wide-ranging. It was often used to include inhibited female orgasm, which is certainly incorrect. Females with orgasmic dysfunction often become quite excited during sexual relations and, consequently, are poorly described with the word *frigid*.

Male erectile disorder is associated with the excitement and plateau stages of the sexual-response cycle, but primarily the latter. Often the male with this disorder becomes excited, has an erection, but cannot sustain it long enough during sexual intercourse to maintain contact of sufficient duration. A formal distinction is made between *primary* and *secondary* erectile disorder. In primary erectile disorder, the male has never sustained an adequate erection. In secondary erectile disorder, the male has a past history of successful intercourse but is presently having difficulties. The second condition is much more common than the first. The traditional term for male erectile disorder is *impotence*, which means "lack of power." Although this term is still often used in popular language, it lacks precision and is avoided in clinical settings.

In *vaginismus*, the muscles that allows entry into the vagina do not relax adequately. Instead, they contract on their own and make sexual intercourse difficult or impossible. If penetration is achieved, the sexual act is very painful.

Premature ejaculation is characterized by brevity of penetration and penile stroking before the ejaculatory reflex is elicited. The time period called "brief" cannot, of course, be exactly defined. Some experts suggest that this is two to four minutes. However, the research of Masters and Johnson suggests that the average span of time required for a woman to reach orgasm with penile stroking alone is 10 to 20 minutes. Obviously, from the female's point of view, any ejaculation prior to her orgasm is "premature."

Inhibited female orgasm is a dysfunction in which the female seldom achieves an orgasm, achieves one with great difficulty after much stimulation, or both. In inhibited female orgasm, there is no implication that the female is "frigid." Often there is excitement, pleasurable sensations, and ample lubrication. If a female has never had an orgasm, even with seemingly adequate stimulation, the condition is referred to as *primary orgasmic dysfunction*. In the majority of cases, at least a few orgasms have been experienced in the past, and this condition is referred to as *secondary orgasmic dysfunction*.

In *inhibited male orgasm*, the male has an erection and can readily sustain sexual intercourse for an extended period. Unfortunately, the ejaculatory reflex is not easily elicited, and, in some cases, the ejaculation will not happen at all. Eventually, the penis will become flaccid, and the sexual exchange concludes under frustrating circumstances to both partners.

Dyspareunia is the clinical name given to painful intercourse. In the case of vaginismus, there is also obviously dyspareunia. However, pain is not associated only with vaginismus and can, in fact, be part of the experience of either males or females.

Causes and Explanations

In some cases, a sexual dysfunction can be explained at the biological level. If a male has atherosclerosis in various arteries, for example, this can adversely affect his capacity to have or maintain an erection. In the same way that coronary arteries can be blocked, penile arteries can also be blocked. In both sexes, low levels of hormones produced by the gonads (i.e., the testes in the male and the ovaries in the female) can adversely affect interest in erotic stimuli and excitement. If a person suffers from chronic fatigue syndrome, libido (i.e., sexual drive) will be diminished. Also, one of the adverse side effects of some high-blood-pressure medication is the diminishing of libido. Sensitive chancres caused by genital herpes can be the principal factor in dyspareunia for either sex. Consequently, it is clear that all sexual problems cannot be understood in psychological terms.

If organic factors are ruled out, then it is reasonable to seek explanations for sexual dysfunctions in psychological factors. Keep in mind that more than one psychological factor may be involved in a particular case. When this happens the factors *interact*, meaning their joint effects are complex and the result is a magnification of symptoms. Also, keep in mind that the explanations offered are general. A sexual dysfunction affects a specific individual, *this* person, and can be understood completely only in the context of that individual's life history and present situation.

If one takes an overview of sexual dysfunctions, assuming an absence of an organic problem, it can be seen that the basic theme is *inhibition* of behavior. (The very word *inhibited* appears in connection with two of the disorders.) The exception to this general thesis is premature ejaculation in which there is excessive *disinhibition* of behavior. This point will be covered later.

In classical psychoanalysis, explanations of sexual dysfunctions tend to revolve around negative childhood experiences. These experiences possibly produce what can broadly be called a *sexual neurosis*, anxiety surrounding sexual ideas as well as the act itself. Four examples of how childhood experiences can play a role in sexual dysfunctions will be offered.

First, it is possible that some individuals have an unresolved *Oedipus complex*, a repressed wish for sexual intercourse with the parent of the opposite sex. (The term *Electra complex* is sometimes used in connection with females.) An Oedipus complex has its roots in a child's incest fantasies around the age of five or six. Assume that a parent is seductive or suggestive in an erotic way toward a child. Also assume that the child is very emotionally upset and guilty because of his or her sexual fantasies. It is possible that confused images at the unconscious level may give rise to the general feeling that having sex with *any* member of the opposite sex is, in a way, having sex with one's parent. The incest taboo is activated, and, even when one becomes an adult, he or she is unable to let go and enjoy sex. It is important to add that the unconscious perception of one's partner as a father or mother is a factor in *some* sexual dysfunctions, not all. Freud tended to overgeneralize the importance of the Oedipus complex.

Second, in some instances there is actual sexual molestation of a child or an adolescent by a parent or stepparent. If there is sexual abuse of this kind during the developmental years, it is easy to understand how the individual might look upon sex as dirty, disgusting, or frightening. If there was pain or humiliation during sexual abuse, the individual will associate such negative emotional states with sexual activity even in adulthood.

Third, some children witness their parents engaging in sexual intercourse during early childhood, and this can be an emotional trauma. In one of Freud's most famous cases, the case of the Wolf-man, the child saw his parents engaged in intercourse in the rear entry position. It made him think of sex as a low, animal activity and left him with a distorted attitude toward sexual contact.

Fourth, many children are raised by parents who are authoritarian and who also have a very strict, moralistic attitude toward sex. In various ways, a general message is conveyed that suggests the sex act is something "nasty," something to be ashamed of, and certainly not to be enjoyed. If the child incorporates these attitudes into his or her personality, then it becomes subsequently difficult to "let go" and discover the pleasures of sexual behavior.

It is possible, of course, to look to other viewpoints than the psychoanalytic one for causes and explanations of sexual disorders. The behavioral viewpoint is particularly worthwhile and defines sexual disorders in terms of maladaptive habits. Inability to respond to erotic stimulation with pleasure and in a relaxed way is seen as the result of unfortunate distortions in the general conditioning process. There may be in the individual's developmental history, for example, a high frequency of punishment for either autoerotic play as a preschooler or for the expression of sexual interest as an adolescent. Anxiety in the presence of sexual stimuli or sexual opportunity is the psychological fallout, and this is a conditioned emotional response.

From the cognitive viewpoint, it is possible that a person has some irrational or illogical ideas about sex. Amelia K., for example, believed that there was something "inferior" about an orgasm attained with the aid of manual clitoral stimulation. She thought that she should be able to climax with penile stroking only and was convinced that she was frigid or sexually inadequate in some way. Jason R. believed in his first year of marriage that he should initiate sexual contact at least four or five times a week. He developed "performance anxiety" and, in consequence, erectile difficulties. Both Amelia and Jason were the victims of their own illogical ideas. In Amelia's case, the research of Masters and Johnson suggests than an orgasm is an orgasm no matter how it is induced. Most sexologists today do not "grade" orgasms on the basis of whether or not they are "clitoral" or "vaginal." In the case of Jason, he was imposing an unrealistic, idealistic image of masculinity on himself with unfortunate consequences.

Taking an interpersonal viewpoint, it can readily be seen that a sexual disorder can be a reflection of a troubled relationship. Latent hostility toward one's partner is a common problem. The first partner does not want the second partner to experience pleasure. One way to deny pleasure to another is to deny pleasure to oneself. If, for example, a female does not have an orgasm, it is likely that the male will feel inadequate. Conversely, if a male has erectile problems, the female's self-image and sense of attractiveness will suffer.

Habituation is a problem in relationships. Members of a couple become too familiar with each other. They know what to expect. Novelty is gone. Consequently, excitement is diminished. The curiosity drive is set in motion, and one begins to wonder if a sexual disorder would disappear with a different partner. Often individuals act on the curiosity drive and seek an outside relationship. Both hostility and the search for novelty play important roles in "cheating" on one's partner.

Psychosocial stressors can be causal factors in a sexual disorder. Examples are loss of a job, loss of an important friendship, the illness of a child, an excessively large mortgage payment, and, for students, a too-heavy academic load. Thcsc, and similar stressors, will tend to dampen the capacity for sexual arousal.

Returning to the subject of premature ejaculation, you will recall that the point was made that it is unlike the other sexual disorders in that it involves not inhibition, but excessive disinhibition. The early psychoanalysts explained premature ejaculation in terms of anxiety and guilt feelings. The psychoanalytic approach may have value in some cases. However, another formulation is possible. It can be argued that premature ejaculation is frequently caused by an above-average level of excitement. One would expect this when the partner is a new one, particularly attractive, or when the male is quite young. More than one study indicates that premature ejaculation tends to be much more common in younger, rather than older, males. Common sense suggests that not all distressing behavior has to be explained in terms of unconscious motives and emotional conflicts.

Coping

If you suffer from a sexual difficulty, you may find value in the following list of coping strategies.

• Pay attention to physical health. As indicated earlier, such conditions as atherosclerosis and chronic fatigue can adversely affect various stages of the sexual-response cycle. A diet low in saturated fats will help prevent and/or control atherosclerosis. Moderate and regular exercise will encourage the production of endorphins in the brain, which have a positive effect on mood and responsiveness to erotic stimuli. In view of the fact that the orgasm is an induced reflex involving nerves and muscles, it is only logical that it be based solidly on a foundation of physical health.

• Reflect on your childhood. It is quite possible, as psychoanalysis suggests, that you had experiences in your developmental years that traumatized you. You can gain a better understanding of these experiences and the emotions attached to them by writing about them. Keep a personal journal that is for your eyes only. The insights you produce by your own efforts can have great value and may, to some extent, set you free from the influence of the past.

• Develop a positive attitude. Start to think of the sexual act as a pleasant aspect of human behavior. Define it in your own mind as a normal aspect of God's will or of nature, depending on your personal theological or philosophical perspective. Realize that there is nothing inherently sinful or "dirty" about the sexual act in and of itself.

• Examine your ideas about sexual behavior. You may find that illogical ideas are interfering with sexual satisfaction. A female, for example, may have the idea that she should have an orgasm every time that she has sexual intercourse. The fact of the matter is that if the female has an orgasm 70 to 80 percent of the times that she has intercourse, she falls well within the normal range. Fatigue, psychosocial stressors, not being in the mood, fear of pregnancy, and so forth, can all be inhibiting factors during a given sexual exchange. In the case of the male, he may have the illogical idea that he should be able to perform well any time, every time, and even on demand. Even a man with a high sexual drive is not a machine. And, for that matter, sex is not a "performance." Excitement and orgasm are not "acts" or "roles" that one can play. They are expressions of states of mind and feeling. Unrealistic expectations, expressed at the conscious level in terms of illogical ideas, need to be evaluated and modified.

• Do not use sex as a way to express hostility. The denial of your partner's pleasure is very destructive to a relationship. If you think that latent hostility is inhibiting your own sexual response, look for constructive ways to improve your overall relationship. You may need to acquire more effective communication skills. (For more about interpersonal difficulties, see Chapter 13.)

• Find ways to reintroduce novelty into a sexual exchange. There are several ways in which this can be done. Having sexual relations in new surroundings is a possibility. Many couples find that when they have sexual relations on a trip or vacation in a different room, excitement is enhanced. Budget allowing, it is sometimes a good idea to take a mini-vacation for one night to a hotel or motel within easy driving distance. A couple can vary sexual positions. If an individual who is overweight slims down, not only is his or her body more attractive, the change introduces an element of novelty. You can change somewhat as a person by learning new things, and your partner may find you "different" and more exciting. In general, the principle is to find ways to make the sexual relationship less predictable. It should not be allowed to grow stale.

• Reduce self-demand in the face of unavoidable psychosocial stressors. If, for example, you have recently lost a job or if your child is ill, it is really too much to expect of yourself that you also continue to invest psychological energy in the sex act. If the time is not right, then the time is simply not right. Without forcing yourself, wait for the external crisis to pass, and sexual desire will reassert itself in a natural way.

• Learn the skills involved in inducing the female orgasm. In the vast majority of cases, a female will have frequent orgasms if she receives adequate stimulation of a high quality. Unfortunately, penile stroking alone is seldom sufficient to induce the female orgasm. One reason for this is because, according to the research of Masters and Johnson, when a male engages in unrestricted sexual intercourse, he will ejaculate within two to four minutes. A typical female will require 10 to 20 minutes to reach a climax. Consequently, a practical strategy is to provide the female with manual stimulation to the clitoral area, bringing her to the threshold of an orgasm. Entry and penile stroking can then be used, alone or in combination with manual stimulation, in order to attain the female orgasm. On the whole, it is a good idea to induce the female's orgasm before the male's. Older sex manuals used to recommend a couple try to attain a simultaneous climax. Today's sexologists consider this to be antiquated advice.

• Use pragmatic techniques to cope with premature ejaculation. A male can masturbate two or three hours before anticipated intercourse, and this will probably give him better self-control of the ejaculatory reflex during the actual exchange. Some couples have intercourse twice during a given sexual session. The first time is "for the male." The second time is "for the female," during which the male will be able to sustain more prolonged penile stroking. A technique recommended originally by Masters and Johnson is called the *squeeze technique.* When a male approaches the threshold of his orgasm, he informs his partner. She places a thumb and her forefinger just behind the glans penis, with the thumb on the underside. Then she *gently* squeezes, and this inhibits the orgasm. Repeated application of the squeeze technique sets in motion a conditioning process that makes possible greater self-control of the ejaculatory reflex.

• Use alcohol sparingly. Although it is true that alcohol can relax you and your partner as well as release inhibitions, it is also true that alcohol is a central-nervous-system depressant that reduces excitation. From the psychological point of view, a little alcohol may act as an aphrodisiac. From the biological point of view, a little too much alcohol acts as an anti-aphrodisiac.

Professional Help

If you find that you cannot cope adequately with a sexual difficulty, there are a number of ways in which the professions of psychiatry and clinical psychology can help you.

A psychiatrist is also a medical doctor. However, in most cases, if a psychiatrist believes that a sexual problem has primarily organic causes such as atherosclerosis, a chronic illness or infection, or a neurological problem, he or she will probably refer the patient to either a family physician or a specialist. The same is, of course, true of clinical psychologists, who are not medical doctors, and, consequently, not qualified to treat medical problems. The treatment modalities described in this section assume that it has been ascertained that the sexual problem is primarily one involving mental attitudes, emotional conflicts, or maladaptive habits.

Ever since the publication in 1970 of *Human Sexual Inadequacy* by Masters and Johnson, the focus of sex therapy has been on *pragmatic techniques*, that is, techniques "that work." These are the kinds of practical strategies already described, such as manual stimulation of the clitoral area and the squeeze technique. Other pragmatic techniques include (1) *sensate focusing*, involving conscious attention to sensations that bring pleasure, (2) familiarity with the erotic zones, and (3) relaxation exercises. In the vast majority of cases, if a couple is seen together and given guidance by a qualified sex therapist, there will be a significant decrease in the distress associated with a sexual disorder. It should be noted that pragmatic techniques are based on the behavioral approach in which more attention is paid to maladaptive habits than to unconscious motives and emotional conflicts.

This is not to say, however, that the psychodynamic approach, and other approaches, play no part in the treatment of sexual disorders. If a sexual disorder resists pragmatic treatment, it may be necessary to probe deeper into the personality in order to discover ways to help the sexually troubled person. Taking a psychodynamic approach, a therapist may help the individual discover that emotional wounds inflicted during the early years of development have created both sexual inhibitions and somewhat abnormal attitudes. Using such techniques as free association, hypnotherapy, or even just a relaxed, random discussion about one's past and childhood, long-repressed painful memories will surface. Once brought to consciousness, they can be dealt with in new, effective ways. And they lose much of their malevolent influence.

Taking a cognitive approach, a therapist can help you examine specific irrational, illogical ideas. Such ideas abound in the area of sexual behavior. Some examples have been given earlier, such as "I should have an orgasm every time" or "I should be ready for sex whenever my partner wants it." Other illogical ideas may include "I am ashamed of my body when my partner sees me in a full light," "I have climaxes, but I'll bet other people have better ones," "If I do not have an orgasm, I can't get pregnant," and "My partner must be a pig because he (or she) asks for things that I think are awful."

Finally, taking an interpersonal approach, a therapist can help a couple develop better communication skills. If sexual inhibition is being used as a way to express latent hostility, this can be examined and discussed. Ways will be sought to reduce the frustration and, consequently, the level of hostility in the relationship. Also, it is important in sexual behavior to know how to ask for the kind of stimulation that one needs and desires while at the same time not being offensive to one's partner. Issues such as those identified can be discussed, and solutions can be sought, in the supportive atmosphere of interpersonal therapy.

Key Points to Remember

· *Sexual dysfunctions* are problems in the area of sexual response characterized by such experiences as lack of excitement, inability to attain an orgasm, or painful intercourse.

· The four stages of the sexual-response cycle are (1) excitement, (2) plateau, (3) orgasm, and (4) resolution.

· The principal sexual dysfunctions are (1) hypoactive sexual desire disorder, (2) sexual aversion disorder, (3) female arousal disorder, (4) male erectile disorder, (5) vaginismus, (6) premature ejaculation, (7) inhibited female orgasm, (8) inhibited male orgasm, and (9) dyspareunia.

· In some cases, a sexual dysfunction can be explained at the biological level. Biological factors include atherosclerosis, low levels of hormones produced by the gonads, chronic fatigue syndrome, the effects of high-blood-pressure medication, and genital herpes. Consequently, physical health deserves attention.

· The basic theme in sexual dysfunctions is *inhibition* of behavior.

· In classical psychoanalysis, explanations of sexual dysfunctions tend to revolve around negative childhood experiences. You may find it of value to reflect on your childhood.

· The behavioral viewpoint defines sexual disorders in terms of maladaptive habits.

· The cognitive viewpoint defines sexual disorders in terms of irrational or illogical ideas about sex. Examine your ideas about sexual behavior.

· A sexual disorder can be a reflection of a troubled relationship. Do not use sex as a way to express hostility.

· Habituation, or loss of novelty in sex, is a problem in relationships. Find ways to reintroduce novelty into a sexual exchange.

· Reduce sexual self-demand in the face of unavoidable psychosocial stressors.

· Learn the skills involved in inducing the female orgasm.

· The focus of today's sex therapy is on pragmatic techniques, that is, techniques "that work."

· If a sexual disorder resists pragmatic treatment, it may be necessary to take a psychodynamic approach in therapy and probe more deeply into the personality.

· Taking a cognitive approach, a therapist can help you examine specific irrational or illogical ideas that contribute to sexual difficulties.

· Taking an interpersonal approach, a therapist can help a couple develop better communication skills. This will help them to stop using sexual inhibition as a way of expressing hostility.

Chapter 26

Shyness: Painful Self-Consciousness

He suffered to some degree from shyness all of his life. In childhood and young adulthood, it was both chronic and excessive. In middle and old age, he learned to temper the effects of his sensitive disposition with a set of relatively effective coping strategies. He became one of the world's most well-known authors. The novels *The Razor's Edge* and *The Moon and Sixpence* are among his works. He wrote about his temperament and his reactions to being raised by an authoritarian uncle and an emotionally withdrawn aunt in his acknowledged masterpiece, the autobiographical novel *Of Human Bondage*. The name of the author in question is W. Somerset Maugham.

As Maugham's case illustrates, shyness can afflict those who are famous and talented as well as the average person. Like most mental and emotional problems, it has little respect for one's social rank. How common is shyness? The social psychologist Philip G. Zimbardo has given the Stanford Shyness Survey to more than 5,000 persons worldwide. His results suggest, as indicated above, that shyness is a common problem. Approximately 80 percent of his subjects said that they experienced shyness some of the time. About 25 percent reported that they were shy in almost all social situations.

The common experience of being shy in a few social situations is called *situational shyness* and is not considered to be a behavioral problem. Feeling shy in almost all situations is called *chronic shyness*, and it is, of course, a problem. This kind of shyness can also be called *dispositional shyness* because it is a personality trait. The two terms can be used interchangeably with little or no loss of meaning.

It is possible to extend the trait of shyness into a more abnormal realm. *Pathological shyness* is the kind of shyness exhibited by a person who becomes very withdrawn from others and avoids all unnecessary contact with other persons. Also, the term *social introversion* is sometimes used to label the tendency to move away from people and into one's own private psychological world.

The Minnesota Multiphasic Personality Inventory (MMPI), a personality test widely used in psychiatry and clinical psychology to measure pathological traits, has on it a set of *clinical scales*, scales of measurement that report the degree of disturbance an individual has in given personality areas. One of these scales is a measure of social introversion. A high level of social introversion suggests that an individual suffers from either chronic or pathological shyness.

The focus of this chapter will be on chronic, or dispositional, shyness. It should be recognized that pathological shyness may be identified as an extreme kind of chronic shyness.

Here is a useful working definition of *chronic shyness*: a distressing personality trait characterized by maladaptive strategies designed to minimize the sense of being overexposed in social situations. Adjectives often used more or less synonymously with *chronic shyness* are *modest, self-effacing, bashful, retiring, timid,* and *hesitant. Webster's Encyclopedic Unabridged Dictionary of the English Language* (Portland House) even includes the entry *shrinking violet* followed by the definition, "a shy, modest, or self-effacing person."

Some of the signs and symptoms frequently associated with chronic shyness are listed below. Keep in mind that not all of these need to appear in the case of a given individual.

1. Stumbling or awkward speech
2. Very few egocentric statements
3. Avoidance of the limelight or "center stage"
4. Apparent aloofness and emotional coldness
5. Failure to take advantage of opportunities
6. Distinct feelings of inferiority
7. Sexual difficulties
8. Introverted interests
9. A very small circle of friends

The above items merit comment. *Stumbling or awkward speech* is common in persons who suffer from chronic shyness. In some cases, stuttering is a problem. (Maugham often stuttered, particularly as a child and young adult.) In this case, awkward speech is caused by anxiety, and the anxiety comes from the feeling that one is being judged by others or looked down upon in some way. Consequently, speech difficulties become exaggerated in the presence of authority figures.

Egocentric statements are statements about oneself in which the focus of attention is on one's own personal experiences or attitudes. The person thinks, "No one is interested in me or what I have done. Why bore people?" Oddly enough, the person wants to be well liked and believes that modesty is one way to have an attractive personality. This is, of course, true to some extent. But an almost complete absence of egocentric talk will eventually strike others as unbalanced and eccentric.

There will be an effort on the part of the person troubled by shyness to *avoid the limelight or "center stage."* He or she does not want to be the object of study or scrutiny. As indicated in the subtitle of this chapter, there is painful self-consciousness. Talking in a classroom, giving a speech, or being elected the president of a club make the individual feel as if he or she is naked in a psychological fish bowl.

The individual with dispositional shyness may *appear to be aloof and cold* to others. This is a social mask, a pose. Its purpose is to protect the individual against the feeling that one is overexposed. Others are often held at an emotional arm's length because the individual perceives himself or herself as vulnerable. There is the fear that one's ego will be crushed by the adverse opinions and reactions of other people.

Shyness is associated with *failure to take advantage of opportunities.* An example would be the case of promotions, many of which require supervision of other people. Consequently, persons who suffer from shyness will hold back so as to not earn a promotion. If offered one, they may decline with various plausible-sounding excuses. What is more important is that many opportunities in life are self-generated. The effective, assertive person approaches others and "knocks on many doors." Those who suffer from dispositional shyness do nothing to create opportunities because of the emotional threat linked to these opportunities.

Social introversion tends to go hand in hand with *distinct feelings of inferiority.* Often, these feelings are quite specific. A person may feel inferior in terms of stature, facial features, verbal skills, intelligence, creativity, mathematical ability, and so forth. The general attitude toward others is what, in transactional analysis, has been called the "I'm not O.K., you're O.K." life position. The perception is that others are more competent, attractive, and effective than oneself.

Shyness is a contributing factor to sexual difficulties. The individual is often inhibited and, consequently, has trouble relaxing and enjoying both lovemaking and intercourse. Frequently, the person feels ashamed to be seen in the nude. (For more about sexual difficulties, see Chapter 25.)

Introverted interests are one way to reduce contact with others. Such interests are those in which psychological energy flows inward toward one's own personality in contrast to flowing outward toward the external world. Examples of introverted interests are solitary activities and avocations such as writing, painting, composing music, meditating, going for long walks alone, reading novels, and so forth. There is, of course, nothing wrong with the identified activities in and of themselves. Indeed, some of them should be a part of every person's normal repertoire of behavior. But if they dominate one's life as a way of avoiding others, then these activities are certainly maladaptive.

In connection with the above, it will be expected that the person who suffers from shyness will have a *very small circle of friends*. He or she will be comfortable only with people who are "safe" and predictable. Over the years, the number of friends and acquaintances may shrink to a meager number, and the individual will feel very lonely and isolated.

Causes and Explanations

An important causal factor in shyness is parental style. There are two important factors in this. First, during one's childhood and adolescence, one's parents may have been *authoritarian*, meaning they were overcontrolling and critical without sufficient reason. Second, one's parents may have tended to give the tokens of love (i.e., smiles, hugs, approval, and attention) only if *earned* by the child. This is often referred to as *conditional love*. The combination of authoritarianism with conditional love leads the child to believe that he or she is *not* intrinsically loveable or worthwhile. Instead, the individual feels that "I am worth something *only if* I live up to expectations." The sufferer from chronic shyness has often been, during the developmental years, hypersensitized to criticism and the judgments of others. Trait shyness is, in a sense, an urge to hide from others.

An *inferiority complex* is a set of ideas revolving around one's own ego that state that one is inadequate, unattractive, or ineffective in some way. The concept in this form was first put forth by Alfred Adler, founder of a school of psychotherapy known as *individual psychology*. Today, the terms more likely to be heard are *low self-esteem* or the "I'm not O.K., you're O.K." life position. All of these labels point to the same basic process—the one that Adler identified. Where does an inferiority complex come from? As already indicated, one source can be a parental style characterized by the two attributes of authoritarianism and conditional love. In addition, Adler identified *sibling rivalry*, the jealousy and consequent emotional contest experienced by brothers and sisters, as a major causal factor in an inferiority complex. Imagine that one has an older sibling who is perceived to be the "star" in the family. He or she is seen by the younger child as stronger, more self-confident, more well coordinated, and so forth, than the younger sibling. One cannot "hold a candle" to the big brother or big sister. The problem can be made worse if the older sibling frequently teases or discounts the younger child. And the problem can be compounded still more if the parents dote on the older child. In Adler's language, a full-blown inferiority complex, carried over from childhood, often is the key to understanding chronic shyness in an adult.

It should be noted that the development of an inferiority complex does not begin and end in the home. Erik Erikson, a psychoanalyst and originator of an important psychosocial theory of development, notes that the school-age years (i.e., approximately from ages 6 to 12) are particularly sensitive ones in terms of the acquisition of inferiority feelings. If one has troubled relations with peers, if one is looked upon by them as unattractive or incompetent, this will contribute to the formation of an inferiority complex.

Up until now, this section has focused primarily on the kind of experiences that contribute to chronic shyness. However, it is important to note that the seeds of these experiences are much more likely to produce their undesirable sprouts if they are planted in a fertile soil. This soil is the child's temperament. More than one researcher has concluded that temperament is to some extent inborn, perhaps determined by one's genetic structure. Carl Jung, who introduced the concept of introversion into psychology, believed that it was basically an inborn trait, part of the individual's nature. Some children are primarily disposed toward introversion; others are primarily disposed toward extraversion. It is children in the first category who are made excessively shy by the kinds of experiences already described, as well as those that follow.

From a behavioral viewpoint, it is easy to see how shyness begets shyness. The troubled person is distressed in the presence of others. Avoidance of, or withdrawal from, others brings relief from anxiety. This strengthens the shy behavior, reinforcing what becomes, little by little, a strong maladaptive habit.

Interpersonal factors play a role in causing chronic shyness. Persons who efface themselves tend to lack assertiveness skills. They do not know how to stand up for themselves and ask for their rights in a relationship. They allow themselves to be used and abused by partners, relatives, and friends. Consequently, they shrink from others and avoid realistic encounters whenever possible. They tend to grant to others too much personal power because they feel, as noted earlier, inferior in some way to others.

As is the case in phobias, the person who suffers from chronic shyness has a very active imagination and is often a person with high levels of creative ability. (Keep in mind that there is such a thing as a *social phobia*, and pathological shyness falls into this clinical category. For more about phobias, see Chapter 14.) The sufferer can easily imagine the kinds of negative judgments and criticisms of his or her behavior or appearance that might be running through the minds of others, and this makes the individual feel ashamed and confused.

Coping

If you suffer from chronic shyness, you may find value in the following list of coping strategies.

• Explore your childhood experiences. If you keep a dated, running journal, you will find that many of your early memories will return to consciousness. You will see how some of today's attitudes toward yourself were shaped by interactions with parents and peers. Understanding the early roots that nurtured a contemporary trait such as chronic shyness can liberate you from it to some extent.

• Examine your inferiority feelings. Keep in mind that a "complex," as originally used in early psychology, was a group of self-referential ideas. These ideas in and of themselves are neither true nor false and, indeed, are often false. They are frequently fictions you hold about yourself. If you examine them in the light of your adult intelligence, often you will be able to reject them. And they will in turn have less influence on you.

• Do not demand too much of yourself too quickly. If you are by temperament somewhat disposed toward shyness, it is unrealistic to think that you are going to convert yourself into a jolly extravert with a large circle of friends. Do not idealize the outgoing style of life and develop unrealistic expectations. Take *small*, effective steps in the right direction. Work on a few specific behaviors and situations, coping at first with the least threatening, most manageable ones.

• Keep in mind that habit is a factor in chronic shyness. Habits are learned. What can be learned can be unlearned. Be aware of how avoidance-and-withdrawal behavior on your part strengthens shyness by providing relief from anxiety. Whenever you feel you have the ego strength, stand your ground and learn to tolerate anxiety. It will diminish because of a phenomenon known as *habituation*, which means that you gradually adapt to a situation. What is being described here is *in vivo* (i.e., "in life") de-sensitization. But again, remember to practice the recommended behaviors *gradually*, and only in social situations that you logically recognize to be manageable ones.

• Give yourself voluntary countersuggestions. It can be argued that the negative ideas you have about yourself are somewhat like posthypnotic suggestions. They derive from attributions that were made about your personality when you were too young to evaluate them. Today, they may be identified as *involuntary suggestions* arising from the subconscious and unconscious levels of your personality. Say to yourself, "I'm as attractive as the next person," or, "I'm as effective as the next person," or, "I reject the 'I'm not O.K., you're O.K.' life position." If these voluntary countersuggestions seem to lack power at first, be sure to *repeat* them, and they will gain in strength and power. Another good idea is to write them down and read them to yourself from time to time with conviction and meaning. Consciously recognize that the involuntary suggestions you have been living with may very well be *wrong* and that the countersuggestions may very well be *right*.

• Do not make an effort to be witty or clever in your speech. Persons who suffer from chronic shyness often mistakenly think that the key to effective human relations resides in adroit, charming self-introductions and the ability to display an agile mind with amusing remarks. Nothing could be farther from the truth. It is far, far better to be straightforward and sincere. You will be less threatening to others and more well liked. Also, there is less of a demand and burden on you. You do not have to keep writing a script for yourself.

• Acquire assertiveness skills. Learn to ask for what you want, to place yourself first some of the time. Realize that you have as much right to be "Number One" as other people. Several popular books list specific assertiveness skills such as *I-messages* and *broken record*. An example of such a book is *When I Say No, I Feel Guilty* by psychologist Manuel Smith. (For more about assertiveness, see Chapter 13.)

• Take up acting as an avocation. This may seem like an odd suggestion in view of the fact that those who suffer from chronic shyness avoid the limelight. However, more than one victim of shyness finds himself or herself able to act in a play. This is because the person's ego can hide behind the character of the role. Now one can play "peek-a-boo" with the world. One is center stage, but one is also hiding. Such experiences can gradually build self-confidence and help a person overcome dispositional shyness.

• Talk about yourself once in a while. You will recall that sufferers from shyness make very few egocentric statements. Although it is true that in social situations people who talk only about themselves are considered to be boring, it is also true that people who almost never talk about themselves are thought to be somewhat odd and too self-concealing. If you seldom talk about your life, your interests, and your attitudes, people will think of you as remote and emotionally isolated. There is nothing wrong with egocentric speech if it is kept within reasonable bounds.

Professional Help

If you find that you cannot cope effectively with chronic shyness, there are several ways in which the professions of psychiatry and clinical psychology can help you.

Clinical data suggest that one of the most fruitful ways to approach the treatment of chronic shyness is through the use of behavior therapy technique pioneered by the psychiatrist Joseph Wolpe. The specific technique is *systematic desensitization*, a process that brings about anxiety reduction through counterconditioning. First, the therapist induces guided fantasies in which the patient is the central character in mildly threatening social situations. If anxiety rises to an uncomfortable level, suggestions that induce muscle relaxation are given. Muscle relaxation is antagonistic to anxiety and brings about desensitization to the anxiety-arousing images. Gradually, it is possible to introduce somewhat more socially demanding fantasies as the patient adapts to the less threatening ones. (For more on desensitization therapy, see the "Professional Help" section in Chapter 14.)

The next treatment to be described is, like systematic desensitization, a kind of behavior therapy because it focuses first on actions, not feelings. *Assertiveness training* is characterized by the learning of a set of effective communication skills designed to help the individual avoid passive, reactive responses to the power tactics of others. The basic thesis is that one can act better *before* one feels better. Acting better is facilitated by the acquisition of some well-defined skills. This is accomplished in terms of the social learning process, a process of modeling and imitation in which the therapist or admired peers act as role models. Effective action feeds back on moods and emotions, helping the patient overcome shyness. In view of the fact that shyness takes place in a social context and is to a large extent an interpersonal problem, assertiveness training is of particular value in treatment.

Although there is no question that behavior therapy is the first line of treatment against chronic shyness, this does not rule out other modes of therapy. They can give a boost to the effects of behavior therapy.

Taking a psychodynamic approach, a therapist will help you gain greater insight into the emotional roots of your chronic shyness. By exploring childhood experiences and the way in which they affected your development, you are likely to find that you will have greater conscious control over dispositional shyness. Understanding the nature of a problem is not sufficient of and in itself to bring about its effective management, but it can give you ideas that will help you cope.

A psychodynamic approach can assist you in comprehending how a social mask can be an ego defense mechanism. It was earlier noted, for example, that such manifest traits as aloofness and emotional coldness were often protective devices designed to deflect the criticisms, real or imaginary, of others. If, in therapy, you can be brought to see how this approach is counterproductive in the long run, how it plunges you increasingly into isolation and loneliness, you may be motivated to give it up.

Finally, taking a cognitive approach, a therapist can work with you to examine your *personal constructs*, ideas you have developed about yourself. These ideas may or may not reflect social reality. However, if you *think* that they are true, they become self-fulfilling prophecies and *acquire* a kind of pseudotruth. You and your therapist can "rewrite" negative personal constructs in such a manner that they will fit better with the actual facts of your life. A cognitive modality will show you that you do not have to be the victim of your own, possibly false, ideas about yourself.

Therapy should bring about the realization that, even if you are somewhat introverted by nature, chronic shyness is *acquired* by experience, and is, on the whole, learned. As noted earlier, what has been learned can be unlearned.

Key Points to Remember

· *Situational shyness* refers to the common experience of feeling shy in some social situations. *Chronic shyness* refers to feeling shy in almost all situations. Chronic shyness can also be called *dispositional shyness*.

· When a person becomes very withdrawn from others and avoids all unnecessary contact with other persons, this person suffers from *pathological shyness*. Also, the term *social introversion* is sometimes used to label the tendency to move away from people and into one's own private psychological world.

· Here is a useful working definition of *chronic shyness*: A distressing personality trait characterized by maladaptive strategies designed to minimize the sense of being overexposed in social situations.

· Some of the signs and symptoms frequently associated with chronic shyness include stumbling or awkward speech, avoidance of the limelight, apparent aloofness, introverted interests, and a small circle of friends.

· The sufferer from chronic shyness has often been, during the developmental years, hypersensitized to criticism and the judgments of others.

· An *inferiority complex* is a set of ideas revolving around one's own ego that state one is inadequate, unattractive, or ineffective in some way.

· An introverted temperament may contribute to shyness.

· Persons who efface themselves tend to lack assertiveness skills. Work on acquiring such skills.

· Examine your inferiority feelings. They may be buttressed by false ideas about yourself.

· Whenever you feel you have the ego strength, stand your ground and learn to tolerate anxiety arising from threatening social situations. The anxiety will eventually diminish because of a phenomenon known as *habituation*.

- Do not make an effort to be witty or clever in your speech.

- Clinical data suggest that one of the most fruitful ways to approach the treatment of chronic shyness is through the use of behavior therapy.

- Taking a psychodynamic approach, a therapist will help you gain greater insight into the emotional roots of your chronic shyness.

- Taking a cognitive approach, a therapist can work with you to examine your *personal constructs*, ideas you have developed about yourself.

Chapter 27

Sleep Difficulties: The Long and Restless Night

Rod Serling, host of the highly praised fantasy and science fiction television series "The Twilight Zone" and author of many of its stories, suffered from persistent insomnia for many of his adult years. This passage from a full-length biography by Joel Engel is instructive:

> So what attracted Rod Serling, the writer, to the world of the fantastic? Bob Serling says that his brother told him "The Twilight Zone" sprang from his frequent insomniac nights, when his active imagination—fed by his lifelong love of horror films, his war experiences, and the stories of such writers as Robert Heinlein, Ray Bradbury, and H. P. Lovecraft—contrived fantastical plots that somehow seemed plausible in the predawn. (*Rod Serling: The Dreams and Nightmares of Life in the Twilight Zone*, p. 103)

It seems certain that Serling would have been more than happy to have had fewer ideas in exchange for more nights of refreshing sleep. Few events in life are more miserable than wanting to sleep, indeed *needing* to sleep, and instead finding that one simply cannot go to sleep no matter how hard one tries.

Insomnia, the focus of this chapter, is one of several sleep disorders recognized by the American Sleep Disorder Association (ASDA). The term *insomnia*, briefly defined, simply means "sleeplessness or inability to sleep." On a more formal level, insomnia is a disturbed or abnormal pattern of sleep. Four of the more common distressing patterns are (1) resistance to falling asleep at all, (2) difficulty in staying asleep, (3) sleep of poor quality, and (4) waking up too early in the morning.

The first pattern described above in which there is great resistance to falling asleep is often accompanied by worries, overstimulation, excitement, and involuntary flights of ideas.

Under these conditions the restless state is referred to as *hyperarousal insomnia*. (This seems to be the kind of insomnia from which Rod Serling suffered.) The term *learned insomnia* is used when maladaptive habits play a role in sleeplessness. The role of conditioning appears to be important in this kind of insomnia, and more will be said about this later. *Hypersomnia* is a sleep disorder that is, in a sense, the opposite of insomnia. People who suffer from hypersomnia seem to be sleepy all of the time. They suffer from chronic drowsiness.

Three other disorders that can be specified are sleep-clock disorder, narcolepsy, and sleep apnea. A *sleep-clock disorder* exists when one's 24-hour wake-sleep cycle is disturbed. A temporary version of this disorder exists when one suffers from jet lag after traveling across several time zones. The individual's "sleep clock" has not yet reset, and he or she wants to sleep or be active at the wrong times in the new time zone. Persons with a chronic sleep-clock disorder cannot seem to conform to the pattern that most people follow, and they suffer significantly if their vocations and responsibilities demand a wake-sleep cycle other than the one demanded by their biological clock.

Narcolepsy is a disorder characterized by falling asleep abruptly and unexpectedly during the daytime hours. The individual does not wish to fall asleep, and the behavior goes against his or her will. To some extent, narcolepsy overlaps with insomnia and hypersomnia because the person who suffers from narcolepsy often also suffers from both of the other two disorders. Narcolepsy is not a frequently encountered condition in clinical work. In spite of its name, it is *not* a kind of epilepsy.

The word *apnea* itself means "a temporary cessation of the respiratory process." Consequently, *sleep apnea* refers to brief interludes during the night when the individual stops breathing. The length of these interludes can usually be measured in seconds, not minutes. The person does not wake up, but the quality of sleep is damaged, and there may be hypersomnia during the day.

Although, as already indicated, the principal focus of this chapter is on insomnia proper, it is evident that it overlaps to some extent with the other sleep disorders. Consequently, in the subsequent discussion of signs and symptoms and in the section on causes and explanations, some light will be shed on sleep disorders in general.

Other signs and symptoms frequently related to the major symptom of persistent insomnia are identified below. Keep in mind that not all of these will necessarily be displayed in the case of a given individual.

1. Fatigue
2. Grouchiness and irritability
3. Inability to concentrate
4. Interference with short-term memory
5. Drowsiness
6. Abuse of stimulants
7. A driven, strong-willed personality
8. Nightmares

The above items merit comment. *Fatigue* is to be expected in persons who suffer from insomnia. One of the important purposes of sleep is to provide an opportunity for the body to rest and restore itself. Frequent loss of sleep acts as a stressor and does not allow normal biological processes to undo the wear and tear experienced by the individual on the prior day.

Loss of sleep affects the individual's personality in an adverse way. Consequently, *grouchiness and irritability* are frequently associated with insomnia. The person who is chronically sleep-deprived often is "touchy" and has a "short fuse." One such individual said, "It's as if I had raw nerves." Some of the grouchiness and irritability can be related to general fatigue. And some of the general touchiness is due to loss of rapid eye movement (REM) sleep. There will be more about this particular point later.

Inability to concentrate refers to an impairment of the voluntary attention. William James, a principal founder of American psychology, spoke of voluntary attention as the ability to focus one's thoughts and problem-solving abilities on a particular topic or target by an act of will. An impairment in this ability makes it difficult to work effectively and meet many of one's obligations during the day. The individual may complain that his or her "mind wanders."

Short-term memory is also known as "working memory." It is the kind of mental process you use when you want to remember where you parked a car, what you had for breakfast, or that you intend to stop at the market on the way home and buy a carton of milk. *Interference with short-term memory* refers to the fact that the person who suffers from persistent insomnia frequently finds that there are little lapses in the ability to recall mental information and a forgetting of intentions that make day-to-day functioning somewhat difficult. (For more about memory problems, see Chapter 17.)

Drowsiness during the day is a common sign of insomnia at night. If this creates a long-standing problem in functioning, the individual may be diagnosed as suffering from *hypersomnia*. (A fictional example of hypersomnia is provided by the dwarf named Sleepy in the Disney version of *Snow White and the Seven Dwarfs*.) It is possible to suffer from daytime drowsiness without suffering from insomnia. However, the reverse case is unlikely. The person who suffers from significant insomnia will be likely to suffer bouts of daytime drowsiness.

Insomnia is often associated with the *abuse of stimulants*. Stimulants are drugs that have the effect of increasing alertness or arousal. They are frequently taken either to help a person "keep going" during the day or for recreational purposes. Examples of commonly abused stimulants include caffeine, nicotine, amphetamines, and cocaine. It is to be expected that if a person abuses stimulants, particularly during the evening hours, he or she will find it hard to "come down" and relax sufficiently for high-quality sleep. (For more about drug abuse, see Chapter 9.)

A person with a *driven, strong-willed personality* will often suffer from insomnia. Such individuals tend to generate a high state of arousal and excitement even without stimulants. (If they also abuse stimulants, the high arousal effect is magnified.) A person with a long agenda of personal dreams, goals, and tasks may think of sleep as a "waste of time." In bed, the person is thinking of tomorrow, what needs to be done, and so forth. He or she finds it hard to let go of the commitment to daily life and just mentally drift for a while.

Nightmares are often associated with insomnia. A nightmare is a vivid dream that induces an emotional state of fear, terror, or general anxiety. Almost all adults have an occasional nightmare. However, if one has frequent nightmares, there are at least two ways in which they may interfere with sleep. First, the individual may be afraid to go to sleep at all because of the anticipated nightmare. Second, when one awakes from a nightmare in the middle of the night, there is usually a high level of arousal (e.g., one's heart may be beating rapidly), and the individual often finds that it is difficult to relax sufficiently to fall asleep again.

Causes and Explanations

Biological factors can play an important part in insomnia. The list of biological factors that may interfere with sleep is long and includes heart disease, high blood pressure, "heartburn" associated with a hiatal hernia, chronic breathing problems linked to such conditions as asthma and emphysema, nagging pain from rheumatoid arthritis, kidney disorders, abnormal thyroid functioning, and adverse side effects to medications.

One of the biological factors not mentioned above is *minimal brain dysfunction (MBD).* This is a condition characterized by such cognitive and behavioral disturbances as hyperaggressiveness, problems in concentration, short attention span, and restlessness. The assumption is that these disturbances are caused by a slight amount of damage in the brain stem, the region of the brain that controls arousal. It is hypothesized that, in most cases, the damage was caused during the birthing process. An infant deprived of oxygen, for example, may suffer such damage. It is not at all uncommon to diagnose the condition in children, and it is believed to be a principal factor in many cases of *attention deficit disorder*, characterized by such behavioral problems as seldom completing tasks, not listening, being distracted easily, impulsiveness, and sometimes aggressiveness. Minimal brain dysfunction may carry over and affect an adult to some extent and can play a role in insomnia because the "arousal center" of the brain has inadequate control over attention and the wake-sleep cycle. The condition does not affect one's intelligence. Minimal brain dysfunction is a treatable condition by the medical profession, particularly by specialists such as neurologists.

In spite of the length of the list of biological factors, the majority of cases of insomnia lack any obvious physical basis. Consequently, psychological factors are considered as important agents. Anxiety can be an important causal factor in insomnia. This is particularly true of individuals who suffer from *free-floating anxiety*, a kind of anxiety that follows a person around all day like a formless cloud. The overall feeling is one of vague apprehension and dread. Such persons are likely to continue to worry and feel anxiety when they are trying to fall asleep. And this, of course, keeps them awake. (For more about chronic anxiety, see Chapter 5.)

Anger can keep a person "on alert." If one goes to bed mad at someone else, particularly one's partner, it will be difficult to fall asleep. Feeling that one has been taken advantage of or believing that one was used and abused by someone else will cause an individual to ruminate and mentally travel the same psychological territory over and over again. The result can be sleeplessness. In the cases of both anxiety and anger, there is *hyperarousal*. One's thoughts keep one in a state of agitation and excitement that is antagonistic to falling asleep. (For more about anger, see Chapter 4.)

It is common to hear it said or to read that depression can play an important role in insomnia. This is not exactly correct because depression suggests *hypoarousal*, or a reduction in the general level of excitement. Persons suffering from long-lasting depression often suffer from hypersomnia, or chronic drowsiness. In fact, they often sleep too much— as many as 10 or more hours per day. However, depression sometimes alternates with periods of *mania*, a condition characterized by great excitement, agitation, aggressiveness, and a flight of ideas. Under these conditions, the individual will, of course, manifest insomnia. The prior observations apply primarily to a behavioral disturbance known as *bipolar disorder*. (The traditional name for bipolar disorder is *manic-depressive psychosis*.)

The lack of regular sleep habits is frequently a causal factor in insomnia. Suppose that a person keeps irregular hours, follows a disorderly schedule, and, in general, has a chaotic, disorganized life style. He or she has no regular bedtime. Under these circumstances, it is understandable that there will be problems with resting and sleeping. To be more specific, lack of a predictable pattern appears to disrupt the action of the *pineal gland*, an endocrine gland that secretes the hormone melatonin. Melatonin regulates *circadian rhythms*, biological rhythms that take place in 24-hour periods. The wake-sleep cycle is one of these rhythms. (In this case, it can be seen that a psychological factor interacts with a biological one.)

A highly active imagination can interfere with the capacity to fall asleep. Debra R. is a single, high school English teacher, 28 years of age, who aspires to a second career as a romance novelist. She often writes two or three hours in the evening, and when she goes to bed, she is still vicariously living the adventures of her heroine. As Debra tries to go to sleep, she continues to get ideas and visualize scenes. She is afraid that if she does not get up from bed and make some notes, she will forget good ideas. She is in a state of self-induced excitement, and this state is antagonistic to sleep.

Also, it should be noted that in the discussion of signs and symptoms, three additional factors were identified that can be causal agents in insomnia. The first of these was the abuse of stimulants. The second was a driven, strong-willed personality. And the third was a tendency to have nightmares.

Coping

If you suffer from persistent insomnia, and if you believe that its principal causes are either psychological factors or behavior patterns within your own control, you may find value in the following list of practical coping strategies.

• Do not abuse stimulants. This includes *all* stimulants, including such common ones as caffeine and nicotine. Stimulants increase the level of overall arousal, make the central nervous system more active, and interfere with the letting down and letting go that is associated with sleep.

• Drink 4 to 8 ounces of slightly warmed milk about one-half hour before you go to bed. If you protest, "I'm lactose intolerant," it is important to be aware that lactose-reduced milks are now available in many markets. Warm milk acts to help you sleep in two ways. First, something that has food value and is also slightly warmed in your stomach activates the parasympathetic division of your autonomic nervous system. This lowers central-nervous-system arousal. In brief, this means that warm milk acts as a natural tranquilizer. Second, there is evidence suggesting that one of the amino acids in milk, tryptophan, regulates the firing of neurons in the cerebral cortex and, in consequence, tends to induce sleepiness.

· Attend to your sleep habits. Practice what is sometimes called *sleep hygiene*. This means that you go bed at the same time most nights, that you have a bedtime routine, that you arise at the same time most mornings, that you usually sleep in familiar surroundings, and so forth. Sleep hygiene will help you to regulate your biological clock.

· Do not overexcite yourself before bedtime. On the whole, for about two hours before bedtime, keep the level of stimulation relatively low. Reading an action-adventure novel, getting into a fight with a partner, and working on a project that requires attention and creative thinking are all examples of behaviors that will make you excited and, in turn, interfere with relaxation and sleep.

· Keep illumination at moderate or low levels for an hour or two before you retire. There is evidence suggesting that high light levels inhibit the pineal gland's production of melatonin. Consequently, overexposure to too much light may make it difficult to sleep or to keep one's sleep-clock regulated.

· If you are restless during the middle of the night, do not suffer, tossing and turning. Get out of bed for about 15 or 20 minutes. Do not do anything demanding or anything that will overly excite you. A good strategy is to read a poem or a psalm that offers a soothing, positive outlook on life. This can have a tranquilizing effect. Again, you can drink a little warm milk.

· Do not try to will yourself to sleep. Falling asleep is an involuntary response and is not under the direct control of the will. In fact, the more you try to will yourself to fall asleep, the more aroused and alert you are likely to become. Sleep can, of course, be *induced*. This is done by creating the conditions that make it possible for you to let go of the day's concerns and slip automatically into sleep. The will, or decision-making ability, plays a part in this process. However, note that the will's effect is indirect, not direct.

· Learn the art of mental entertainment. It is not at all abnormal to take 10 to 20 minutes to fall asleep. If you are bored by the fact that you have nothing to do during this time period, you may feel that it is intolerably long. The art of mental entertainment is characterized by the ability to give yourself either controlled experiences or little tasks that can occupy your attention. Douglas V., for example, is able to give himself the controlled experience of "listening" to music. He has memorized the music and lyrics of many popular songs, and he can "play" them at will. Phoebe T. gives herself the little task of spelling familiar words backwards. She thinks of a word at random, such as *entrance*, and then tries to spell it backwards, reciting mentally, "e-c-n-a-r-t-n-e." She says that the task is interesting and that it occupies her attention. She also indicates that it must not be too exciting because she usually falls asleep easily while engaged in it.

· Be sure that you are warm enough. A common problem is that one feels a little chilly while trying to fall asleep. Warmth induces muscle relaxation, and muscle relaxation induces relaxation in general. Also, muscle relaxation has been found to be antagonistic to anxiety. The old practice of wearing a covering on the head to keep it warm has something to recommend it. (Clement Moore's famous poem "A Visit from St. Nicholas," published in 1823, has in it the lines, "And ma in her kerchief and I in my cap/ Had just settled down for a long winter's nap.")

· Obtain moderate aerobic exercise. Such exercise during the day helps to induce sleep at night. It does this in more than one way. First, moderate exercise facilitates long-range muscle relaxation. Second, moderate exercise helps your central nervous system to form *endorphins*, natural substances that give you a sense of well-being and help you to sleep at night. The word *endorphin* is a contraction of the two words *endogenous* and *morphine*. *Endogenous* means "arising from within." *Morphine* is an opiate, a substance that induces sleep. And it is particularly instructive to note that the word *morphine* itself is derived from the Roman poet Ovid's designation approximately 2,000 years ago of the name Morpheus for the son of sleep and the god of dreams. Do *not* exercise closer than two hours before retiring because this will induce increased central-nervous-system arousal, not relaxation.

Professional Help

If you find that you cannot cope adequately on your own with persistent insomnia, you should seek professional treatment. Because, as earlier indicated, there are many biological factors that can play a role in sleep difficulties, the first thing that you should do is consult a physician. It may be that your problems will require medical treatment and help from medical specialties such as endocrinology and neurology.

Assuming that your problem is not primarily medical in nature and, instead, is of psychological origin, there are several ways in which the professions of psychiatry and clinical psychology can help you.

The first line of psychological treatment for insomnia is usually a behavioral approach. Your sleep habits are behaviors that are accessible, can be clearly defined, and, to some extent, are voluntarily altered. Consequently, they afford the best avenue for attacking your problem. You and your therapist can work together to make a functional analysis of your sleep patterns. The concept of *sleep hygiene*, introduced earlier, plays an important role in modifying your habits. The therapist will help you pinpoint the environmental cues that either tend to keep you awake or induce sleep. Usually, you will be asked to keep a daily record of habits and practices that relate to sleep. The behavioral approach is a problem-solving one that is both practical and direct. It often brings good results with brief therapy.

Although the behavioral approach is of paramount value in the treatment of insomnia and related sleep disorders, this does not mean that other therapeutic approaches cannot be used in combination with it. Other approaches can increase the effectiveness of therapy. Taking a psychodynamic approach, a therapist will focus on the problem of chronic anxiety, a common causal factor in insomnia. Constant worry combined with vague apprehensiveness makes it difficult to relax and go to sleep. The therapist will explore the roots of chronic anxiety and help you find ways to reduce its intensity. (For more about anxiety, see Chapter 5.)

Taking a cognitive approach, a therapist will focus on the kinds of irrational and illogical ideas that tend to keep some people awake. Emil C., for example, two years after his divorce was final, would frequently go to bed and start thinking about his ex-wife, Delia. He frequently repeated to himself such thoughts as, "She was completely unfair to me. She took everything. She never loved me." In therapy, he was helped to see that these thoughts were overgeneralizations and oversimplifications. Emil eventually grew to realize that Delia was not *completely* unfair to him. She was very understanding about sharing time with their children. She had taken her half of the community property, not "everything." And he was able to recall more than one tender moment in the early years of their relationship.

Cognitive therapy often includes training in two related skills called thought stopping and thought substitution. *Thought stopping* teaches the individual ways to "turn off" useless thought sequences. Thought stopping can get a boost from *thought substitution*. It teaches the individual to voluntarily substitute a new, productive, and useful idea in place of an older, self-defeating idea. The two techniques can be applied to Emil's case. Suppose he starts thinking one night, "Delia never loved me." Using thought stopping, he then says to himself, "All right, Emil. I want you to stop this. You're just going on a mental merry-go-round. This kind of circular thinking is pointless." Now, using thought substitution, he says to himself, "I cannot say that Delia never really loved me. I still remember how caring and concerned she was that time I had surgery. And I'll never forget the good time we had on our honeymoon."

If you are a member of a couple, taking an interpersonal approach, a therapist will focus on communication patterns and emotional exchanges associated with your ongoing relationship. If these patterns are self-defeating, as they often are, they can induce anxiety and anger, and these emotional states may cause or aggravate insomnia. A therapist will help you and your partner discover better ways of relating to each other, ways that bring you greater emotional closeness, while at the same time preserving the autonomy of each individual. (For more about the interpersonal approach, see Chapter 13.)

It is common for physicians, including psychiatrists, to prescribe drugs for insomnia. *Diphenhydramine* is an antihistamine, and it is available in some over-the-counter medications. In stronger doses, a prescription is required. Some of the trade names used to market diphenhydramine are Benadryl, Insomnal, Nytol, and Sominex. Antihistamines do not appear to create a physiological dependency, and they do induce sleep. There are a group of drugs known as sedative-hypnotic agents, and these usually require a prescription. Some of these drugs are sodium butabarbital, flurazepam hydrochloride, phenobarbital, and temazepam. Tranquilizers, because they reduce anxiety, are also frequently prescribed for sleep.

Drugs have some significant drawbacks in the treatment of insomnia. First, there are sometimes adverse side effects. Second, there is evidence suggesting that some of the drugs interfere with rapid eye movement (REM) sleep. This is the kind of sleep associated with dreaming, and it appears to be important in maintaining mental health. The data surrounding the effects of drugs on REM sleep is somewhat contradictory. Nonetheless, there is some concern. Third, a drug tolerance often builds up. Then the individual is not helped much by the drug but has a very difficult time sleeping during any period of withdrawal. On the whole, drug therapy is useful for dealing with some acute sleep problems. However, drug therapy is seldom a long-term treatment of choice for persistent insomnia of psychogenic origin. In general, it can be expected that such insomnia will respond well to both the self-management coping strategies and the psychological therapies presented earlier.

Key Points to Remember

• *Insomnia*, briefly defined, simply means "sleeplessness or inability to sleep."

• *Hyperarousal insomnia* is characterized by resistance to falling asleep, worries, overstimulation, excitement, and involuntary flights of ideas.

• The term *learned insomnia* is used when maladaptive habits play a role in sleeplessness.

• Three sleep disorders in addition to those listed above are sleep-clock disorder, narcolepsy, and sleep apnea.

• Signs and symptoms frequently related to the major symptom of persistent insomnia include fatigue; inability to concentrate; drowsiness; and a driven, strong-willed personality.

• A number of biological factors may interfere with sleep. Consequently, you may find it necessary to consult a physician for help.

• Such emotional problems as chronic anxiety and persistent anger can be important causal factors in insomnia.

• The lack of regular sleep habits is frequently a causal factor in insomnia.

• A highly active imagination can interfere with the capacity to fall asleep.

• Do not abuse stimulants. They increase the level of overall arousal.

• Drinking 4 to 8 ounces of slightly warmed milk about one-half hour before going to bed can often help you sleep.

• Practice sleep hygiene.

• Do not overexcite yourself before bedtime.

• Taking a behavioral approach, a therapist will help you pinpoint the environmental cues that either tend to keep you awake or induce sleep.

• Taking a psychodynamic approach, a therapist will focus on the problem of chronic anxiety.

• Taking a cognitive approach, a therapist will focus on the kinds of irrational and illogical ideas that tend to keep some people awake.

• Drug therapy is common in the treatment of sleep disorders. However, drugs have some significant drawbacks.

Chapter 28

Workaholism: Prisoners of Success

Otto C. is a hard-driving businessman who owns two family restaurants, 50 miles apart. He spends a total of 70 to 80 hours a week managing his two establishments. Kathleen M. is a California community college English professor. She teaches a full load of five classes plus two extra evening classes, is under contract to research a composition textbook, and is writing a novel that she hopes to have published. It is not unusual for her to work until 1:00 A.M., writing or grading papers. Both Otto and Kathleen suffer from a pathological psychological symptom that can be called *workaholism*. They are intelligent, ambitious, successful persons—and they are prisoners of their own success.

Workaholism is certainly not a mental disorder and is not listed as such in the American Psychiatric Association's handbook of such disorders. Nonetheless, it is a disturbing behavioral trait with substantial costs, as shall be seen, to the individual. As such, it can be regarded as a psychological symptom. The concept of workaholism has arisen as an informal one among people in general, and it is obviously derived from the word *alcoholism*. Although *workaholism* has no precise clinical meaning, it can be broadly defined as "a stable behavioral pattern in which an individual is psychologically addicted to work." Like an alcoholic, the individual cannot readily resist the "drug" of work. Work draws the person like a magnet.

The concept of workaholism does not apply to individuals who must work long hours as a necessity. A small farmer with livestock that must be tended to every day may work 60 or 70 hours a week, but he or she is not suffering from workaholism. A single parent who works long hours and takes college classes in the hope of becoming a better provider is not a victim of workaholism.

On the whole, it can be said that persons who display workaholism tend to perform either challenging or creative work, not routine drudgery. They tend to be people who (1) own businesses or have management positions in a business, (2) have professions in such fields as medicine, law, and teaching, or (3) have careers in the fine arts, such as writing, composing, or performing.

Signs and symptoms associated with the focus symptom of workaholism are listed below. Not all of these need appear in the case of a given individual.

1. Working 50 percent or more over the standard 40-hour work week
2. Talking about work "constantly"
3. Working even when ill
4. Being bored and restless when on vacation
5. Obtaining almost all psychological and emotional gratification from work
6. Feeling vaguely guilty when not working
7. The "I'm doing this for you" rationalization
8. The conviction that others are incompetent
9. The early-death syndrome

The above items merit comment. *Working 50 percent or more over the standard 40-hour work week* is common among those who suffer from workaholism. It is not at all unusual for persons who display the trait to work 12-to-16-hour days or to work 7 days a week. The great inventor Thomas Alva Edison comes to mind; he worked around the clock and slept by taking catnaps only when he had to.

Some people *talk "constantly" about work*, driving the subject into the ground. A general conversation is going on, and they will somehow turn the topic toward their own vocation. If a tape recording were to be made, if might be found that 80 to 90 percent of their remarks were work related.

Victims of workaholism tend to *work even when ill*. A cold, cough, pains in the chest, or fever will not keep them in bed or at home. It is not that they are insensitive to pain or without distress. It is just that there is a feeling that the work *must get done* at almost any cost.

Being bored and restless when on vacation is one of the more reliable symptoms of workaholism. The individual keeps thinking about all that needs to be done, makes phone calls back to the place of business or employment, and makes extensive notes even when sightseeing. It is not uncommon for the person to feel in ill health while on vacation. In the case of businesspersons, they often suffer from anxiety about the course of the business while they are away, and this can be a factor in such disorders as peptic ulcers.

When people are addicted to work, they *obtain almost all of their psychological and emotional gratification from work.* Coworkers and employees often provide more recognition than do partners or children. Work provides its addicts with feelings of competence; this in turn enhances self-esteem. Work keeps persons active and helps them avoid boredom. Obviously, the immediate psychological payoffs can be substantial and may help the person compensate for a family situation that does not offer either enough affection or approval.

Persons addicted to work often *feel vaguely guilty when they are not working*. At a rational level, they know that they have earned a rest, that there is nothing wrong with recreation. But the voice of conscience whispers, "You're wasting time. You're not accomplishing anything. You ought to be doing something productive."

The *"I'm doing this for you" rationalization* is an ego defense mechanism offered to partners who feel neglected. The driven person argues that he or she is trying to provide a higher standard of living, build an estate for a partner or the children, and so forth. And it is true that the troubled person is usually a good provider. Consequently, like all rationalizations, the one in question has a superficial plausibility. Nonetheless, it *is* a rationalization and only a cover over deeper motives and a hidden agenda.

The victim of workaholism often has *the conviction that others are incompetent*. There is the firm belief that "no one can do the job quite as well as I can." This is particularly true if the individual owns a business or supervises others. There is the frequent complaint that underlings are "blockheads," "out of it," "daydreamers," "lazy," and so forth.

The *early-death syndrome* is a well-known pattern to stress researchers. It goes by the more formal name *the general adaptation syndrome* and was first identified by the Canadian researcher Hans Selye. The three stages of the syndrome are (1) alarm, (2) resistance, and (3) exhaustion. The alarm reaction is set off when an individual encounters heavy stress and must find a way to cope with it. Arousal and alertness increase; the "fight-or-flight" reaction is triggered, and the body begins to secrete additional adrenal hormones. The second stage, resistance, is a plateau of considerable duration. In human beings who are addicted to work, there is chronic stress often lasting for years. The person appears to be coping relatively well— lives, works, solves problems, reproduces, has relationships, and so forth. Nonetheless, the chronic stress takes a heavy toll. The third stage, exhaustion, often appears suddenly and seemingly unexpectedly. The individual develops heart disease, bleeding ulcers, a lung infection, cancer, or another illness that on the surface may not seem to be related to stress. However, it can be argued that the individual has become highly susceptible to disease and infection because the immune system has been greatly weakened by chronic stress. In the case of the workaholism, the stress is self-induced. A premature death is often the result.

Causes and Explanations

One of the basic themes that runs through the behavior of those who suffer from workaholism is *avoidance*. In particular, such persons often arrange their lives in such a manner that they can move away from or put psychological distance between themselves and a partner. There is often a troubled relationship to be found at home, and the person feels more important, more competent, and more gratified at work.

If there is repressed hostility toward the partner, hostility that cannot stand open admission or expression, then being away from home in order to work accomplishes two purposes: it allows for the gratification indicated above, and it also is a way of punishing a partner via the means of neglect without admitting that there is, in fact, any actual neglect. Indeed, the addicted person can use the "I'm only doing it for you" rationalization to reinforce the denial that the behavior in question is punitive toward another.

A neurotic need for power is frequently a causal factor in workaholism. The need for power is one of the basic social motives, and, within reason, it is a normal one. The need for power propels people toward accomplishments and motivates them to become both effective and competent. However, when the need for power is excessive, it may express itself in compulsive, rigid ways. Thus, a high need for power may drive the individual to ruthlessly dominate employees or underlings. The troubled person may feel like a small god when working, when telling others what to do, and when his or her hands are at the controls of a career. Away from work, there is a sense of emptiness, a power vacuum.

Everyone has a need to structure time. The need to structure time expresses itself as the desire to have something to do and someplace to go. It is because of the need to structure time that many people have to "make plans" on weekends and are unable to just relax and enjoy leisure time without a timetable. The importance of the need to structure time was stressed by the psychiatrist Eric Berne, father of transactional analysis. Persons addicted to work appear to have an above-average need to structure time. Every spare minute must be filled with a goal, a task. They hate to have "time on their hands." The intense need to structure time is met to a large extent by working. The days are full. Now they have somewhere to go and something to do.

One of the motives studied by psychologists is called *the need for achievement*. A person with a low need for achievement suffers from the "amotivational syndrome." He or she sets a low level of aspiration, does not have well-defined goals in life, and seems, much of the time, to be just drifting. On the other hand, a person with a high need for achievement sets a correspondingly high level of aspiration, has well-defined goals in life, and seems to be always "on track" toward a destination. A high need for achievement is admirable. However, the person addicted to work probably has a need for achievement that is too high. The level of aspiration is frequently unrealistic. If "impossible dreams" do not come true, there is often bitter disappointment.

In traditional psychoanalytic terms, a high need for achievement may be a component in a strict *superego*, the moral agent of the personality. The superego sets goals and standards like a harsh taskmaster. It says, "Jump," and the individual jumps. Work-addicted persons often report that they feel somewhat like robots, that they *have to* work. It is possible in such cases that during their developmental years they were subjected to a parental style that was characterized by two factors. First, it was authoritarian. The parents were overcontrolling and dominating. Second, the parents controlled the child through the use of *conditional love*, love that had to be earned. The idea was communicated that "we will love you *if* you are a little angel, are good, and do whatever Mommy and Daddy tell you to do." If such an attitude is assimilated into the personality—and it often is—the long-range effect is that even in adulthood the individual will compulsively work and strive in a blind effort to keep pleasing the internal image of one's parents of the past. Work and more work makes the person feel psychologically comfortable, approved of in some nebulous, half-understood way. And, conversely, the individual tends to feel guilty when not working because the superego says, "You must work harder. You ought to be working now."

Overattachment to a vocation can be explained to a certain extent by reference to a principle known as the *functional autonomy of motives*. The principle was first formulated by the Harvard psychologist Gordon W. Allport, a personality theorist. The principle states that behavior patterns often become detached from their original motives or incentives. The behavior becomes self-gratifying, intrinsically valuable to the individual even though it does not necessarily bring any objective reward or satisfy any biological or social need. A sort of psychological perpetual motion takes place. So the person goes on working and working and working when all others shake their heads and ask, "Why?"

Many people feel that life has no real meaning or purpose. This state of affairs is termed an *existential vacuum*, a vague feeling that our mortal being is at its core empty. Understandably, an encounter with an existential vacuum is frightening, and there is a strong tendency to run from it. Burying one's self in work is one of several ways to, in a synthetic way, fill up the hole in one's existence. (For more about meaninglessness, see Chapter 16.)

Coping

If you suffer from workaholism and find its costs are greater than its benefits, you may find value in the following list of practical coping strategies.

• Find ways to stop running. A German proverb says, "What is the use of running when we are not on the right road?" The "I have to hurry because I have so much to do" attitude toward life characteristic of work-addicted individuals is frequently counterproductive. A nervous froth is not the best way to get things done. Remember the fable of the tortoise and the hare— the tortoise won the race because it paced itself and did not get too excited.

• Decide to give up the rationalization that "I'm only doing it for you." Whatever it is you are doing in the way of overwork, you are almost certainly doing it for yourself. If it is depriving a person you care about of your time and affection, you are doing your relationship more harm than good. Face facts. Ask yourself, "Am I really doing this in order to provide a better standard of living? Or am I really doing it because of other motives?"

• Question your need for power. Ask yourself if it is excessive. Is it a way of dominating others? If so, you should recognize that an excessive need for power has the long-term effect of isolating you from others. It will eventually make you feel very, very lonely. Say to yourself, "I do not need or want this much personal power. It's not worth it." Make an effort to exert less power. Instead, negotiate with others in a rational way.

• Look for ways to cut back on the hours you invest in work. You cannot do this all at once, but you should think of it as a worthy goal. Try to shave four hours off the first week, for example. At first, you will have "withdrawal symptoms." You may feel bored, restless, dissatisfied, and empty. You may even develop a headache or suffer some other low-grade physical symptom. Therefore, do not cut back an additional four hours until you have found a way to cope with the first four hours of leisure, or unstructured, time. If you feel you must work more than 40 hours a week, try to get your total time down to no more than 48 to 50 hours.

• Commit yourself to taking off at least *one complete day* each week. Essayist Clarence Day, author of the book that inspired the famous play *Life with Father*, wrote, "The ant is knowing and wise; but it doesn't know enough to take a vacation." Do not be like the unthinking ant, a sort of work-robot.

• Take on no more than one or two important projects at a time. This recommendation is contained in the familiar advice "Don't bite off more than you can chew." People who are addicted to accomplishment will often simultaneously involve themselves in three, four, five, or more assignments, ventures, or enterprises. One successful author, for example, signed four different book contracts with four different publishing companies and found himself working 16-hour days six and seven days a week. Think ahead, and do not impulsively jump into deep psychological water.

• Cultivate the capacity for experiential meaning. *Experiential meaning*, as described by the psychiatrist Viktor Frankl, is the capacity to derive intrinsic satisfaction from a passive experience, one that is not an objective accomplishment. Examples are the joys associated with watching a child take his or her first steps, reading a novel, looking at a painting, gazing upon a sunset, tasting good food, petting a dog, and so forth. Work-addicted persons tend to get almost all of their sense of value out of assertive activity that ends in accomplishment. As you can see from the above, meaning does not begin and end with constructive behavior alone. Reject the idea that all of your time has to be used in a productive way. Nonproductive existence also has its place.

• Avoid self-labeling. Do not say to yourself, "I am a workaholic." This simple statement, seemingly a constructive admission, has its risks. It associates your very being with the trait of workaholism. Psychologically, workaholism and you become hopelessly connected. Instead, separate the trait from yourself. Say, "I'm a person who suffers from workaholism," or, "I'm addicted to work," or "I'm a work-addicted person." (These are the usages adhered to in this chapter.) If workaholism is not an intrinsic part of your personality but instead something that is looked on as a kind of affliction, then there is hope for change, and there is also the hope that you can rid yourself of the affliction.

• Confront the issue of meaninglessness. Ask yourself, "Is addiction to work a way of filling an existential vacuum?" If the answer is yes, you will only compound the problem by burying yourself in the activities associated with a career. Instead, begin to think about the meaning of your life, why you exist, and what is of real, enduring, long-term value to you. Look for avenues of behavior that will give your life greater meaning. (For more about meaninglessness, see Chapter 16.)

Professional Help

If you find that you are unable to adequately cope on your own with the maladaptive trait of workaholism, there are several ways in which the professions of psychiatry and clinical psychology can help you.

Taking a psychodynamic approach, a therapist may help you gain insight into how a punitive, demanding superego acts as a taskmaster, keeping you like a slave at the job day after day. The *superego* is the moral agent of the personality and often reflects the attributions and wishes of one's parents. It is quite possible that some persons are still carrying out "orders" given long ago, orders that are no longer functional.

A therapist will also help you examine your ego defense mechanisms. One of these, the "I'm only doing it for you" rationalization, has already been discussed. The therapist will assist you in developing greater insight into how you may use and abuse it. Also, the therapist will help you to understand, and in turn neutralize, some of the effects of other defense mechanisms. It is common to employ the mechanism called *denial of reality*. When Richard C. started therapy, he insisted that "everything" was perfect between him and his wife. Gradually, he was able to see that he was using work as a way of running away from his sense of ineffectiveness at times when his wife expressed a desire for greater emotional closeness.

Taking a behavioral approach, a therapist may assist you in examining the ways in which workaholism is sustained as a maladaptive habit by reinforcers. Examples of reinforcers associated with work are already familiar. They include recognition, relief from boredom, the structuring of time, an opportunity to express personal power, and so forth. Applying behavior therapy, a functional analysis is made in which you and the therapist determine together *specific* cues that trigger a habitual, unreflected response. Kathleen M., the community college English professor introduced in the first paragraph of this chapter, discovered that she signed up for extra committee work after an incident with her mother left Kathleen feeling slighted and unimportant. Once the connection between the cue of the incident and the recognition provided by committee members and the college president was revealed, Kathleen was free to give consciously weighed responses to adverse incidents involving her mother instead of running toward more work.

Taking a cognitive approach, a therapist will help you to see the ways in which irrational ideas may play a role in workaholism. As earlier indicated, a common cognitive distortion is self-labeling in which an individual says, "I am a workaholic." The adverse aspects of this proposition have already been discussed and will not be repeated at this point. However, assume that the individual continues to think such associated thoughts as, "It's hopeless. I'll never change." Cognitive therapy will reveal that these statements also contain cognitive distortions. The proposition "It's hopeless" is based on overly simplified either-or thinking. A dichotomy is made between total hope and lack of hope. A more realistic interpretation of a psychological state of affairs is to recognize that hope resides on a gradient with a number of degrees between its two extremes. As dismal as it seems at first, converting the "hopeless" statement to something such as "I do not have much hope" is an advance. The existence of hope in some small degree has been granted. Now there is something to build on.

The "I'll never change" proposition can also be shown to be based on a well-known logical error known as *hasty generalization* or *jumping to conclusions*. Based on the inconclusive evidence of the past limited experiences of one's own life, the individual has reached a final, self-defeating conclusion about the future. The reality is that people learn, grow, change, and take new directions. Life is an open system, not a closed one. These kinds of understandings can be attained in the context of the cognitive approach.

Taking a humanistic approach, a therapist will help you explore the ways in which such factors as the search for meaning and the need for self-actualization play a role in workaholism. As earlier indicated, excessive work may be filling an existential vacuum with pseudomeaning. Applying a humanistic mode, a therapist will help you discover what is of real value to you.

In the case of self-actualization, it is common for work-addicted persons to be chasing goals and dreams that are not their own, but those that were both suggested and imposed by parents in one's developmental years. The troubled person feels that "I ought to be a physician because that's what Dad always wanted for me." Oddly, as indicated earlier by a quoted German proverb, people often run faster when they are on the wrong road. A humanistic orientation in therapy makes a distinction between ego-ideal actualization and self-actualization. *Ego-ideal actualization* consists of working toward false goals that really belong to other people, often one's parents. *Self-actualization* consists of the kind of work and avocations that bring to fruition one's own unique aptitudes and talents. Therapy will help a person suffering from workaholism to make new, adult choices based on the natural need for self-actualization.

Key Points to Remember

• Although *workaholism* has no precise clinical meaning, it can be broadly defined as "a stable behavioral pattern in which an individual is psychologically addicted to work."

• On the whole, it can be said that persons who display workaholism tend to perform either challenging or creative work, not routine drudgery.

• Signs and symptoms associated with the focus symptom of workaholism include working 50 percent or more over the standard 40-

hour work week, talking "constantly" about work, being bored and restless when on vacation, and the early-death syndrome.

• One of the basic themes that run through the behavior of those who suffer from workaholism is avoidance of significant others, such as a partner.

• A neurotic need for power is frequently a causal factor in workaholism.

• Persons addicted to work appear to have an above average need to structure time.

• Overattachment to a vocation can be explained to a certain extent by reference to a principle known as the *functional autonomy of motives.*

• Find ways to stop running. Remember the German proverb that asks, "What is the use of running when we are not on the right road?"

• Question your need for power. Ask yourself if it is excessive.

• Commit yourself to taking off at least *one complete day* each week.

• Cultivate the capacity for *experiential meaning,* the capacity to derive intrinsic satisfaction from a passive experience, one that is not an objective accomplishment.

• Taking a psychodynamic approach, a therapist may help you gain insight into how a punitive, demanding superego acts as a taskmaster, keeping you like a slave at the job day after day.

• Taking a behavioral approach, a therapist will help you to examine the ways in which workaholism is sustained as a maladaptive habit by reinforcers.

• Taking a cognitive approach, a therapist will help you to see the ways in which irrational ideas may play a role in workaholism.

• Taking a humanistic approach, a therapist will help you explore the ways in which such factors as the search for meaning and the need for self-actualization play a role in workaholism.

Chapter 29

Concluding Remarks: Symptom-Free Living

Is symptom-free living possible? If symptom-free living is living without ever being sad, bored, or anxious, always being comfortable in all social situations, and so forth, then, of course, it is not possible. The kinds of experiences identified are part and parcel of the human condition. However, this is *not* what is meant by symptom-free living.

Symptom-free living is the capacity to live without the plague of chronic mental, emotional, and behavioral problems. It refers to the capacity to think clearly in most circumstances, to spontaneously experience emotions that are appropriate to the majority of occasions, and to act in an effective manner in order to lead a constructive, satisfying life. This definition of *symptom-free living* gives rise to a "yes" answer to the chapter's opening question.

As was mentioned in Chapter 1, it now appears from both research evidence and experience with psychotherapy that the natural emotional state of a human being without significant psychological symptoms is a general feeling of mental and emotional well-being—comparable to the way your body feels on good days when you have no aches or pains.

Some suffering in life is inevitable. As already indicated, it is the *chronic* suffering that you should seek to defeat. And this is within the realm of possibility.

The aim of this chapter is to briefly identify seven master principles of symptom-free living. This is, of course, the concluding chapter. Consequently, these principles summarize much of what has been both implicit and explicit in prior chapters.

Principle 1

Take care of your physical health. It is an often missed point, although obvious, that mental health is built on a bedrock of physical health. A person who abuses refined sugar may suffer from hypoglycemia, and symptoms such as anxiety and depression can mistakenly be thought to be psychological in origin. A male who overeats saturated fats may eventually suffer from atherosclerosis, and this can be a complicating factor in erectile dysfunction. A person who is undernourished may suffer from chronic fatigue, and this can contribute toward a nagging state of depression. Other similar examples were given in earlier chapters. The fact of the matter is that the *soma*, or body, and the *psyche*, or mind, are intertwined. They interact and affect each other in a complex way.

Before you decide that there is something seriously wrong with your mental and emotional life, make sure that you are taking care of yourself at a fundamental, biological level.

Principle 2

Know your own motives. For almost every human action, there is an answer to the question "*Why* did you do it?" Human beings have primitive biological drives, such as hunger, thirst, the need to escape from pain, and the impulse toward sexual behavior. Under some circumstances, they may have a need to be aggressive and even destructive. Evidence suggests that human beings have an inborn curiosity drive and an inborn need for activity and also have complex social motives such as the need for power, the need for achievement, and the need for affiliation.

To complicate matters, some motives are unconscious. This was one of Freud's basic points. Motives are repressed that are forbidden in terms of one's moral self or in light of the values of one's family and culture. As a consequence, these motives often act as invisible agents, and the person becomes their pawn and victim. In particular, these motives often consist of forbidden sexual and aggressive impulses.

The complex interplay of both conscious and unconscious motives can reside behind a wide range of psychological symptoms. Motives as factors were identified and discussed in most of the prior chapters under the heading "Causes and Explanations."

It is in the realm of motivation that the ancient dictum *know thyself* is most applicable. Some principal means and avenues for knowing oneself are personal reflection, discussions with nonjudgmental friends, keeping a journal of thoughts and dreams, meditation, and free association in psychotherapy.

Principle 3

Learn how to modify maladaptive habits. Habits are learned responses. One of their striking features is that they involve little or no conscious reflection.

Something triggers the habit, and this event activates a predictable behavioral chain. Events that trigger habits are called *cues* or *conditioned stimuli*. Habits themselves are maintained by *reinforcers*, or "payoffs" for the behavior. These payoffs can be objective in nature, such as food, water, money, or praise; or they can be subjective, such as reduction of anxiety, avoidance of pain, satisfaction of the curiosity drive, or domination over another person. Reinforcers strengthen and maintain habits.

The importance of habits in human behavior was stressed by such psychologists as John B. Watson, the father of behaviorism, and B. F. Skinner, a researcher who did much to stimulate the interest in behavior modification.

The key to modifying habits is to know both the cues that trigger the habit and the reinforcers that strengthen it. One can then effectively modify the habit either by avoiding the critical cues or by finding other ways to obtain its associated reinforcers. When you set out to modify a habit, it helps greatly to make in writing a *functional analysis* of your behavior. The functional analysis should (1) break the habit down into its individual components, (2) identify cues or triggers, (3) identify reinforcers, and (4) include your ideas for ways to cope with the cues and reinforcers.

A Spanish proverb says, "Habits are at first cobwebs, then cables." It is unfortunate that one's maladaptive habits can come to exert a strong grip. Nonetheless, there is real hope. Habits, as earlier indicated, are *learned*. They are not a part of the inborn, unchangeable programming of your brain and nervous system. They were not there when you were an infant and a toddler. What was learned can be unlearned. It takes some time, some effort, and some know-how, but it can be done.

Principle 4

Avoid cognitive distortions. Cognitive distortions are illogical, irrational ways of thinking, and they often play a role in both adverse emotional reactions and self-defeating actions. Cognitive distortions are the target of related approaches to both self-help and therapy. The three most familiar such approaches are *rational-emotive therapy*, pioneered by the psychotherapist Albert Ellis; *cognitive therapy*, often associated with the psychiatrist Aaron T. Beck; and *cognitive-behavior modification*, linked to the teachings of social learning theorists such as Albert Bandura.

Examples of common cognitive distortions include all-or-nothing thinking, overgeneralization, jumping to conclusions, magnification, and personal labeling. These were discussed and identified earlier in various chapters under the heading "Coping."

The key to avoiding cognitive distortions is *reflection*. One must stop and think and take a hard look at one's automatic thought chains. Unfortunately, people have a strong tendency to take their own thoughts as correct and true merely because they are *their* thoughts. This tendency can be thwarted, however, to some extent. You have the capacity to think and then to *think again*. Almost everyone has heard the term *second thoughts*. One might say, "I changed my mind. I had second thoughts." This is what it takes to cope with cognitive distortions. A tendency toward second thoughts in which cognitive distortions are challenged and examined can itself become an adaptive mental habit.

Principle 5

Seek ways to improve your personal relationships. Human beings are social beings. Consequently, many psychological symptoms are caused or aggravated by disturbances between oneself and others. An argument or a falling out with a partner may trigger an episode of depression. Lack of comfort in a marriage may induce one of its members to avoid prolonged contact by developing a trait such as workaholism. A feeling of latent hostility toward a partner may play a role in a sexual dysfunction. And people often play pathological, self-defeating "games" with each other. This viewpoint is emphasized in the writings of the psychiatrist Eric Berne, father of transactional analysis.

One of the key ways to improve relationships is by becoming assertive. *Assertiveness* is the happy medium in a social response between extreme passiveness and extreme aggressiveness. If you are too passive, you will feel used and abused. And this is often a complicating factor in depression. If you are too aggressive, you will push others away, and you will end up feeling emotionally isolated and unloved. Assertiveness as a social skill helps you to retain control over your own behavior, stand up for your rights, avoid shyness, and establish emotional closeness. It is a behavioral trait well worth developing.

Principle 6

Give a high priority to uniquely human needs. According to humanistic and existential psychology, two of these needs are (1) the need for self-actualization and (2) the need for meaning in life. Abraham Maslow, a principal founder of humanistic psychology, defined the need for self-actualization as the need to make the most of one's talents and potentialities. People want at some deep level to become what they are meant to become. If this need is frustrated, depression is often the result.

The psychiatrist Viktor Frankl has called attention to the importance of the need for meaning in life. He asserts that this is an inborn need and that it really is possible to satisfy it. The way in which this is done is by discovering values, those experiences or accomplishments that appear to you to have intrinsic, real importance. If the need for meaning is frustrated, the result will be an existential vacuum. An *existential vacuum* exists when a person believes that nothing is worth doing and that life is pointless. Feelings of great despair and demoralization accompany an existential vacuum.

Principle 7

Assert your autonomy. Autonomy is the capacity for self-direction, experienced as the conviction that you are in charge of your life and can make effective decisions. Traditionally, in the history of philosophy and psychology, there are two opposed viewpoints relating to the subject of autonomy. The first viewpoint is termed *determinism*, and it assumes that all behavior is determined—it is caused by known or potentially knowable factors such as genetic structures, motives, conditioned responses, early-life experiences, or the social environment.

The second viewpoint is termed *voluntarism*, and it assumes that the experience of autonomy is real. The traditional name for the mind's power to direct behavior is *free will*. William James, often called the dean of American psychologists, suffered from depression as a younger man. He had accepted determinism, and he felt somewhat like a pawn of circumstances beyond his control. He read an essay by the French philosopher Charles Renouvier that convinced him of the reality of voluntarism. James said that his first act of free will was to decide that he had a free will. And this played an important part in the lifting of his depression.

Studies conducted by the psychologist Julian Rotter make a distinction between external control and internal control. Some persons tend to see their behavior as primarily under *external control*. External agents or forces are perceived as alien to the personality. Examples of such agents or forces are other people, abusive childhood experiences, the impersonal organization, luck, the lack of an insider's favored position, the state of the economy, and so forth. Other persons tend to see their behavior as primarily under *internal control*. Internal agents or forces are perceived as belonging to the personality. Examples of such agents or forces are one's positive ambitions, one's talents, one's aptitudes, one's likes and dislikes, the capacity to dream about the future, and the perception that indeed one really has a free will. Rotter's studies suggest that *locus of control* is an important factor in mental health. If one locates sources of control outside of one's personality, one feels helpless and life seems hopeless. This tends to be associated with anxiety and depression. On the other hand, if one locates sources of control within one's personality, one feels effective and competent. This tends to be associated with a sense of well-being and a generally optimistic outlook. Rotter's research confirms James's more informal and personal observations.

It should be clear that neither Rotter's research nor James's experience resolves age-old philosophical issues revolving around determinism and voluntarism. However, that is why Principle 7 says you should *assert* your autonomy. It is not necessary to prove something is true in order to assert it. If you assert that you have free will, then you act *as if* you have free will. And this itself will be a positive force in freeing you from the plague of chronic psychological symptoms.

A Last Word

In brief, this is a book built on a foundation of *hope*. You have been shown in numerous ways, based on solid psychological principles, how you can avoid being a victim of either others or yourself. No one needs to endure chronic mental and emotional suffering. If you feel trapped, be assured that there are ways out. You need to look for them and make an effort. They are there and you will find them. If you cannot do it on your own, the professions of psychiatry and clinical psychology offer real help.

Again, there is hope.

There is help.

Glossary

The Glossary provides brief definitions of all psychological terms used in the book. You can also consult *The Family Mental Health Encyclopedia*, also by this author, for additional definitions and discussions of terms that have particular reference to psychological symptoms.

A

Abreaction. In psychoanalysis, the discharge of an emotion associated with a memory that is both repressed and painful.

Accident proneness. The tendency to have a series of injuries in which either standard safety precautions are disregarded or there is an element of carelessness.

Acute suicide. See *chronic suicide*.

Agoraphobia. An anxiety disorder characterized by a set of related fears including the fear of being alone, the fear of public places, and a fear of traveling any significant distance from home.

Ahedonia. See *anhedonia*.

Alcohol. See *sedatives*.

Alcohol abuse. A chronic self-destructive pattern of heavy drinking that produces significant damage to one's health, career, and family relations.

Alcohol amnestic disorder. A disorder characterized by damage to the central nervous system and by memory impairment. The traditional name for alcohol amnestic disorder is *Korsakoff's psychosis*.

Alcohol dependence. The inability to free oneself at will from a pattern of heavy drinking; can be thought of as an addiction to a drug.

Alcoholic. A person who is dependent on alcohol or who manifests a pattern of chronic alcohol abuse.

Alienation. A psychological symptom associated with the belief that one is alone, is an emotional stranger to others, and does not fit into one's family, society, or other reference group in a meaningful way.

All-or-none (either-or) thinking. A cognitive distortion characterized by the tendency to sort all events and experiences into only two categories.

Alzheimer's disease. A disease involving degeneration of neurons in the frontal portion of the brain. Signs and symptoms of Alzheimer's disease include memory impairment, bewilderment, lack of trust, useless activity, and agitation.

Amobarbital (Amytal) interview. The use of the drug amobarbital in therapy as a means of gaining access to repressed memories.

Amphetamines. See *stimulants.*

Amytal. The brand name of the drug amobarbital. See also *amobarbital interview.*

Anal-retentive character. In classical psychoanalysis, a personality type characterized by excessive orderliness, stinginess, and obstinacy.

Angel dust. See *phencyclidine.*

Anhedonia (ahedonia). Chronic, pathological loss of pleasure in existence.

Anhedonic-apathetic syndrome. A mental and emotional syndrome characterized by a combination of loss of pleasure and loss of interest in life.

Anorexia nervosa. A mental disorder characterized primarily by the refusal to eat enough food for the maintenance of a normal body weight.

Antianxiety drugs. Drugs capable of reducing excessively high levels of anxiety. Such drugs are also referred to as a *minor tranquilizers.*

Antidepressant drugs. Drugs used primarily to relieve depression. There are two broad general classes of antidepressant drugs: (1) tricyclic agents and (2) monoamine oxidase (MAO) inhibitors.

Antipsychotic drugs. See *major tranquilizers.*

Antisocial personality disorder. A kind of personality disorder characterized by an inadequate set of moral and ethical standards.

Anxiety. If no qualifying adjective is used, a feeling of dread or apprehension lacking a specific well-defined source. The emotional state is similar to fear. *Realistic anxiety* is identical in meaning to fear. However, such terms as *chronic anxiety* or *pathological anxiety* suggest the presence of a neurotic process.

Anxiety neurosis. See *generalized anxiety disorder.*

Apnea. A temporary cessation of the respiratory process. *Sleep apnea* refers to brief interludes during the night when the individual stops breathing.

Approach-avoidance conflict. A conflict in which a goal, or object of desire, has both positive and negative value to the individual.

Assertiveness training. A kind of behavior therapy designed to enhance one's social skills. Basic aims include learning how to (1) say no to unreasonable demands, (2) stand up for one's rights, and (3) cope with others without becoming unnecessarily aggressive.

Attention deficit disorder. A disorder in children characterized by such behavioral problems as seldom completing tasks, not listening, being distracted easily, impulsiveness, and sometime aggressiveness.

Authoritarian parent. A parent who tends to be bossy, overcontrolling, critical, and highly judgmental.

Autonomy. The capacity for self-direction, experienced as the conviction that one is in charge of one's own life and can make effective decisions.

Aversive conditioning. A behavior therapy procedure in which an unpleasant stimulus such as a mild electric shock is administered, often on a random basis, when an individual is engaged in an undesirable action.

B

Bad faith. According to the philosopher Jean-Paul Sartre, a quality of interpersonal behavior suggesting that one is manipulative and without conscience in one's dealings with others.

Barbiturates. See *sedatives.*

Basic anxiety. According to the psychoanalyst Karen Horney, an unverbalized impression that the world is unsafe and threatening. In some adults, this may play a part in a neurotic process. Basic anxiety is presumed to have its roots in adverse experiences associated with early childhood.

Behavior modification. A kind of behavior therapy based on principles of operant conditioning. The consequences of actions are altered in such a way as to bring about the extinction, or modification, of maladaptive habits.

Behavior therapy. A general approach to therapy that focuses primarily on learned aspects of behavior. The general assumption underlying behavior therapy is that much maladaptive behavior is acquired by conditioning and observational learning. Consequently, behavior therapy seeks to employ various methods to help a troubled individual unlearn, or modify, pathological habits.

Behavioral viewpoint. The viewpoint that no valid distinction can be made between a psychological symptom and an underlying illness. The behavioral viewpoint asserts that symptoms are learned through a conditioning process.

Beta method of extinction. See *negative practice.*

Bipolar disorder (manic depressive psychosis). A severe mood disorder with two extremes, mania and depression. A related, but less intense and not as disabling condition as bipolar disorder, is identified with the more or less exchangeable terms *cyclothymia, cyclothymic disorder,* and *cyclothymic neurosis.*

Blackout. A period of amnesia that spans a few hours or several days, sometimes experienced in connection with alcohol abuse.

Bulimarexia. See *Bulimia nervosa.*

Bulimia nervosa. A mental disorder characterized primarily by binge eating. The binge is frequently followed by purges such as self-induced vomiting or the taking of a laxative. The informal term *bulimarexia* is sometimes used to identify an eating disorder that alternates between self-imposed starvation and binge eating.

C

Caffeine. See *stimulants.*

Cannabis (or "marijuana"). See *hallucinogens.*

Character analysis. In psychotherapy, interpretations to the patient of the meaning of personality traits.

Charmed-life fallacy. The unconscious assumption that an aura of luck follows the individual into all situations.

Chronic (dispositional) shyness. A distressing personality trait characterized by maladaptive strategies designed to minimize the sense of being overexposed in social situations. If a person becomes very withdrawn and avoids all unnecessary contact with others, this can be spoken of as *pathological shyness.*

Chronic fatigue syndrome. A syndrome characterized by, as its name suggests, chronic fatigue. Other symptoms may include depression, sleep problems, disturbances in appetite, and a pervasive apathy. The convention is to reserve the term *chronic fatigue syndrome* for a condition in which the suspected causal factors are primarily organic in nature, not psychological.

Chronic suicide. According to the psychiatrist Karl A. Menninger, a process of gradual self-destruction. Chronic suicide stands in contrast to *acute suicide,* which is characterized by direct and quickly lethal acts of self-destruction. Another, more recently coined term for chronic suicide is *indirect self-destructive behavior.*

Circadian rhythms. Circular biological processes complete in one day. The wake-sleep cycle is the prime example.

Clinical psychologist. A psychologist who specializes in psychotherapy and psychological testing.

Clinical psychology. A field of psychology concerned with the diagnosis and treatment of mental disorders.

Cocaine. See *stimulants.*

Codeine. See *narcotics.*

Codependent. As originally formulated, a family member who obtains secondary psychological gratifications from another family member's abuse of, or dependence on, alcohol or other drugs. The basic concept is that the codependent person is addicted to the irresponsible behavior of the other person.

Cognitive-behavior therapy. A kind of behavior therapy that treats thoughts and ideas as learned behavior.

Cognitive distortion. As formulated in the context of cognitive therapy, a warped thought process associated with such errors as lack of logic, overgeneralization, personal labeling, and either-or thinking.

Cognitive therapy. An approach to psychotherapy that focuses on replacing maladaptive automatic thoughts with adaptive voluntary ones.

Compensation. According to Alfred Adler, a kind of ego defense mechanism characterized by an effort to maximize one's strengths in order to psychologically minimize one's weaknesses. Compensation is often used in an effort to counterbalance real or imagined feelings of inferiority.

Compulsion. A ritual, tinged with either an irrational or a magical quality, designed to reduce the anxiety associated with an obsession.

Compulsive eating. A maladaptive behavior pattern characterized by the eating and digestion of calories significantly beyond one's metabolic needs.

Conditional love. Love that must be earned.

Condensation. In classical psychoanalysis, the unconscious combining of two or more images into a single one.

Confabulation. A tendency to respond to questions by making up information. Confabulation is different from conscious lying and is frequently associated with organic mental disorders.

Consensual reality. The way in which a well-defined group, such as a family or a tribe, perceives the world.

Conversion disorder (hysteria). A kind of disorder characterized by an impairment of physical capacities without an organic basis. Imaginary neurological impairments are often associated with conversion disorders.

Counterconditioning. A method used to extinguish conditioned responses. In counterconditioning, a natural response is elicited that is antagonistic to an unwanted conditioned response.

Counterphobic behavior. Paradoxical behavior that is the logical opposite of the common-sense response to a fear. Instead of avoiding a feared situation or object, the individual displaying counterphobic behavior *seeks* contact.

Creative self. According to Alfred Adler, an inborn ability to take charge of life and become autonomous.

Crossed transactions. In transactional analysis, a transaction in which there is conflict between, for example, two people. In such transactions, each person tries to shove the other one down to a lower psychological level.

Cyborg complex. An informal term suggesting a tendency to make a subconscious identification of the ego with a machine or device such as a car, a hang-glider, or a motorcycle.

Cyclothymia. See *bipolar disorder.*
Cyclothymic disorder. See *bipolar disorder.*
Cyclothymic neurosis. See *bipolar disorder.*

D

Delirium tremens. A kind of delirium caused by withdrawal from the heavy use of alcohol. The state is characterized by an elevated temperature, agitation, delusions, and hallucinations.

Delusion. A belief that most members of an individual's family or culture regard as irrational or false.

Delusional (paranoid) disorder. A mental disorder characterized by a highly organized, consistent delusional system.

Demoralization. A negative mental and emotional state characterized by the conviction that life is worthless.

Denial of reality. An ego defense mechanism characterized by a refusal to face unpleasant facts.

Depersonalization. A psychological symptom characterized by distortions in the perception of the self. The individual may have the impression that one is a thing, an object, or a robot or that the personality is outside of the body.

Depression. A negative emotional state characterized by sadness, self-doubt, and a loss of interest in daily living. The clinical term *major depressive episode* is used to refer to severe, chronic depression.

Depressive neurosis. See *dysthymia.*

Desensitization therapy. See *systematic desensitization.*

Despair. A negative mental and emotional state characterized by a general sense of hopelessness.

Destrudo. In classical psychoanalytic theory, the energy associated with Thanatos, the death instinct. Destrudo is aggressive, destructive, and self-destructive in nature.

Determinism. The point of view that all behavior is caused by known, or potentially knowable, factors, such as genetic structures, motives, conditioned responses, early life experiences, or the social environment.

Detoxification. A process requiring medical supervision in which a patient is removed from physiological dependency on a drug.

Diphenhydramine. An antihistamine that tends to induce sleep.

Dispositional shyness. See *chronic shyness.*

Dopamine. One of the neurotransmitters, or chemical messengers, present in the brain and nervous system. There is evidence suggesting that there is excessive dopamine activity in the brains of schizophrenic patients.

Drug abuse. The use of a drug in such a manner that it interferes with everyday functioning and takes a toll on one's body and life.

Drug addiction. A state characterized by (1) abuse and (2) dependence on a given drug. The dependence can be physiological or psychological.

Drug therapy. In the context of psychiatry and abnormal psychology, the use of drugs to treat mental and emotional disorders.

Drug use. The use of a drug for either therapeutic or recreational purposes.

Duplex transactions. In transactional analysis, transactions characterized by messages at two levels. The first level is the *social level* and consists of the meaning communicated by the actual words that are spoken. The second level is the *psychological level* and consists of the meaning communicated by tone of voice, facial expression, and body language.

Dyspareunia. A sexual dysfunction characterized by pain during sexual intercourse.

Dysthymia (depressive neurosis). A mood disorder characterized primarily by depression. Secondary symptoms include fatigue, sleeping problems, loss of self-confidence, loss of interest in friends and family, and a generally negative outlook on life.

E

Ego. In psychoanalytic personality theory, the "I" of the personality. The ego is reality-oriented and mediates between the conflicting demands of the id and the superego.

Ego-ideal actualization. In the framework of humanistic therapy, working toward false goals that really belong to other people, often one's parents.

Egocentric thinking. Thinking characterized by the attitude that the whole world revolves around oneself.

Ego analysis. In psychotherapy, an evaluation of the positive and negative aspects of a given patient's ego in order to help that patient employ ego functions more realistically and effectively.

Ego defense mechanism. An involuntary psychological process that protects the individual against the harsher aspects of reality. A defense mechanism, used unconsciously by the ego, provides a buffer between unpleasant facts and threats to the integrity of the personality.

Either-or thinking. See *All-or-none thinking.*

Electra complex. See *Oedipus complex.*

Electroconvulsive therapy (ECT). A kind of biological therapy in which a brief, low-intensity electrical current is passed through the frontal part of the brain.

Emotional insulation. An ego defense mechanism characterized by withdrawal and a lack of ability to consciously experience a given emotion, such as grief or anger.

Emotional isolation. A condition characterized by loneliness and a sense that there is no real human contact with others, including partners and children.

Emotional modulation. A voluntary self-control process that helps the individual reduce the intensity and range of mood swings. Emotional modulation is to a large extent accomplished by replacing cognitive distortions with rational thoughts.

Empathy. In psychotherapy, the ability on the part of the therapist to have a sensitive appreciation for the thoughts, attitudes, and feelings of the troubled person.

Endorphins. Morphinelike substances, produced by the body's normal chemistry, with the capacity to relieve pain and induce a wholesome sense of well-being.

Eros. In classical psychoanalysis, the life instincts such as hunger, thirst, and sex.

Existential anxiety. Anxiety revolving around one's very being. Such anxiety is experienced as dread and apprehension associated with the fact everyone is vulnerable to accidents and disease as well as the reality that everyone ages and dies.

Existential neurosis. A neurosis characterized by chronic anxiety and despair in connection with the nature of existence itself.

Existential therapy. An approach to therapy that focuses on the nature of one's unique life as it is both lived and experienced. The therapist helps the individual resolve questions pertaining to one's identity and the meaning of life. This kind of therapy has its roots in European existential philosophy, and it is very similar to humanistic therapy.

Existential vacuum. A negative mental and emotional state characterized by the belief that one's life is empty of meaning.

Existentialism. In philosophy, the point of view that the starting place for understanding life is the *inner outlook*, life as it is actually lived and experienced, not as it is studied objectively by biology and academic psychology.

Experiential meaning. As described by Viktor Frankl, the capacity to derive intrinsic satisfaction from a passive experience (e.g., watching a sunset), one that is not an objective accomplishment.

External locus of control. See *locus of control.*

Externalization. In the case of a phobia, the conversion of a fear of a forbidden impulse or wish held at an unconscious level into a fear of an object or situation outside of the self. The ego defense mechanism of projection makes the conversion possible.

Extrovert. According to Carl Jung, a personality type characterized by the flow of libido, or psychological energy, toward the outer world.

F

Feeling-intuition type. According to Carl Jung, a personality type characterized by the making of decisions on the bases of moods, emotions, hunches, and "gut reactions."

Female sexual arousal disorder. A sexual dysfunction associated with the excitement stage of the sexual response cycle. Although willing to participate in sexual relations, a female with the disorder does not in fact become excited by any of the stimuli commonly associated with erotic arousal. A traditional term for the disorder, now considered obsolete in clinical language, is *frigidity.*

Fetal alcohol syndrome. A set of related symptoms present in an infant and child associated with alcohol abuse by the mother during pregnancy.

Fight-or-flight reaction. According to the physiologist Walter B. Cannon, a primitive emotional response in which the body prepares itself, when threatened, for the actions of either becoming aggressive or running away. There is an increase in the momentary production of adrenal hormones, the pumping of additional blood to the extremities, and the mobilization of glucose for the striated muscles.

Food abuse. Excessive eating and otherwise responding to food in pathological and self-defeating ways.

Free association. A technique used in psychoanalysis to explore the unconscious aspects of a patient's mental life. Free association requires that the patient relate to the therapist anything and everything that comes to mind without regard to logic.

Free-floating anxiety. A kind of anxiety that is attached to nothing and seems to have no source. It can be described as a cloud that follows the person everywhere as if on a string. Free-floating anxiety is a symptom of a neurotic process.

Free-floating hostility. A kind of hostility characterized by being mad at everybody and everything. The hostility may manifest itself by the making of frequent biting remarks, by insults, or by sarcasm. Free-floating hostility tends to be associated with Type A behavior.

Free will. See *voluntarism.*

Frigidity. See *female sexual arousal disorder.*

Frustration. A state that occurs when (1) the motivated individual is unable to attain a desirable goal or (2) the motivated individual is unable to escape from, or avoid, an unpleasant situation.

Frustration-aggression hypothesis. The hypothesis that frustration induces aggressive behavior.

Functional analysis. In the context of behavior therapy, a technique in which a general pattern of maladaptive behavior is analyzed into a set of specific habits.

Functional autonomy of motives. As formulated by Gordon W. Allport, a psychological principle stating that behavior patterns often become detached from their original motives or incentives.

G

Game. In the framework of transactional analysis, a self-defeating pattern of social behavior involving two or more persons.

General adaptation syndrome. As described by Hans Selye, a predictable three-stage response pattern to chronic stress.

General paresis. An organic disorder caused by syphilis. General paresis is characterized by memory impairment, motor-coordination difficulties, paralysis, and a decline in functional intelligence.

Generalized anxiety disorder. A kind of anxiety disorder characterized primarily by the constant feeling that some sort of unfortunate or terrible event is about to take place. An older term, no longer in vogue, is *anxiety neurosis.*

Good faith. According to the philosopher Jean-Paul Sartre, a quality of interpersonal behavior suggesting that one is honest and authentic in one's dealings with others.

H

Habituation. A process of gradual adaptation to a stimulus or a situation.

Hallucination. A false perceptual experience that carries the force of reality. Kinds of hallucinations include those that are visual, auditory, olfactory, tactile, and gustatory.

Hallucinogens. Drugs capable of producing hallucinations. Hallucinogens are also known as *psychedelics. Mescaline, psilocybin, lysergic acid diethylamide-25 (LSD),* and *phencyclidine (PCP or "Angel dust")* are kinds of hallucinogens. *Cannabis (or "marijuana")* is classified as a somewhat weaker hallucinogen than the prior ones identified.

Hasty generalization (jumping to conclusions). A logical error, or cognitive distortion, characterized by drawing a general conclusion on the basis of insufficient evidence.

Hedonism. As presented in the writings of the philosopher Aristotle, the point of view that pleasure and pain are the main motivational factors in human behavior.

Heroin. See *narcotics.*

Hidden message. A message that is communicated at a psychological level by an expression, a tone of voice, or a position of the body. The hidden message is both contradicted and masked by spoken words.

Humanistic therapy. An approach to therapy that focuses on the theme of self-actualization. Humanistic therapy aims to help the person grow and to become the individual he or she was meant to be. This kind of therapy owes much to the teachings of the psychologist Abraham Maslow.

Humanistic viewpoint. A viewpoint emphasizing the unique behavioral qualities of human beings in contrast to other organisms. This viewpoint holds that a psychological symptom comes into being when one finds it difficult to attain certain crucial human values.

Hyperarousal. A state characterized by excessive alertness and excitement.

Hyperarousal insomnia. See *insomnia.*

Hyperesthetic (oversensitive) memory. A memory process characterized by involuntary recollections.

Hypersomnia. See *insomnia.*

Hypnotherapy. The use of hypnosis in psychotherapy to treat disorders.

Hypoactive sexual desire disorder. A sexual dysfunction characterized by little or no desire for sexual relations.

Hypoarousal. A state characterized by an abnormally low level of alertness and a reduction in the general level of excitement.

Hypochondria. A tendency toward irrational and excessive worry about one's health.

Hypoglycemia. Low blood sugar. If hypoglycemia is chronic, the condition can induce or complicate psychological symptoms such as mental confusion, anxiety, and depression.

Hypoglycemic rebound. A sudden drop in blood sugar caused by the immediately prior consumption of a large quantity of food or an excessive amount of refined carbohydrates.

Hypomania. See *mania.*

Hysteria. See *conversion disorder.*

I

Id. In psychoanalytic personality theory, the foundation of the personality. The id is the primal, or "first," self. It consists of basic biological drives such as hunger, thirst, pain, and sex. It is pleasure-oriented. Pleasure is perceived by the id as relief from the tension of inborn drives.

Idealization-frustration-demoralization (I-F-D) syndrome. As described by the semanticist Wendell Johnson, a common pattern in troubled relationships. The first stage of the pattern is characterized by unrealistic expectations and perfectionistic thinking. The second stage is characterized by disappointments and misunderstandings. The third stage is characterized by hopelessness and demoralization.

I-F-D Syndrome. See *idealization-frustration-demoralization syndrome.*

I-it relationship. According to the theologian Martin Buber, a relationship in which a first person feels like an "I"—a living self—but does not, in fact, recognize or realize that this is true of a second person.

Implosive therapy. As developed by the therapist Thomas G. Stampfl, a rapid version of desensitization therapy. A guided fantasy induced by the therapist brings anxiety to a high level very quickly, and the individual is "flooded" with anxiety.

Impotence. See *male erectile disorder.*

Indirect self-destructive behavior. See *chronic suicide.*

Individual psychology. The name given by Alfred Adler to his system of psychology and therapy. Individual psychology tends to focus on understanding the role that such concepts as the will to power, sibling rivalry, and the inferiority complex play in neurotic processes.

Inferiority complex. According to Alfred Adler, a constellation of negative ideas about oneself. An inferiority complex makes a person feel extremely ineffective, unattractive, or inadequate.

Inhalants. See *stimulants.*

Inhibited female orgasm. A sexual dysfunction in which the female either seldom achieves an orgasm or achieves one with great difficulty after much stimulation, or both.

Inhibited male orgasm. A sexual dysfunction in which the ejaculatory reflex is either not easily elicited or not elicited at all. The male suffering from the dysfunction is capable of an erection and can readily sustain extended sexual intercourse.

Insomnia. A disturbed, or abnormal, pattern of sleep. *Hyperarousal insomnia* is a kind of insomnia characterized by great resistance to falling asleep; often accompanied by worries, overstimulation, and excitement. *Learned insomnia* is a kind of insomnia in which it is believed that maladaptive habits play a significant role in sleeplessness. *Hypersomnia* is characterized by chronic drowsiness.

Instinct. In American psychology, an inborn tendency to manifest a complex chain of related behaviors. In classical psychoanalysis, a biological drive such as hunger, thirst, or sex. The word *instinct* has a long history of somewhat conflicting usages.

Internal locus of control. See *locus of control.*

Interpersonal difficulty. A difficulty characterized by self-defeating patterns of behavior between two or more persons.

Interpersonal viewpoint. A viewpoint that explains psychological symptoms and maladaptive behavior in terms of ineffective patterns of communication, lack of emotional closeness, and similar problems in a relationship.

Introvert. According to Carl Jung, a personality type characterized by the flow of libido, or psychological energy, toward the inner, or psychological, world.

I-thou relationship. According to the theologian Martin Buber, a relationship in which a first person respects a second person as a living being, a living self.

J

James-Lange theory of emotions. A theory suggesting that actions induce the physiological changes, such as increased arousal and muscle tension, that in turn induce emotions.
Jumping to conclusions. See *hasty generalization*.

K

Korsakoff's psychosis. See *alcohol amnestic disorder*.

L

LCU. See *life change unit*.
Learned helplessness. A tendency to generalize actual helplessness experienced in a first situation to a second situation in which the individual is not helpless.
Learned insomnia. See *insomnia*.
Learned optimism. An acquired state of mind and general attitude characterized by self-enhancing generalizations, adaptive personal constructs, and positive expectations.
Libido. As introduced by Freud, combined psychological and sexual (i.e., psychosexual) energy. The term *libido* is derived from a Latin root meaning "lust."
Life change unit (LCU). As formulated by the psychiatrists T. H. Holmes and R. H. Rahe, a unit of measurement assigning a numerical value to stressful changes in one's life. These changes can be in either a positive or a negative direction.
Life script. In transactional analysis, an unconscious plan for an individual's personal future written by one's Child ego state.
Limerance. A mental and emotional state characterized by elevated mood and the conviction that a partner, or potential partner, will satisfy all of one's psychological and emotional needs.
Locus of control. As formulated by Julian Rotter, the perception that one's own behavior has either an external or internal origin. *External locus of control* tends to be associated with anxiety, depression, and helplessness. *Internal locus of control* tends to be associated with autonomy, feeling effective and competent, and an optimistic outlook.
Logotherapy. A kind of psychotherapy pioneered by the psychiatrist Viktor

Frankl. The aim of logotherapy is to help an individual restore meaning in life. This is accomplished by discussions with the aim of rediscovering values.

LSD. See *lysergic acid diethylamide-25.*

Lucid dream. A dream in which one becomes aware that one is dreaming. It is sometime possible to break out of such a dream or to gain voluntary control of it.

Lysergic acid diethylamide-25 (LSD). See *hallucinogens.*

M

Magnification. A cognitive distortion characterized by a tendency to enlarge in personal perception events that are small in the perception of others.

Major depressive episode. See *depression.*

Major tranquilizers (antipsychotic drugs). Tranquilizers that have a beneficial effect on psychotic disorders, disorders characterized by severe thought distortions. These drugs help ameliorate delusions, hallucinations, and agitation in mental patients.

Male erectile disorder. A sexual dysfunction characterized by the inability to sustain an erection long enough during sexual intercourse to maintain contact of sufficient duration. The traditional term, now considered obsolete in clinical language, for the disorder is *impotence.*

Mania. A state of agitation and excitement so intense that behavior becomes irrational. Mania is also characterized by euphoria, elation, and hurried speech. When mania is moderate in intensity, it is referred to as *hypomania.*

Manic-depressive psychosis. See *bipolar disorder.*

Masochism. A behavioral trait in which a person seeks either physical or psychological pain. There is an element of paradox in masochism because the person appears to extract pleasure from pain.

MBD. See *minimal brain dysfunction.*

Medical viewpoint. As applied to mental, emotional, and behavioral problems, the viewpoint that a constellation of psychological symptoms represents an illness in either organic or functional terms.

Megavitamin therapy. See *orthomolecular psychiatry.*

Mescaline. See *hallucinogens.*

Minimal brain dysfunction (MBD). A set of related cognitive and behavioral disturbances assumed to be caused by a slight amount of damage in the brain stem, the region of the brain that controls arousal. MBD is a possible contributing factor to both chronic aggressiveness and hyperactivity in children and possibly some adults.

Minor tranquilizer. See *antianxiety drug.*

Mnemonic device. A conscious strategy designed to improve the functioning of one's memory processes. A mnemonic device is a memory aid.

Mood. A transient, involuntary emotional state. A mood has either a negative or a positive tone.

Morphine. See *narcotics.*

Motivated forgetting. See *repression.*

N

Narcissism. A kind of ego defense mechanism characterized by self-absorption. The term *narcissism* can also be used to identify a personality trait characterized by preoccupation with one's own self and one's personal needs.

Narcoanalysis. The use of a narcotic drug to assist in the exploration of a patient's unconscious mental life.

Narcolepsy. A disorder characterized by a tendency to fall suddenly and involuntarily asleep.

Narcotics. In general, drugs that tend to induce drowsiness, stupor, and a reduction in the ability to feel pain. *Opium, morphine,* and *codeine* are kinds of narcotics. *Heroin* is a synthetic narcotic.

Need for achievement. A need, expressed as a psychological motive, to set a high level of aspiration in association with well-defined life goals.

Need for self-abasement. A need, expressed as a psychological motive, to lower one's own worth and status.

Negative practice (beta method of extinction). As formulated by the psychologist Knight Dunlap, a method of extinguishing maladaptive habits calling for the individual to consciously and voluntarily produce the "error" or unwanted behavior associated with the habit.

Neurasthenia. An outdated term once used to label a condition characterized by chronic fatigue. The literal meaning of the word *neurasthenia* is "weakness of the nerves."

Nicotine. See *stimulants.*

Nihilism. In philosophy, the viewpoint that nothing has any value and that, consequently, all human action is ultimately pointless.

Norepinephrine. One of the neurotransmitters, or chemical messengers, found in the brain and nervous system. Low levels of norepinephrine are associated with depression.

O

Obsession. A persistent, invasive idea that is perceived to be illogical by either the subject who holds the thought or an outside observer.

Obsessive compulsive disorder (obsessive compulsive neurosis). An anxiety disorder characterized by the presence of either obsessions or compulsions, or both.

Obsessive compulsive neurosis. See *obsessive compulsive disorder*.

Obsessive compulsive personality disorder. A kind of personality disorder characterized by perfectionistic tendencies and a lack of flexibility.

Oedipus complex. In classical psychoanalysis, a set of unconscious motives and ideas characterized by (1) an incest wish toward the parent of the opposite sex, (2) guilt over the wish, and (3) fear of punishment from the parent of the same sex. The term *Electra complex* is sometimes used as a synonym for the Oedipus complex when talking about women.

Operant conditioning. As formulated by the behavioral psychologist B. F. Skinner, a kind of learning process in which an organism's behavior is shaped by the consequences of its behavior.

Opium. See *narcotics*.

Orthomolecular psychiatry (megavitamin therapy). As pioneered by the biochemist Linus Pauling and the psychiatrist David Hawkins, an approach to the treatment of mental disorders in which large doses of vitamins are prescribed. There is particular emphasis on the B-complex vitamins.

Oversensitive memory. See *hyperesthetic memory*.

P

Paradox of hedonism. The contradiction inherent in the observation that pleasure often escapes persons who pursue it directly and that it frequently emerges as a side effect when people lead responsible lives.

Paranoid disorder. See *delusional disorder*.

Parent ego state. In transactional analysis, an ego state tending to be value oriented. The Parent ego state is often judgmental and authoritarian. An ego state is a way in which the personality expresses itself at a given moment. The concept of the Parent ego state is very similar to Freud's concept of the superego.

Paresthesia. A condition characterized by a disturbance in the sense of touch. Symptoms include tingling, numbness, or heat in the fingers or toes.

Passive-aggressive behavior. The expression of hostility in an indirect manner. The aim of such behavior is to mask or deny the existence of hostility.

Passive-aggressive personality disorder. A personality disorder characterized by masked hostility and its expression in disguised form.

Pathological conditioned emotional reactions. Emotional reactions that are both maladaptive and learned.

Pathological shyness. See *chronic shyness*.

PCP. See *phencyclidine*.

Peak experience. According to Abraham Maslow, a moment of genuine joy or ecstasy. A peak experience is usually experienced in the context of the self-actualization process.

Perfectionism. A personality trait characterized by a compulsive effort to eliminate all flaws and blemishes from one's behavior and the products of that behavior.

Personal construct. According to the personality theorist George Kelly, a well-defined conscious idea about oneself. Personal constructs determine behavior, and they tend to become self-fulfilling prophecies.

Personal labeling (self-labeling). A cognitive distortion in which negative names are attached to either oneself or to others. Personal labeling represents oversimplified judgments.

Phencyclidine (PCP or "angel dust"). See *hallucinogens*.

Phobia. An anxiety reaction characterized by an irrational fear or an obsessive dread.

Pineal gland. An endocrine gland that appears to be involved in the regulation of biological rhythms.

PMS. See *premenstrual syndrome*.

Premack's principle. A principle stating that if a high probability action is made contingent on a low probability action, the high probability action will act as a reinforcer on the low probability one.

Premature ejaculation. A sexual dysfunction characterized by brevity of penetration and penile stroking before the ejaculatory reflex is elicited.

Premenstrual syndrome (PMS). A cluster of symptoms believed to be caused by the female's physiological state a few days prior to the beginning of her regular menses. Symptoms include cramps, headaches, illogical thinking, depression, and excitability. PMS should not be confused with *premenstrual tension*, a milder condition that possibly affects most women to some degree.

Premenstrual tension. See *premenstrual syndrome (PMS)*.

Procrastination. Postponing the actions required to complete a task, attain a goal, or rise to the challenge of an opportunity.

Progressive relaxation. A way of inducing muscle relaxation. One systematically progresses from attention to muscles in the arms to those in the legs. The key to the method is voluntarily tightening muscles for a number of seconds at a time. This makes it easy to then let go of tension and induces automatic muscle relaxation.

Projection. A kind of ego defense mechanism in which a repressed idea or motive is unconsciously placed on an external source, such as a person or a thing.

Psilocybin. See *hallucinogens*.

Psychedelics. See *hallucinogens*.

Psychiatrist. A medical doctor (M.D.) who specializes in treating mental disorders.

Psychiatry. A field of medicine concerned with the diagnosis and treatment of mental disorders.

Psychoanalysis. Both a personality theory and a method of psychotherapy created by Sigmund Freud. A principal assumption of psychoanalysis is that there is an unconscious level to the personality.

Psychodynamic approach. A general term suggesting an approach to both therapy and human behavior loosely based on Freud's basic assumptions such as unconscious motivation, the ego defense mechanisms, and internal psychological conflict.

Psychogenic amnesia. Memory impairment without a clear-cut biological basis. It is common for a person suffering from psychogenic amnesia to lose the ability to remember any information that will reveal his or her identity. A condition related to psychogenic amnesia is *psychogenic fugue,* in which the symptoms of psychogenic amnesia are combined with a flight from home. Both conditions are thought to have roots in psychological and emotional conflicts.

Psychogenic fugue. See *psychogenic amnesia.*

Psychology. The science that studies the behavior of human beings and other organisms. As commonly used today, the word *behavior* includes thoughts, emotions, and actions.

Psychosis. An extreme mental or emotional derangement of either biological or emotional origin. The individual suffering from a psychosis is out of touch with reality as it is usually understood.

R

Rapid eye movement (REM) sleep. The kind of sleep associated with dreaming. During rapid eye movement, or REM, sleep, the eyes actually move about erratically under the eyelids as if the individual is watching a motion picture.

Rational-emotive therapy. As formulated by the psychologist Albert Ellis, an approach to therapy that helps the patient replace irrational thoughts with rational ones. The key assumption is that rational thoughts will modulate excessive reactions associated with emotions such as anger, anxiety, and depression.

Rationalization. A kind of ego defense mechanism in which either an irrational idea or irrational behavior is made to seem rational through the use of a chain of superficial logic.

Reaction formation. A kind of ego defense mechanism in which a repressed idea reappears at the conscious level in an opposite form.

Realistic anxiety. See *anxiety.*

Reality therapy. As formulated by the psychiatrist William Glasser, an approach to therapy that helps the patient become aware of the long-term consequences of important life decisions. Reality therapy helps the individual to make responsible choices.

Reinforcer. A consequence, or outcome, of an action that has the effect of increasing the likelihood that similar actions will be repeated in the future. Informally, a reinforcer is a valued "payoff" for behavior.

Relaxation response. As described by medical researcher Herbert Benson, a natural response induced by meditative techniques. The relaxation response is antagonistic to the fight-or-flight reaction associated with anxiety.

REM sleep. See *rapid eye movement sleep.*

Repression (motivated forgetting). A kind of ego defense mechanism in which unpleasant memories and forbidden motives are blocked from consciousness and directed toward the unconscious level of mental life.

S

SAD. See *seasonal affective disorder.*

Sado-masochistic relationship. A relationship in which a first person dominates and controls a second person. The first person extracts psychological pleasure from domination, and the second person extracts psychological pleasure from submission. The relationship may be, but is not necessarily, sexual in nature.

Schizophrenia. A mental disorder characterized by a gross impairment in the ability to think in logical and rational terms. Related symptoms frequently include delusions, hallucinations, odd use of language, and loss of touch with reality as it is usually understood.

Seasonal affective disorder (SAD). A variety of either bipolar disorder or major depression in which the appearance of symptoms can be linked to a given season of the year. There are alternations of mood such that there is emotional elevation in the summer and depression in the winter.

Sedatives. Drugs that decrease central-nervous-system arousal. Both *alcohol* and *barbiturates* are sedatives.

Self-abasement. See *need for self-abasement.*

Self-actualization. According to Abraham Maslow, an inborn tendency to maximize one's talents and potentialities.

Self-alienation. A psychological symptom characterized by (1) a loss of a robust sense of identity and (2) depersonalization.

Self-esteem. An evaluation of the self, an informal self-ranking in terms of personal worth. Persons with a negative overall view of themselves tend to have low self-esteem. Persons with a positive overall view of themselves tend to have high self-esteem.

Self-labeling. See *personal labeling.*

Senile dementia. A deterioration in functional intelligence and mental ability; associated with old age.

Sensate focusing. As used in sexual therapy, a technique characterized by paying conscious attention to sensations that bring pleasure.

Sexual aversion disorder. A sexual dysfunction characterized by generally negative behavioral and emotional reactions to the idea of sexual contact. Images of participating in sexual activity are likely to induce disgust, anxiety, nausea, or a headache.

Sexual dysfunctions. Problems in the area of sexual response characterized by such experiences as lack of excitement, inability to attain an orgasm, or painful intercourse.

Short-term (working) memory. A mental process characterized by the ability to remember facts and ideas that one needs to use in the present.

Simple (specific) phobia. An anxiety reaction in which the source of an irrational fear or an obsessive dread can be readily defined and identified.

Sleep apnea. See *apnea.*

Sleep-clock disorder. A disorder characterized by a disturbance in an individual's 24-hour wake-sleep cycle.

Social interest. According to Alfred Adler, an inborn tendency to care about both other people and the state of humankind.

Social introversion. A tendency to move away from people and into one's own private psychological world.

Social phobia. A kind of anxiety disorder characterized by the fear of placing oneself in situations where others have an opportunity to observe or judge one's behavior.

Sociocultural viewpoint. A viewpoint asserting that many psychological and emotional problems are reflections of, as its name indicates, a troubled society and culture.

Somatization disorder. A disorder characterized by symptoms of physical illness without organic basis.

Specific phobia. See *simple phobia.*

Squeeze technique. A technique used in sexual therapy for the treatment of premature ejaculation.

Stimulants. Drugs that have the effect of increasing alertness or central-nervous-system arousal. Some specific kinds of stimulants are *amphetamines, caffeine, cocaine, inhalants,* and *nicotine.*

Stimulus generalization. A tendency to give a conditioned, or learned, response to stimuli (i.e., situations or objects) that are similar to an original conditioned stimulus.

Stoicism. In classical philosophy, the viewpoint that it is possible, within rational limits, to develop an attitude of cool, calm indifference toward one's own suffering.

Stress-inoculation training. A cognitive-behavior modification technique that involves preparing oneself ahead of time to cope with a stressful situation. One way to accomplish this is to voluntarily run a mental movie of an anticipated event. This will tend to induce anxiety. Anxiety will diminish each time the mental movie is replayed.

Substance abuse. The imprudent use of alcohol or of other drugs, such as cocaine and amphetamines.

Superego. In psychoanalytic personality theory, the moral agent of the personality. It sets standards of right and wrong, as well as pointing to goals in life.

Systematic desensitization (desensitization therapy). As developed by the psychiatrist Joseph Wolpe, a kind of behavior therapy designed to help a troubled person adapt to stimuli that produce maladaptive emotional reactions. This is accomplished by either presenting the stimuli in guided fantasies or *in vivo* (i.e., in life).

T

Thanatos. In classical psychoanalytic theory, the death instinct.

Thinking-sensation type. According to Carl Jung, a personality type characterized by the making of decisions on the bases of (1) a rational analysis and (2) what can be seen and heard.

Thought stopping. A cognitive therapy technique characterized by the ability to disrupt useless thought sequences.

Thought substitution. A cognitive therapy technique characterized by the voluntary substitution of a new, productive idea in place of an older, self-defeating one.

Time urgency. A general attitude characterized by impatience and constant hurrying. Life is lived under the rule of deadlines and the clock.

Tip-of-the-tongue phenomenon. The frustrating experience of (1) knowing that at some level one remembers an item of information and (2) the inability to voluntarily recall the item.

Transactional analysis. As formulated by the psychiatrist Eric Berne, both a personality theory and a method of therapy. Transactional analysis explains personal problems in terms of flawed communication patterns.

Type A behavior. As described by the cardiologists Meyer Friedman and Ray H. Rosenman, a pattern characterized by such behaviors as chronic anger, time urgency, free-floating hostility, and rapid motions. Meyer and Friedman suggested that Type A behavior is a possible risk factor in heart disease.

U

Unconscious motives. According to Freud, repressed motives containing a forbidden wish. Such a wish tends to be of either a sexual or an aggressive nature and often has an adverse impact on emotions and behavior.

V

Vaginismus. A sexual dysfunction characterized by an involuntary contraction of the muscles around the vagina.

Voluntarism. The viewpoint that one's subjective experience of autonomy is real, that human beings can take responsible charge of their own lives. *Free will* is the traditional name given to the mental faculty associated with voluntarism.

W

Will to power. According to Alfred Adler, an inborn tendency directed toward becoming competent and effective. Also, the will to power plays a role in the desire to gain ascendancy over others. Adler derived the concept of the will to power from the writings of the philosopher Friedrich Nietzsche.

Workaholism. An informal term suggesting a stable behavioral pattern in which an individual is psychologically addicted to work.

Working memory. See *short-term memory.*

INDEX

McLuhan, H. M., 183
Medical viewpoint, 2
Megavitamin therapy, 50
Melanin, 138
Memory, 127
Menninger, K. A., 64, 188
Mescaline, 47, 63
Minimal brain dysfunction (MBD), 24, 222
Minnesota Multiphasic Personality Inventory (MMPI), 210
Minor tranquilizer, 36
Mnemonic device, 131–132
Monoamine oxidase (MAO) inhibitors, 59
Monophobia, 103
Montaigne, M. de, 135
Mood, 135
Moore, C., 226
Morpheus, 226
Morphine, 63, 226
Motivated forgetting, 130
Mowrer, O. H., 91
Mysophobia, 103

N

Nabakov, V., 126
Narcissism, 190
Narcoanalysis, 133
Narcolepsy, 220
Narcotics, 62–63
Need for achievement, 233–234, 241
Need for activity, 241
Need for affiliation, 241
Need for power, 182, 233, 241
Need for self-abasement, 190
Need to avoid failure, 174
Need to structure time, 233
Negative practice, 148
Neurasthenia, 164, 167
Neurasthenic syndrome, 164
Neuropathy, 164
Nicholson, J., 15

Nicotine, 62, 224
Nietzsche, F., 119
Nightmares, 222
Nihilism, 118–119, 122
Norepinephrine, 54
Nyctophobia, 103
Nytol, 228

O

Obsession, 143–144
Obsessive compulsive disorder, 144
Obsessive compulsive neurosis, 144
Obsessive compulsive personality disorder, 144, 153
Ochlophobia, 103
Oedipus complex, 201
O'Neill, E., 7
Operant conditioning, 78
Ophidiophobia, 103
Opium, 63
Oral stage, 71
Organic approach, 140
Organic causes, 129
Orgasm, 198
Orthomolecular psychiatry, 50
Orwell, G., 157
Overgeneralization, 242
Oversensitive memory, 128
Ovid, 226

P

Pandora's box, 197
Paradox of hedonism, 115
Paranoid disorder, 44
Parent ego state, 156
Paresthesia, 163
Parker, R. B., 183–184
Passive-aggressive behavior, 130, 166
Passive-aggressive personality disorder, 173